☆

The Saints and the Union

THE SAINTS
AND THE UNION
Utah Territory during the Civil War

E. B. LONG

UNIVERSITY OF ILLINOIS PRESS
Urbana   Chicago   London

Library of Congress Cataloging in Publication Data

Long, Everette B 1919–
The saints and the Union.

Bibliography: p.
Includes index.
1. Utah—History—Civil War, 1861–1865.   I. Title.
E532.95.L66   979.2′02   80-16775
ISBN 0-252-00821-9

For Barbara

Contents

Acknowledgments

It is impossible adequately to express appreciation to the many people and institutions who have aided in the preparation of this book, or to acknowledge the many who have furnished help over the years to me in my general field, the Civil War. Of primary importance was Barbara Long, editor extraordinary and map artist. David Crosson, formerly Research Historian at the University of Wyoming Archives and now Director of the Allen County–Fort Wayne, Indiana, Historical Society, gave constant help in research, and suggestions. Various personnel of the University of Wyoming were of invaluable assistance, particularly Coe Library's Inter-Library Loan Department headed by Kelly Patterson, and Gene M. Gressley, Esther Kelley and Eunice Spackman, of the Western History Research Center.

Of particular importance were institutions and individuals in Salt Lake City, Utah. The Historical Department of the Church of Jesus Christ of Latter-day Saints was unparalleled in its cooperation and painstaking assistance. Church Historian Leonard J. Arrington, Church Archivist Earl E. Olson, Church Librarian Donald T. Schmidt, and their staff-members, including Marilyn Siefert, Lauritz Petersen, and Ronald Watt, were unstinting in making materials available. It would have been impossible to write this book without their generous aid and suggestions.

The personnel of the Utah State Archives and the Utah Historical Society, Melvin T. Smith, Director, Jay M. Haymond, Librarian-Historian, were always willing to assist. Dr. Everett Cooley of the University of Utah Library must also be recognized, as well as Dr. Robert Chandler, San Francisco, California, Theron Luke, Provo, Utah, and Thomas Lindmier, researcher for Bear River.

The staffs of a number of major institutions are deserving of thanks. These include the Beinecke Rare Book and Manuscript Library, Yale University, New Haven, Connecticut; the Manuscript Division, Library of Congress, Washington, D.C.; the Henry E. Huntington Library, San Marino, California; the National Archives, Washington, D.C.; and the Federal Archives and Records Center, Denver, Colorado.

It would be remiss indeed not to include the help of the late Dr. Allan Nevins, who gave me access to his splendid collection of books and research notes; Harold Schindler of the Salt Lake City *Tribune*; David Bigler of Salt Lake City, Utah; Professor R. David Edmunds of Texas Christian University, Fort Worth, Texas; and Professor Peter M. Wright of Fort Lewis College, Durango, Colorado. In the search for materials regarding General Patrick Connor, I wish to thank Ken Rollandelli, President of the Redwood City Heritage Association, Redwood City, California, and Mrs. Gladys Woodhams, who operates the Lathrop House, one-time residence of General Connor. Also of help were Ned Himmel and the Redwood City Public Library, Herbert Garcia and the San Mateo County Historical Association, and General Connor's granddaughter, Mrs. Paul Fay of San Francisco. Finally, I wish to express my appreciation to the University of Illinois Press and its staff, including its director, Richard L. Wentworth, the managing editor, Elizabeth Dulany, and my manuscript editor, Doris J. Dyen.

E. B. LONG

Introduction

☆

THE AMERICAN CIVIL WAR, 1861 to 1865, can be and often is studied without reference to the vast western frontier, thus giving an incomplete account of that struggle. And central to the American West during the Civil War is Utah Territory. The story of this region during the conflict is a good deal more than a sideshow, though it receives scant mention in Civil War histories and only a little more in volumes on the American West.

Utah Territory would have been important because of its geographical position astride transportation and communications arteries even if it had not been an anomaly. And it was also unprecedented in this country, being both a civil and a religious entity of considerable size and influence.

In addition, there developed during the Civil War years in Utah Territory an amazingly effective leadership on one hand and an equal but frustrating lack of leadership on the other. Brigham Young, President of the Church of Jesus Christ of Latter-day Saints, was already a powerful civil and religious figure. And then Patrick Connor, a determined soldier of fortune, arrived in the territory. Both were successful in their endeavors, both were men of substance and ability, and both possessed forceful personalities.

Brigham Young and Patrick Connor overshadowed all other men in Utah Territory and in the Rocky Mountain West of the 1860s. On the other hand, the federal civilian leadership in the area was largely, though not entirely, an often extreme example of inability and ineptitude.

There was, in addition, a small and interesting host of supporting characters in Utah, a stage full of as varied people as ever gathered in such an isolated and remote area. From northern Europe, from the eastern and midwestern United States came the Mormons, a heterogeneous group bonded together by a new-found and compelling faith. From California came the volunteer federal soldiers, and of course there was the usual breed of tough, independent westerners unattached to religion or the army. Furthermore, and significantly, were those who had been there for a while—the Indians.

The question was how these divergent people would be molded into the national ethic, the national political, social, and economic picture. For molded they were to be; one way or another it was inevitable, facing as they did the development of the West and the advance of so-called "progress." Intruding into this process was a new and further disruptive factor: the Civil War.

There were questions of military operations, army occupation, politics, religion, philosophy, economics, leadership, and, perhaps paramount, personalities. At times it almost seemed that on the deserts of Utah another side to the Civil War was being enacted.

History as it is lived weaves a narrative, and the events, controversies, and words of those in Utah Territory during the Civil War and those watching the territory from afar make an exciting and meaningful story of adventure, intrigue, and clashing egos.

Almost from the organization of the Church of Jesus Christ of Latter-day Saints a vast and controversial literature, most of it almost fanatically polarized, has been written about it. There are hundreds of violently anti-Mormon articles, books, and memoirs, and many exposés of polygamy. Much of this is sensational trash, but some of it is based on fact and at least partial truth. Perhaps lesser known are the scores of books and articles, often church-sponsored or written by participating Mormons defending the faith, explaining polygamy and idolizing Brigham Young. There are on the subject only a few serious, objective studies.

The Saints and the Union is neither another anti-Mormon screed based on sensationalism nor an apologia. The conclusions herein are based on a very considerable amount of original research in manuscripts and primary printed sources. I have deemed it best to let the participants speak their minds as much as possible. Therefore, direct quotations from letters, newspapers, reports, and speeches have been used liberally. Those on the spot wrote and spoke of the events, viewpoints, and their own efforts with a verisimilitude, emphasis, and weight of repetition that cannot be captured by a secondary historian writing today. It is the historian's job to record and then interpret the words and deeds of those who "were there." Almost more important is the historian's task of attempting to understand what happened, what was said and written, and why, and to throw light upon the complex interrelation of events and the interplay of diverse and influential personalities on the developing patterns of history.

Analysis of that intricate interrelation is especially necessary when dealing with the Mormon Church, the U.S. Army, the Indian, the "opening of the West"—so intimately intertwined and at once so inexorable, the often misunderstood and underestimated parts of the much greater Civil War raging far to the East.

E. B. LONG

Laramie, Wyoming
1980

☆

The Saints and the Union

CHAPTER

I

Facing the Crisis of Secession

ALL THE TERRITORIES and states of the American West had their differences and their unique qualities. Of the established territories or states at the outbreak of the Civil War, Utah Territory was unique in that it was both a civil and a religious entity; it had a civil and religious government, or really two governments; it was inhabited almost entirely by those who had what elsewhere was often labeled a "peculiar" faith; it had a moral code that was in part repugnant to most other Americans; it had a charismatic leader who held over it an almost undisputed sway. Utah Territory was the only state or territory that in its maturing years was largely a religious state. It had been founded not because of a mining boom, or because of numerous and long-established settlers, or because it offered obvious agricultural benefits, but because it was the homeland of a religious sect. Utah was located, by an accident of geography, astride the principal communication lines between the eastern and western states. Across its land went the great and vulnerable emigrant roads, the Overland Trail to California, the Pony Express, stage lines, the telegraph—all becoming even more vital when Civil War came and the southern routes were disrupted. Utah, it was generally held, would likely be crossed by the first transcontinental railroad.

Salt Lake City was the only major city between far western Missouri and California. It was a base for civilization, for repairing the wear and tear of western travel, for resupplying. It was a marketplace, an oasis of considerable size in the midst of the vast and arid reaches of the American West. Soon it would be sending its agricultural products and its supplies to new mining camps in Idaho and Montana.

The people of Utah had made a naked valley flower; they had created a good deal of something out of almost nothing by hard work, obedience to their faith, and a sizable share of common sense about independent survival.

In 1850 Utah Territory had been officially listed as having a population of only 11,330. In the 1860 census it could boast of 42,273 people, most of whom dwelt in a narrow north-south littoral along the western side of the Wasatch Mountains, with a few living in outlying settlements. This figure may be on the low side. In the mountain West this was surpassed only by New Mexico Territory, which still included the soon-to-be-separated territory of Arizona. Colorado Territory counted 34,277, and Nevada Territory only 6,857.[1] Furthermore, Utah was continuing to grow. New recruits to the Church of Jesus Christ of Latter-day Saints were arriving with regularity every summer. Of the more than 40,000 Utah residents, it was said that Salt Lake City had 14,000.[2]

For a western territory in 1860 Utah showed a surprisingly close balance between male and female whites, with 22,224 male whites and 19,990 female whites. There were 13 free male "colored" and 17 female "colored" for a total of 30 free blacks. Of slaves only 29 were listed compared with 26 in 1850: 18 male and 11 female. The Indian population was put at 20,000 but the accuracy of that figure is in doubt.[3]

Easterners were already greatly excited by the supposed opportunities of the West, and became especially enthusiastic when news, reliable or not, of finds of precious metals came in from the mountain regions. They were also intrigued and titillated by the novel and enigmatic Mormons, and were responsive to "news" from these strange-sounding people with their "odd" faith. Much of this "news" was spurious, erroneous, exaggerated, and based on rumor, gossip, and misunderstanding. There were already numerous exposés and "eyewitness" accounts of the Mormons focusing on their dominating leader Brigham Young, and on their unusual and much condemned institution of polygamy. Books, magazines, and newspapers found avid readers of sensational and, by Victorian standards, libidinous, "truth" about the Mormons.

Even the most literate Americans seem to have had a very fuzzy idea of the Church of Jesus Christ of Latter-day Saints. The faith had a small beginning in rural New York State in 1830 when it was organized by Joseph Smith and five others. By 1860 many Americans and many foreigners knew of Joseph Smith's claim that he heard the voice of the Lord in 1820 while he was praying in the woods. Later there were more revelations, and, he said, a heavenly messenger, the angel Moroni, appeared to him in 1823. Moroni told Smith of plates of gold, buried on a hill near his home, which were the sacred writings of ancient prophets. According to Smith, he obtained the plates and other writings, which he published in 1830 as the *Book of Mormon*.

The religion Smith established grew rapidly and, instead of fading away like so many new faiths, gathered unto it a dedicated group of men and women who began long years of trial, suffering, and persecution. The headquarters of the Church moved slowly west, first to Kirtland, Ohio, and then to Jackson County in western Missouri. After several moves within that state, where the Mormons were often reviled and driven from their homes, they went back to the eastern shore of the Mississippi River at Nauvoo, Illinois. Here, by dint of hard work and dedication, the Church continued to grow and the community flourished, arousing even more animosity from outsiders.

Joseph Smith and his brother were murdered at Carthage, Illinois, in June, 1844, while being held for trial on charges brought by their numerous enemies. On the death of Smith, the spiritual leader and prophet, the Mormons found their temporal leader in the young, ambitious, brilliant, energetic, enthusiastic, and able Brigham Young. After more persecution, the Mormons crossed the winter-bound Mississippi early in 1846 and once more headed west. Across Iowa, what became Nebraska, and out on the Oregon Trail they went, seeking a place where they could live unmolested. Their trials seemed only to strengthen the Church both in faith and in numbers.

The first party of Mormons reached the Valley of the Great Salt Lake in July of 1847. They were not necessarily trying to leave the United States but were looking for a homeland isolated from the furies that had attended them. The famed Mormon Battalion had loyally served the United States with distinction in the Mexican War. But even in Utah there were still troubles—with the Indians, with other whites, or "Gentiles" as the Mormons called them, and occasionally with apostates from the faith. The Mormons had generally received a bad press. Much of the criticism against them, even now that they were somewhat removed, was not so much because of their creed, but because of their polygamy, which engendered increasing outrage from many and lewd snickers from others outside the Church.

The Mormons were fervently busy in Utah creating a well-planned city, tilling their fields, and making their barren land green with crops, for Young and his followers were keen businessmen and excellent administrators and organizers. And, at the same time, Mormon missionaries were spreading out into the United States and to Europe and converts were coming in, some of whom trundled painfully westward over the wastelands of the "Great American Desert" pushing their famous handcarts.

The Mormons were not involved directly in the rising tensions between North and South. They wanted to be left alone and they were prospering. On the other hand, their precious isolation was threatened as the westward human tide quickened. They were right in the path of the emigrants, and could not avoid the march of what was believed to be progress: they were involuntarily being dragged back into the mainstream of the nation. This became abundantly clear when President James Buchanan and his administration became incensed over alleged violations of the law by the Mormons and Brigham Young. Misunderstandings arose over policies on land and Indians, mail contracts, and probate courts, and dissatisfaction grew over Brigham Young as territorial governor. So in 1857–58 came the so-called Mormon Expedition of the federal army and the falsely named "Mormon War." In 1857 a force of 1,500 U.S. troops and artillery was sent from Fort Leavenworth, Kansas Territory, to bring the Mormons to terms. Other soldiers followed. The whole expedition was commanded by an experienced officer, Colonel Albert Sidney Johnston, who was to die in April, 1862, at Shiloh, Tennessee, while commanding the Confederate forces in that bloody battle on the banks of the Tennessee River.

The federal troops spent the winter of 1857–58 around Fort Bridger, which is now in western Wyoming but was then in Utah Territory. They had serious difficulties obtaining sufficient supplies, and Mormons attacked some federal supply trains. But there was little bloodshed and Johnston's expedition marched into Utah in 1858 without major incident. While military action was limited, the Mormon War created bitter feelings and left the Utah community with an increased distaste for what was perceived as the overbearing tyranny of the United States.

Many Mormons, fearing the worst, evacuated their homes and fled at the approach of the soldiers, but eventually they came back to find their homes and barns unburned and their fields unmolested. The federal troops established Camp Floyd, by early 1861 known as Fort Crittenden, some thirty miles southwest of Great Salt Lake City. At times the camp had 3,000 soldiers and the nearby town of Fairfield as many as 7,000 people, together comprising the third largest city in Utah. Here the soldiers protected the Overland Trail and kept an eye on the Mormons, though they were not close enough to Salt Lake City to be really distressing.

The construction of Camp Floyd (or Crittenden) involved building a large number of buildings of adobe and wood. The Mormons, and Brigham Young himself, profited from the sale of lumber and other supplies to the post. It appears that Gentiles also profited from this construction, and the post stimulated Utah's economy. There was some friction, mainly local, between soldiers and the Mormons.

In 1860 command of the camp was taken over by Colonel Philip St. George Cooke when Johnston was transferred to command the Department of the Pacific. By November of that year the post was cut back to 700 men and disposal of equipment, which had started in 1859, continued. On May 17, 1861, a month after the Civil War began, the War Department ordered Cooke to take his remaining command and leave. He was to dispose of everything and it is estimated that $4,000,000 worth of supplies were sold for $100,000. Cooke blew up surplus ammunition, tore down unsold houses and buildings, and by July 27, 1861, pulled out completely.[4] The fort's flagpole ironically went to grace the brow of a hill east of Brigham Young's residence, a gift of officers of the post.[5] President Young's business manager, H. B. Clawson, purchased about $40,000 worth of government "surplus." Flour for which the government had paid $28.40 sold for 52¢ for a hundred-pound sack. The Mormon settlers were able to obtain hardware, tools, wagons, harness, tents, clothing, and many other items.[6] Colonel Cooke, though a Virginian, was strongly devoted to the Union, and remained in that Union to fight for the North.[7]

The army also pulled almost completely out of the strategically located Fort Bridger. An important trading and military post on the Oregon Trail and the major fort west of Fort Laramie, Bridger had a long and controversial history. Jim Bridger, still an active guide and mountain man by the time of the Civil War, claimed rights to the property. The Mormons also had claims to the fort. After an active role as a military post in the Mormon War, Fort Bridger became a junction point and relay station for the new transcontinental telegraph. In May, 1861, Captain Jesse A. Gove took over with a small garrison. On August 9 the army withdrew most of its troops, leaving only a small force remaining on orders of Colonel Cooke to sell most of the fort's supplies. The Mormons once more laid claim to the post. The garrison was reduced even further in the fall of 1861.[8]

Politically the Mormons remained largely unto themselves. Most were not greatly interested in the political alignment of the United States except as it affected them, and desired merely to be left alone to make their own decisions. And, as the residents of Utah Territory, they had no national vote. Largely from New England and the Middle West, as well as from abroad, they had not associated themselves en masse with the Democrats, especially the Southern Democrats, or with any other party except when expedient. After all, it had been the Democratic administration of President Buchanan that had sent troops to invade them. Even the popular-sovereignty position of Illinois Democratic Senator Stephen A. Douglas, which would seem to fit the Mormons' aims of independence and state and territorial rights, did not entirely suit them. This dissatisfaction can be understood when Douglas's attitude toward the Mormons is considered.

At Springfield, Illinois, on June 12, 1857, Douglas spoke on the vital subjects of the time in relation to popular sovereignty, Kansas, Dred Scott, and Utah. In this address he was extremely critical of the Mormons, accusing them of being "bound by horrid oaths and terrible penalties, to recognize and maintain the authority of Brigham Young." Douglas felt the Mormons were resisting federal authority and attempting to subvert the United States. He charged them with cooperating with the Indians in robberies and murders. According to Douglas, "the knife must be applied to this pestiferous, disgusting cancer." If other measures failed he would dissolve the Territory because the Mormons "are alien enemies and outlaws, unfit to be citizens of a territory, much less ever become citizens of one of the free and independent states of this confederacy."[9]

Young undoubtedly remembered this later when he commented on the June, 1861, death of Senator Douglas. The Church leader reportedly said that "he [Douglas] should be president in the lower world and Tom Benton [late Senator from Missouri] should be his first counsellor."[10] Later, however, on August 5, Young tempered his criticism when he remarked that "Stephen A. Douglas was a far better man than President Abel [sic] Lincoln for he knew his feelings were hostile to this people."[11] It is not quite clear whether Young meant that Douglas or Lincoln was hostile.

The new Republican party certainly could not attract many Mormons. In 1856 the first Republican platform adopted at the National Convention proclaimed that it was the duty of Congress to "prohibit in the Territories those twin relics of barbarism, polygamy and slavery. . . ."[12] As for Lincoln, he had been an Illinois legislator and active in Whig party affairs at the time of the Mormon troubles in Illinois. Both Whigs and Democrats had courted the Mormons.[13] What support the Mormons gave had vacillated from one party to the other. But there seemed to be no especial animosity toward or advocacy of the Mormons by Lincoln. There is no known close relationship between Mormon leaders and Lincoln in the Illinois years.[14]

In his answer to Douglas's Springfield speech of 1857, Lincoln, on June 26, 1857, in the Illinois capital, did refer to the Mormons, but mainly in the context of his arguments with Senator Douglas over state sovereignty. He was critical of Douglas's suggestion to divide up Utah, as that would not be in line with the senator's view of popular sovereignty. Lincoln said: "I begin with Utah. If it prove to be true, as is probable, that the people of Utah are in open rebellion to the United States, then Judge Douglas is in favor of repealing their territorial organization, and attaching them to the adjoining States for judicial purposes. I say too, if they are in rebellion, they ought to be somehow coerced to obedience. . . ." He

was mainly attacking Douglas rather than supporting or criti-
cizing the Mormons, although his statement can be considered
critical despite his dexterous use of the word "if." He did add
that there was nothing in the U.S. Constitution or law against
polygamy.[15]

On April 10, 1860, at Bloomington, Illinois, Lincoln, still mainly
involved with Douglas, again referred to Utah. He pointed out
that a bill had passed the House of Representatives against polygamy, but had failed in the Senate. In the newspaper account of the
speech, "Mr. Lincoln said he *supposed* that the friends of popular
sovereignty would say—if they dared speak out—that *polygamy*
was wrong and slavery right; and therefore one might thus be put
down and the other not. . . ."[16] Thus, prior to his presidency, Lincoln did not seem concerned with the issue of Mormonism for its
own sake, but only within the political context of the day.

Another event which added to the Mormons' bad public image
was the Mountain Meadows Massacre, which occurred about
thirty-five miles southwest of Cedar City. The settlers of southern
Utah were upset, as was all of Utah, over the threat of invasion by
federal troops. In late summer of 1857 a group of emigrants
known as the Francher Train came through en route to California.
Among this group were some mounted emigrants who called
themselves the "Missouri Wildcats." The Wildcats set about causing trouble to settlers and Indians alike. Brigham Young issued orders that all emigrants were to pass through in peace. But his order
arrived too late. On Friday, September 11, Indians and men from
the Utah Militia, nearly all Mormons, went to the emigrant camp.
About 120 emigrants were disarmed and murdered, although 17
children were spared. The Mountain Meadows Massacre has been
termed the darkest hour in Utah and Mormon history. It greatly
exacerbated the anti-Mormon feeling throughout the nation.[17]
Thus, by the time the vital national questions were mounting to
the climax of secession there was already a history of great distrust
between Mormons and non-Mormons.

Utah, backed by the Mormon Church, was still struggling for
admission as a state. Its territorial delegates in Washington had
been lobbying for some time for statehood. Congressional Delegate William H. Hooper of Utah Territory wrote to Mormon
leader George Cannon in December, 1860, the month South Carolina seceded:

I think three-quarters of the Republicans of the house would vote for our admission; but I may be mistaken. Many say they would gladly "swap" the Gulf states for Utah. I tell them that *we show our loyalty by trying to get in, while others are trying to get out*, notwithstanding our grievances, which are far greater than those of any of the seceding states; *but that I consider we can redress our grievances better in the Union than out of it*; at least we'll give our worthy "Uncle" an opportunity in engrafting us into his family; and if he doesn't want us, we must then carve out our own future.[18]

What happened to Utah was not in the forefront of the pressing national issues of 1860. Nevertheless, the singular geographical position of the Territory would be a major geopolitical factor, particularly if war came. Many Americans felt the Mormons were disloyal to the United States, but few believed they were really for the South or the Confederacy. There were some, however, who did not make this important distinction. And as the national crisis deepened, the rumors, distortion, and distrust increased on the part of both Mormons and non-Mormons.

By the end of 1860 the majority of the troops at Fort Crittenden had been sent to New Mexico and Arizona. This relieved some of the anxiety in Utah, but there were many incidents there of friction between the federal judges and the Mormons. Utah Territorial Governor Alfred Cumming had a good deal to do with smoothing out some of the rough edges caused by the Mormon War and was at least tolerated by the Mormon hierarchy. Cumming was a native of Georgia and was best known for his role in the peace arrangements which ended the Mormon War. Cumming had had his troubles with General Johnston after arriving in the West as Buchanan's gubernatorial appointee. He is said to have been "simple-minded and credulous, assertive and somewhat pompous in manner and jealous of his personal authority."[19]

Of considerable interest to the outside world was the Mormon stand on slavery, which was never a significant institution or a point of great controversy within the Church or in Utah. In his best-selling volume of western travels, *An Overland Journey*, colorful and influential editor Horace Greeley of the New York *Tribune* reported an 1859 interview he had with Brigham Young. However accurate the actual quotations of the Mormon leader might be, they nevertheless constitute an important statement. When asked what the position of the Mormon Church was with respect to slavery, Greeley quoted Young as saying, "We consider it of divine institution, and not to be abolished until the curse pronounced on Ham shall have been removed from his descendants." Young said there were slaves in the territory, but did not say how many. "If slaves are brought here by those who owned them in the states, we do not favor their escape from the service of those owners," he said. Greeley then asked whether this meant that Utah would be a slave state when admitted to the Union. Young replied, "No; she will be a free state. Slavery here would prove useless and unprofitable. I regard it generally as a curse to the masters. I myself hire many laborers, and pay them fair wages; I could not afford to own them. I can do better than subject myself to an obligation to feed and clothe their families, to provide and care for them in sickness and health. Utah is not adapted to slave-labor."[20]

There seemed to be a sympathetic and paternalistic attitude in Utah toward blacks, although there were very few blacks, free or slave, in the Territory, for at this time there was only a small number of Mormons from the slave states. As has been pointed out, the 1860 census put the number of slaves in the Territory at just 29. The Utah Territorial Legislature in 1851 passed an act assuring that anyone bringing servants "justly bound to them" should be entitled to their service of labor. The legislature, however, provided for their humane treatment. Blacks were not allowed in the Mormon clergy until 1978.[21]

Journalist Greeley had not materially changed his 1859 appraisal of Utah and the Mormons by 1860–61:

In short, the federal judiciary, the federal executive, and the federal army, as now existing in Utah, are three transparent shams—three egregious farces; they cost the treasury very large sums to no purpose; and the sooner the governor, marshall, judges, etc., resign, and the army is withdrawn, the better for all but a handful of contractors. "Popular sovereignty" has such full swing here that Brigham Young carries the territory in his breeches' pocket without a shadow of opposition; for there is no real power here but that of "the church!" and he is practically the church.

Greeley went on to say that despite high spending by the federal government it was "powerless and despised." He urged that Brigham Young be reappointed governor, and that federal office-holders and the army be withdrawn. New trails to California should be opened to the North of Utah. "Let the Mormons have the territory to themselves . . . but cut its area."[22]

Connected with the East by the Pony Express, the citizens and leaders of Utah Territory were avidly and usually pessimistically interested in what was going on there. For instance, Brigham Young in a speech at Box Elder on June 7, 1860, said, "From the States' newspapers one might imagine that 'hell is for noon,' there—that hell is boiling over. They are nigh unto destruction, and it is for us to so live that we can gain the goodness, glory, and mercy of our God."[23] At times the Mormons seemed almost to revel in the turmoil in the East.

While reporting on the election of 1860, the *Deseret News* (the voice of Brigham Young and the Mormon Church) stated on November 7, before election results were known in Utah, ". . . there is and will be less anxiety in relation to what has or may hereafter transpire in the premises in this, than in any other Territory or portion of the Union, as the favors expected, if any, from the successful party are few indeed." The people of Utah learned of the election of Abraham Lincoln in the *Deseret News* of November 14, the paper then being a weekly, which had the "latest by Pony Express." On November 28 the paper editorialized on the "Prospective Dissolution." Interesting news was expected from Washington when Congress assembled:

There will be jolly times at the seat of Government during the session, and the members of Congress have enough business to attend to, in all probability, in which they will be more particularly interested and concerned than in the annihilation of the Saints; and may be expected to be otherwise engaged, than in providing for the overthrow and destruction of those, who by the spirit of inspiration, have long been advised of the calamities that were coming upon the nations, and upon the United States in particular, in consequence of the iniquities and abominations, of the people and their rejection of the gospel which has been proclaimed unto them.

This is only one of the forecasts of doom that had been uttered for months by Mormon leaders, and would be uttered in the years to come. And, of course, the Mormons were not the only ones to make dire predictions, although their twist was a bit different from others. The same editorial predicted that "The day is not far distant, when the United States Government will cease to be, and that the Union, about which the politicians have harped and poets sung, will be no more."[24]

There had been warnings, but the rulers and people "have heeded it not; and the finger of scorn and derision has been pointed at those who believed that the prophetic declarations of the servants of God, concerning the people of the United States, in consequence of their rejection of the principles of truth and the shedding of innocent blood, would be fulfilled." Joseph Smith was not a false prophet and his prophecies were being fulfilled. The Mormons have been "quietly looking on and watching the progress of events below from the tops of the mountains. . . . They have undeviatingly adhered to the principles of the Constitution, and will venerate them after Congress shall have held its last session, and the United States as a nation shall cease to exist."[25]

The *Deseret News* printed on December 24, 1860, the entire text of President Buchanan's "Message to Congress" including his summation of the need to bring Utah under "submission." On January 2, 1861, the paper again proclaimed, ". . . while the people and nations of the earth are warring among themselves, and seeking to destroy each other, peace according to the promise, may be expected to prevail in Utah; and the time may soon be present when those who will not take the sword to destroy their fellow man, shall flee hither for safety."

In a useful chronology of events, the *Journal History*, Young is quoted on September 13, 1860, as telling a meeting of bishops, "You may think that I am hard, but all I ask is, that the Bishops and people see the things of God and His Kingdom as I do." This, of course, was a frank admission of the overall policy of the Church which was thoroughly controlled by the way the leader saw things.[26]

Young, though no longer officially governor, as he had been until the appointment of Cumming, was in close touch with Territorial Delegate William H. Hooper. Hooper, a Democrat, was a native of Maryland, born in 1813. A merchant, he moved to Illinois in 1835 and then to Utah in 1850. He had been secretary of the Territory and served as a delegate to the Thirty-sixth Congress, 1859–61.[27] On November 19, 1860, Young wrote Hooper that the Democrats from outside the borders of Utah were "very much chopfallen at Lincoln's election."[28]

On December 20 Young wrote to Hooper,

By your letters and papers I perceive that the secession question was being violently agitated, but without much definite action. Latest accounts seem to indicate that the South will so far back down as to give "Old Abe" a trial as to what course he will pursue. . . . But while the waves of commotion are whelming nearly the whole country, Utah in her rock fortressess is biding her time to step in and rescue the constitution and aid all lovers of freedom in sustaining such laws as will secure justice and rights to all irrespective of creed or party.[29]

Though there was no way for Brigham Young to know it, South Carolina seceded on the same December 20 and the South of course did not back down.

In the Brigham Young Office Journal for December 30, 1860, the Church president is reported to have in the afternoon "exhorted the people to do right and sanctify themselves, and leave off their drinking. He remarked Br. Jno Taylor has showed us the dissolution of the Union, and the prospect of Zion being redeemed. . . . The President used a few expletives against Jas Buchanan, and remarked he has broken up the government."[30]

In further criticism of the national government, the *Millenial Star*, a Mormon paper espousing Church policy, published in Britain, complained about the quality of federal territorial appointees to Utah: "Generally speaking, the appointments have been made from amongst the personal friends of the Government officers, a large majority of whom had previously become obnoxious even to them, and an outlet was sought whereby they might get rid of them; and Utah has unfortunately been stocked with this class of officials."[31] This probably was not far from the mark as the overall record of territorial appointees in the West has generally been considered a sorry one.

The *Millennial Star* continued that these men were an "eternal disgrace of the Federal Government," and, further,

Their conduct has been so outrageously bad that they have either been removed by the government or induced by their friends to resign to save such disgrace. . . . The judicial dignity of the Federal Judges has been degraded and debased to that of the character of petty Indian traders, which business they have carried on contrary to the law which it was their sworn duty to magnify and make honorable. . . . Those who have not prostituted their commissions and perjured themselves by this unlawful and unholy traffic have fallen into other excesses equally repre-hensible. . . . The treatment of the Federal Government toward the cit-izens of Utah, by persisting to appoint such men to office, will ever be looked upon by them as an unjust and murderous plot for their destruc-tion. We have never asked of the General Government but one thing in the appointment of officers to Utah, which was, to send us good men, statesmen, men of intelligence, men of responsibility at home, men at least of good moral character, and not the rejected scum and rubbish of their political cesspool. But upon the other hand, men of no moral worth—those who could not be trusted at home, and had in every way rendered themselves unworthy of the confidence and esteem of all right-minded and thinking men, have universally been the class selected to hold Government appointments in Utah.[32]

Thus, by the end of 1860, Utah Territory and the Mormons were watching events far to the east with carping criticism, and, in a sense, with glee. This attitude was to strengthen and expand in the months to come.

NOTES

1. *Historical Statistics of the United States* (Washington, D.C.: U.S. Department of Commerce, 1960), p. 13.
2. Hubert Howe Bancroft, *History of Utah, 1540–1887* (San Francisco: History Co., 1890), p. 588.
3. *National Almanac and Annual Record for the Year 1863* (Philadelphia: George W. Childs, 1863), pp. 307, 309–10, 312.
4. The best summary of events during those years is Thomas G. Alexander and Leonard J. Arrington, "Camp in the Sagebrush: Camp Floyd, Utah, 1858–1861," *Utah Historical Quarterly*, 34 (Winter, 1966), 3–21.
5. Edward W. Tullidge, *History of Salt Lake City* (Salt Lake City: Star Printing Co., 1886), p. 248.
6. *Ibid.*
7. Richard W. Etulain, "A Virginian in Utah Chooses the Union: Col. Philip St. George Cooke in 1861," *Utah Historical Quarterly*, 42 (Fall, 1974), 381–85.
8. Fred R. Gowans and Eugene E. Campbell, *Fort Bridger, Island in the Wilder-ness* (Provo, Utah: Brigham Young University Press, 1975), pp. 116–20.
9. George U. Hubbard, "Abraham Lincoln as Seen by the Mormons," *Utah His-torical Quarterly*, 31 (Spring, 1963), 95; Brigham Henry Roberts, *A Com-prehensive History of the Church of Jesus Christ of Latter-day Saints, Cen-tury I* (Salt Lake City: Deseret News Press, 1930), vol. II, pp. 148–58.
10. Brigham Young Office Journal, June 12, 1861, Church Archives, Church of Jesus Christ of Latter-day Saints, Salt Lake City, Utah (hereafter cited as Church Archives).

11. *Ibid.*, August 5, 1861.
12. Edward Stanwood, *A History of the Presidency from 1788 to 1897* (Boston: Houghton Mifflin Co., 1912), vol. I, pp. 271–72.
13. Abraham Lincoln, *The Collected Works of Abraham Lincoln*, ed. Roy Basler (New Brunswick, N.J.: Rutgers University Press, 1953), vol. I, p. 206.
14. For a sound, although pro-Mormon, summary, see Hubbard, "Abraham Lincoln as Seen by the Mormons," pp. 93–108.
15. Lincoln, *Collected Works*, vol. II, pp. 398–99.
16. *Ibid.*, vol. IV, pp. 41–42.
17. Much has been written on the Mountain Meadows Massacre, but probably the leading source is Juanita Brooks, *The Mountain Meadows Massacre* (Norman: University of Oklahoma Press, 1962).
18. Roberts, *Comprehensive History*, vol. V, p. 2. Hooper to Cannon, Dec. 16, 1860, as quoted in *Millennial Star*, vol. 23, pp. 29–30.
19. Allen Johnson and Dumas Malone, eds., *Dictionary of American Biography* (New York: Scribner, 1946), vol. III, pp. 592–93.
20. Horace Greeley, *An Overland Journey from New York to San Francisco in the Summer of 1859* (New York: C. M. Saxton, Barker, 1860), pp. 210–11.
21. Dennis L. Lythgoe, "Negro Slavery in Utah," *Utah Historical Quarterly*, 39 (Winter, 1971), 51–54. Also of importance is Dennis L. Lythgoe, "Negro Slavery and Mormon Doctrine," *Western Humanities Review*, 21 (Autumn, 1967), 327–38.
22. Greeley, *An Overland Journey*, pp. 228–29.
23. *Deseret News*, July 25, 1860.
24. *Ibid.*, Nov. 28, 1860.
25. *Ibid.*
26. Journal History, Church Archives.
27. *Biographical Directory of the American Congress 1774–1961* (Washington, D.C.: Government Printing Office, 1961), p. 1073.
28. Brigham Young Letters, Beinecke Rare Book and Manuscript Library, Yale University, New Haven, Conn., Nov. 19, 1861. Also see Gustive Larson, "Utah and the Civil War," *Utah Historical Quarterly*, 33 (Winter, 1965), 56.
29. Brigham Young Letters, Beinecke Library.
30. Church Archives.
31. "Journal History," from *Millennial Star*, Nov. 10, 1860.
32. *Ibid.*

CHAPTER

11

"There Is No More a United States"

As the year 1861 opened, the Mormon Church through its leaders and its newspaper continued to comment on the momentous events of the breaking of the nation: the secession of the South, the setting up of the Confederacy, the new federal President. Their view differed from that of either the North or the South, although their opinions were not widely disseminated outside Utah. The Mormons were vehemently forthright in their condemnation of both sides in the approaching civil conflict. Circumstances dictated that they could not be as detached as a foreign power would be, but they could take a watchful, waiting, tongue-clacking attitude, while expressing their viewpoints frequently in a sarcastic, often derisive manner. This critical attitude was interpreted by the more radical and ardent Unionists in the East as an indication of the Mormons' basic disloyalty. At such a moment of passion, any group which did not support either side wholeheartedly was suspect by both sides.

News had been received in Utah that the U.S. Army was moving regular units from the western posts. Some malicious satisfaction was expressed over the plight of the army, which so recently had occupied parts of Utah. The *Deseret News* commented, on February 6, 1861,

To evince the sentiments and feelings thus entertained and so often expressed towards the unfortunate beings who became the intended instruments of destruction, as plotted against the people of Utah, by the out-going administration, which has by malfeasance, profaned the constitution, overthrown the government and disrupted the Union, they [the Mormons] have been and still are ready and willing to extend to them any aid and comfort, not in violation of the constitution which they, as citizens, so much revere and ardently support.

Brigham Young early in 1861 set the policy of the Mormons toward the sectional crisis rapidly evolving in the East. At the Tabernacle on February 10, 1861, he told the populace:

Where is there a nation that acknowledges the Supreme God to be their President and their King? The best form of manmade government upon the earth is that of a nation now breaking to pieces. Have they ever acknowledged God? No . . . the nation is ruined and will crumble to pieces. They will destroy themselves. Joseph [Smith] rose up and said—"I will save them, if they will let me." He stepped forth like a man and proffered his services to save the nation that is now breaking; and he would have saved it, if they had permitted him. . . . Is the form of the Government ruined? Has its form become evil? No! but the administrators of the Government are evil. As we have said many times, it is the best form of human government ever lived under; but it has as corrupt a set to administer it as God ever permitted to disgrace his footstool. There is the evil. Can they better the condition of our country? No! they will make it worse every time they attempt to do so.[1]

Young was naturally critical of President Buchanan and even of New York Senator William H. Seward, soon to be Secretary of State. Of the southern leaders he said, "They will prove by their conduct, whether they are capable of forming and sustaining a government for the Southern States that have seceded."[2] The Church president continued on the same theme:

There is no more a United States. Can they amalgamate and form a government? No. Will they have ability to form a government and continue? No, they will not . . . and if a state has a right to secede, so has a Territory, and so has a county from a State or Territory, and a town from a county, and a family from neighborhood, and you will have perfect anarchy. . . . What will King Abraham do? I do not know, neither do I care. It is no difference what he does, of what any of them do. Why? God will accomplish his own purposes, and they may do or not do, they may take the road that leads to the right, or they may take the road that leads to the left, and which ever road they do take they wish they had taken the other. . . . "Mormonism" will live and God will promote it.[3]

Young exhorted the brethren not to boast over the downfall of their enemies for "God has come out of his hiding-place, and has commenced to vex the nation that has rejected us. . . . It will not be patched up—it never can come together again—. . . in a short time it will be like water spilled on the ground, and like chaff upon the summer threshing floor, until those wicked stewards are cut off. If our present happy form of government is sustained, which I believe it will be, it will be done by the people I am now looking upon in connection with their brethren and their offspring."[4] Young continued, "The present Constitution, with a few alterations of a trifling nature, is just as good as we want, and if it is sustained on this land of Joseph, it will be done by us and our posterity. Our national brethren do not know how to do it. They are not capable of controlling their own passions, to say nothing of ruling a nation. . . . We are serving a King who can control his passions."[5]

The theme that the Mormons would inherit the remains of the nation torn asunder and the theme of their belief in the Constitution were expressed often. These two themes were intertwined, with the Divine power being on the side of the Mormons, after others had deserted or had never found the true God and true faith. There was also the understandable condemnation of the Buchanan administration, a lack of confidence in the forthcoming Lincoln presidency, and a skeptical view of both North and South, as well as a continuous thread of "We told you so," as the news from the East became increasingly bleak.

The ubiquitous and adventurous British travel-writer Richard Burton, who was later to translate the *Arabian Nights*, visited "the city of the Saints" in mid-1860. Burton found Great Salt Lake City a pious and generally peaceful community. It was, he wrote, "as safe as at St. James Square, London. There are perhaps not more than twenty-five or thirty constables or policemen in the whole place."[6] There were, of course, some drinking establishments and some typical western devilment which existed despite the Mormons' strict moral code. One source of restraint on behavior, he had been told, was that "Gentiles often declare that the Prophet is acquainted with their every word half an hour after it is spoke. . . . There is no secret from the head of the Church and State; every thing from the highest to the lowest detail of private and public life, must be brought to the ear and submitted to the judgment of the father confessor-in-chief [Young]."[7]

But the Sunday meetings in the Tabernacle or in the partly open-air Bowery were typical of the society of Utah. The Bowery, roofed with bushes and boughs but open on the sides, held some 3,000 people and was often full. The congregation sat on long benches facing the musical ensemble consisting of a violin, bass, and four singers in front of the stage. Most of the women wore sunbonnets and neat but plain calico dresses, though a few affected more citified finery. The men in general wore plain homespun, except for some of the leaders who dressed in solemn black broadcloth. All wore their hats until the main address began.[8]

According to Burton, the highlights of these meetings were the addresses of Brigham Young. As the British writer put it,

The Prophet was dressed as usual, in gray homespun and home-woven; he wore . . . a tall, steeple-crowned straw hat, with a broad black ribbon, and he had the rare refinement of black kid gloves. . . . Mr. Brigham Young removed his hat, advanced to the end of the tribune, expectorated stooping over the spittoon . . . restored the balance of fluid by a glass of water . . . and, leaning slightly forward upon both hands propped on the green baize of the tribune, addressed his followers. The discourse began slowly; word crept titubantly after word, and the opening phrases were hardly audible; but as the orator warmed, his voice rose high and sonorous, and a fluency so remarkable succeeded falter and hesitation, that . . . the latter seemed almost to have been a work of art. The manner was pleasing and animated, and the matter fluent, impromptu, and well turned, spoken rather than preached; if it had a fault it was rather rambling and unconnected. Of course, colloquialisms of all kinds were introduced. . . . The gestures were easy and rounded, not without a certain grace, though evidently untaught. . . . The address was long. God is a mechanic. Mormonism is a great fact. Religion has made him (the speaker) the happiest of men.[9]

After a personal interview, Burton described Young as looking younger than his nearly sixty years, with hardly a gray thread in his thick hair which was parted on the side.

The forehead is somewhat narrow, the eyebrows are thin, the eyes between gray and blue, with a calm, composed, and somewhat reserved expression. . . . The nose, which is fine and somewhat sharp-pointed is bent a little to the left. The lips are close like the New Englander's and the teeth, especially those of the lower jaw, are imperfect. . . . The figure is somewhat large, broad-shouldered and stooping a little when standing. The Prophet's dress was neat and plain as a Quaker's, all gray homespun, except the cravat and waistcoat. His coat was of antique cut, and, like the pantaloons, baggy, and the buttons were black. A neck-tie of dark silk, with a large bow, was loosely passed round a starchless collar, which turned down of its own accord. The waistcoat was of black silk . . . and a plain gold chain was passed into the pocket. . . . Altogether the Prophet's appearance was that of a gentleman farmer in New England. . . . His manner is at once affable and impressive, simple and courteous; his want of pretension contrasts favorably with certain pseudo-prophets that I have seen. . . . He shows no sign of dogmatism, bigotry, or fanaticism. . . . He impresses a stranger with a certain sense of power; his followers are, of course wholly fascinated by his superior strength of brain. . . . His temper is even and placid; his manner is cold—in fact, like his face, somewhat bloodless . . . and, where occasion requires, he can use all the weapons of ridicule to direful effect. . . . He often reproves his erring followers in purposely violent language. . . . Yet he converses with ease and correctness, has neither snuffle or pompousness. . . . He assumes no airs of extra sanctimoniousness, and has the plain, simple manners of honesty. His followers deem him an angel of light, his foes a goblin damned; he is, I presume, neither one nor the other. . . . He has been called hypocrite, swindler, forger, murderer. No one looks it less. . . . Finally, there is a total absence of pretension in his manner, and he has been so long used to power that he cares nothing for its display. The arts by which he rules the heterogeneous mass of conflicting elements are indomitable will, profound secrecy, and uncommon astuteness.[10]

Not only did Brigham Young and the Mormon people attract travelers and avid readers of their writings, but the physical appearance of that far-off "City of the Saints" intrigued those to whom it was as remote as the mountains of the moon. As the city burst on the watchful tourist from the canyons cutting through the Wasatch Mountains, it must have seemed strange indeed. After days and weeks of monotonous, near-desert, suddenly below lay a long belt of rich green between the mountains and the distant shimmering waters of Great Salt Lake. Orchards, fields, and especially gardens gave it the appearance of an immense and anomalous oasis. Many travelers must have consciously or unconsciously inquired, "What hath man wrought," how and why? But most impressive of all was the city itself, with the carefully laid out, broad streets, the large tree-sheltered lots: urban planning at its best, for the day. Here was the proud showplace of the Mormon world. Burton described it as a "modern Athens" without the Acropolis. But the Acropolis, in a sense, was coming. Temple Square was already the focal point of the city and the Temple, the Tabernacle and other buildings soon were to make an Acropolis. None of the houses was whitewashed, except that of the Prophet Young. The building material was principally sun-dried adobe of a "dull leaden blue" deepening to the gray shingles of the roofs. There was a strong suggestion of the "old country," only neater and more organized.[11]

While the streets were unpaved, they were tree-lined, with solidly built private homes of adobe or wood and a few buildings of stone, many barnshaped and unpretentious. It spoke neither of affluence nor of poverty, but of a determined, almost superhuman, energy that had not yet had time for embellishments. After the first impression of possible monotony, the visitor would discover that there were social halls where dances were extremely popular; and an attractive theater was being planned. Everyone had access to the public library, under certain restrictions, and there was a reading room for newspapers and magazines from throughout the world. There were the Universal Scientific Society and the Polysophical Society; the Deseret Philharmonic Society had been in existence since 1855. Other organizations included the Deseret Theological Institute, dedicated to making known "the principles of light and truth," and the Church-run Relief Society, which ministered to the needy, eliminating the necessity for poorhouses.[12]

For many, life was highly organized, often on a serious, almost grim plane. The flavor of northern Europe and Britain was present, for by 1860 about a third of the population was from Great Britain, with a sizeable contingent of Danes, Swedes, and Norwegians, plus those born in America, primarily from New England, the mid-Atlantic states, and the Midwest.[13] Burton summed it up when he wrote: "Upon the whole the Mormon settlement was a vast improvement upon its contemporaries in the valleys of the Mississippi and Missouri."[14] While not wishing to commend the spiritual or leveling materialistic aspects of the Mormon Church, Burton felt that the emigrants to Utah had gained much by their long and arduous transfer from the squalor and wretched conditions of their working-class lives in Britain or on the continent.[15]

In addition to his important published discourses such as that of February 10, Brigham Young is credited with other expressions of attitude in early 1861 as he watched the momentous events to the east. He wrote to Delegate Hooper on January 17: "I perceive from news brought by Pony Express on the 14th that you have presented our petition for admission, constitution, etc., but there is no word as to what action if any has been taken. . . . Tell them that they can do as they please about the matter, but our opinion is that *they had better admit Utah now while* they have the opportunity." [16]

It is recorded in the Office Journal of January 23 that:

The President is usually cheerful, the present distracted state of the affairs of the U.S. following so soon after their wicked attempts to root up the Kingdom of God, and afflict his saints inspires the President with strong hopes for the prosperity of the cause of God. . . . But he occasionally remarks the discovery of a gold mine might be the means of breaking us up. The President's feelings are not those of triumph over a fallen enemy, but merely rejoicing in the hope that their afflictions will bring them nearer to God. His worst wishes are that they may be brought to do right and know right. [17]

It is interesting that Young was worried at that time over the possibility that discovery of precious metals would bring outsiders into Utah and dilute the Mormon community. Just such an attempt was to be made by General Patrick Connor and his soldiers in the next three years or so.

Mormon President Young at this time commented frequently on the news brought to Utah by Pony Express. On January 25 he remarked, ". . . if Abraham Lincoln when inaugurated would coerce the South there would be a pretty fight and if he did not he would be no President at all. . . . The President further remarked that when Anarchy and confusion reigned the Devil's poor prospered." [18] The following day, President Young conversed with the brethren upon the course the government was taking. He observed that "the Lord is taking the Spirit of wisdom from them." [19] On January 28, Young is quoted as saying, "the news from the States would be extremely interesting about the middle of next April." [20] Thus Brigham Young, acute observer that he was, correctly predicted, as did others, several events and trends, although he was mistaken as to the demise of the Union.

Young kept expressing these views during the period of transition of the federal government. "He knew the reason why this Government was in trouble, they had killed Joseph Smith and they would have to pay for it as the Jews did in killing Jesus. . . . The President further remarked there is no union in the North or in the South—the nation must crumble to nothing. They charged us with being rebels and rebels they will have in their Government. South Carolina has committed treason, and if Prest. Buchanan had been a smart man he would have hung up the first men who rebelled in South Carolina."[21] While strong against the Buchanan administration and national policy in general, Young did not spare the incoming Republicans. As to Secretary of State–designate William H. Seward, Young "observed he was not a man of much talent but had been pushed into notice, although he had a capacity to adapt himself to his Company, and present circumstances."[22]

At the Tabernacle in Great Salt Lake City on February 17, Young proclaimed to the public on two of his favorite subjects: "When I hear of the Breathren [sic] and sisters going after gold—the riches and wealth of the earth—I think that if they had it in the spirit-world they could not do anything with it. . . . Those who possess wealth must leave it here for the Saints, and the Saints will become heirs of it. . . ."[23] Young was continually trying to prevent nearly all prospecting, especially for gold and other precious metals, for he felt extensive mining would corrupt his followers. The little mining undertaken was for iron, coal, and lead, and such enterprises were carried out because of the need for industrial minerals. In the same discourse he also forecast, "That Government known as the United States has become like water spilled on the ground, and other governments will follow."[24] In speeches and writings at this time he was continually predicting the destruction of the nations on earth, and implying that the people would eventually have to turn to the Saints.

The Mormons were already cognizant of the 1832 "Revelation and Prophecy" of Joseph Smith, which was used to show the mystic powers of Smith as a "Seer and Revelator." "Verily, thus saith the Lord, concerning the wars that will shortly come to pass, beginning at the rebellion of South Carolina, which will eventually terminate in the death and misery of many souls," began Smith's prophecy. While South Carolina was the first state to secede and was a leader in secession, it should be remembered that at the time of Smith's prognostication, South Carolina was deeply involved in the "nullification crisis" which generated threats of civil war. South Carolina was already marked for radical action when Smith put forth his revelation.[25] Smith continued: "The days will come that war will be poured out upon all nations, beginning at that place; for behold, the Southern States shall be divided against the Northern States, and the Southern States will call on other nations. . . . And it shall come to pass, after many days, slaves shall rise up against their masters, who shall be marshalled and disciplined for war." Smith was correct about the division of states, that was already fairly easy to be seen. But there were never any major slave uprisings in the 1860–61 secession crisis.[26] Smith continued to forecast that the remnants left after this war would gather themselves together and there would be more bloodshed. After this, people would turn to the Saints; the day of the Lord would come for the Mormons.[27] Like all prophecies it was broad enough to be accurate in some details, and general enough to cover quite a spread of events.

Just two days before President Buchanan left office he signed an act which cut off the western portion of Utah and created out of it the Territory of Nevada. Western Utah, while sparsely populated, had been largely Gentile.[28] There were further border adjustments in 1862 and 1866, adding more Utah land to Nevada. On March 2, 1861, Young spoke of the new President as "Abel Lincoln," and remarked, "we cannot tell what he is till circumstances compel him to develop his true character; many supposed that Pres. Buchanan was a pretty fine gentleman before he was made President, but when he came into power his true character was seen in the oppressive course he took towards the Mormons."[29]

The downfall of the Union was predicted by the *Deseret News* on March 6 and again on April 24.[30] Thus, even before actual Civil War broke out, the Mormon position and prophecy were clear. Young kept up the theme, and was still uncertain about and certainly suspicious of President Lincoln, often mocking him with sarcastic words. When Young heard of the President-elect's comments en route to Washington, the Mormon leader laughed heartily and then remarked, "It was a pretty cute remark of Abraham Lincoln comparing the Union to a free love arrangement."[31]

The Church leader kept on speaking out, as in the Tabernacle on March 10: "Brother Hyde has remarked that State after State is leaving the Union, but there is no Union to leave; it is all disunion. Our Government is shivered to pieces—it is all disunion, more to be made manifest. But the Kingdom of God will increase."[32] Not until July did the *Deseret News* report on Brigham Young's March 10 speech, and then it quoted him as saying, "We are, at the present time, the only people in the United States that are willing to be governed by the Constitution, and to grant to all men the same liberties that we ourselves enjoy. . . . To be sure there are a great many who pretend to honor the Constitution, but they are determined in the North and the South that they will fight each other, Constitution or no Constitution."[33] In a gathering of Church officials in the Church Historian's Office on that same day, Young is quoted as saying "he did not wish Utah mixed up with the secession movement."[34]

Brigham Young further commented on the new President on March 15, in conversation:

Abel Lincoln has expressed a determination to keep the Union in as good condition as he received it. He remarked that Abel Lincoln was no friend to Christ, particularly, he had never raised his voice in our favor when he was aware that we were being persecuted . . . time would show what course he would pursue. Abel Lincoln was in the hands of the Lord and He would control him to carry out His designs. He further remarked that President Buchanan had been raised up as much as Pharaoh was. Buchanan was raised up to split the Union.[35]

But by the end of March Young was able to write to Utah Territorial Delegate Hooper in Washington:

We like Mr. Lincoln's inaugural address very well, and wish you to call to his attention that portion in which he claims to be the President of the whole people, and ask him whether he purposes ruling as a father or a tyrant. If he replies "as a father," ask him to appoint our officers from the list in your possession, or else appoint none, and continue none now in office here, except Judge Kinney, and to by no means permit Postmaster Morrell to return here officially. If we cannot have our officers appointed from actual residents among us, which is but right, we had much rather have none.[36]

The letter to Hooper indicates another reason why Young and Utah had almost constant trouble with federal officials, at least until after mid-1863. The Mormons took their popular sovereignty very seriously. Lincoln obviously did not comply with Young's request, and appointed his own men from far to the east of Utah. The results were generally unpleasant for both the Mormons and the officials.

By April 1 Delegate Hooper had presented to the U.S. Senate a list of names of persons from Utah to fill the territorial government offices, including the name of Brigham Young for governor.[37]

In another important message to Hooper on April 11, Young told the delegate:

It was quite proper and correct to suggest to Mr. Lincoln that our appointments belong to us, by every just construction of the spirit of the Constitution. But should he be unwilling or unable to make our appointments from names you may present . . . it will doubtless still be the best policy to patiently bide our time, for plausible pretext against us would tend more than aught else to heal the present breach and unite them in a crusade to Utah, like the Irishman and his wife, who both pitched into the man who parted them when fighting.[38]

Young here expressed in a different context the idea that Secretary of State Seward put forward, of picking a foreign war in order to bring the sections of the United States together in a common cause. But he showed, despite his perception, that he was out of touch with the seriousness of the North-South struggle. It hardly would have been likely in 1861 that the sectional struggle would have been healed or postponed by any second expedition against the Mormons. Young undoubtedly overestimated the national importance of the Mormon question, or the settlements in Utah, despite their strategic geographical position.

At the April Church Conference in Salt Lake City the leaders had an opportunity to expound on the crisis to the east and to set the policy for the Mormons and Utah. In reality, of course, that policy was set by Brigham Young. In a discourse called "True Testimony-Preparation for Coming Events-Corruption of the Government, etc.," Brigham Young in the Tabernacle on April 6 proclaimed,

We are not now mingling in the turmoil of strife, warring, and contention, that we would have been obliged to have mingled in had not the Lord suffered us to have been driven to these mountains—one of the greatest blessings that could have been visited upon us. . . . His wrath will be poured out upon the nations of the earth. We see the nations steadily driving along to the precipice. The Lord has spoken from the heavens, and he is about to fulfil the prophecies of his ancient and modern prophets. . . . Much has been said in regard to the Government in which we live. We say that it is the best form of human government upon the earth. The laws and institutions are good, but how can a republican government stand? . . . There is only one way for it to stand. . . . It can endure, as the government of heaven endures, upon the eternal rock of truth and virtue; and that is the only basis upon which any government can endure. Let the people become corrupt, let them begin to deceive each other, and they will all deceive themselves, as our Government has. . . . Our present President, what is his strength? It is like a rope of sand, or like a rope made of water. What can he do? Very little. Has he power to execute the laws? No . . . I feel chagrined and mortified when I reflect upon the condition of my nation. . . . I feel disgraced in having been born under a government that has so little power, disposition, and influence for truth and right; but I cannot help it. . . . They have left the paths of truth and virtue, they have joined themselves to falsehood, they have made lies their refuge, they have turned aside the innocent from their rights, and justified the iniquitous doers. They have justified thieving and lying and every specie of debauchery; they have fostered those who have purloined money out of the public treasury—those who have plundered the coffers of the people. . . . Shame, shame on the rulers of the nation! I feel myself disgraced to hail such men as my countrymen. . . . The whole government is gone; it is as weak as water. . . . Mobs will not decrease, but will increase until the whole Government becomes a mob, and eventually it will be State against State, city against city, neighbourhood against neighbourhood, Methodists against Methodists, and so on. . . . It will be the same with other denominations of professing Christians, and will be Christian against Christian, and man against man; and those who will not take up the sword against their neighbours must flee to Zion. Where is Zion? Let us be prepared to receive the honourable men of the earth—those who are good.[39]

As he did so often, Young overstated the case, but he wanted to show the people where the Mormons stood. There is a mixture of exaggeration, truth, piety, and politics in most of his addresses.

Also on April 6, Church leader Heber C. Kimball put the Mormons' situation accurately: "President Young is our leader, and has been all the time since the death of Joseph Smith the Prophet. He can govern this people with his hands in his pockets, and they are not governed one whit by the men that are sent here."[40] Kimball at this time was chief counsellor to Brigham Young and, along with John Taylor, one of the most powerful personalities in the faith. On April 14 in the Tabernacle Kimball said, "In this country the North and South will exert themselves against each other, and ere long the whole face of the United States will be commotion, fighting one against another, and they will destroy their nationality. They have never done anything for this people, and I don't believe they ever will. I have never prayed for the destruction of this Government, I know that dissolution, sorrow, weeping, and distress are in store for the inhabitants of the United States, because of their conduct towards the people of God."[41] A forthright statement, but it does not carry the power of the words of Brigham Young, the true head and body of the Church.

In addition to proclaiming the policy of the Church politically and socially and within the context of the Union, Brigham Young often referred to the institution of polygamy. In the Tabernacle on April 7 he asserted that "If the plurality of wives is to pander to the low passions of men and women, the sooner it is abolished the better. . . . The time is coming when the Lord is going to raise up a holy nation. He will bring up a royal Priesthood upon the earth, and he has introduced a plurality of wives for that express purpose, and not to gratify lustful passion in the least. . . . I never entered into the order of plurality of wives to gratify passion."[42]

Elder John Taylor, among others, added to the statements on the Union when, in the Tabernacle on April 28, he proclaimed,

The people of this nation are evidently bent upon their own destruction, and they are full of enmity, hatred, war and bloodshed. To all human appearance, it would seem that they will not stop short of the entire destruction of this great nation. . . . They have neglected righteousness, justice and truth for years that are past and gone; they have allowed the honest, the virtuous, the just, and the true-hearted to be abused and afflicted and they have winked and mocked at their sufferings; and not only so, but they have unblushingly used their force and strength to bring about the destruction of God's people. . . . They have the same God to apply to in the North as in the South, the same kind of religion, but their religion does not teach them to have any confidence in the all-protecting army of Jehovah, for their God has no eyes, no ears, no power, he is without body or parts. . . . Both the North and the South are praying to the same God, that they may have the power to destroy their enemies. Who are their enemies? All good Christians. Therefore, if their God should hear and answer them, they would all be utterly annihilated.[43]

Thus, Mormons were continuously exhorted, and some of the message seeped eastward. This flow of highly colored rhetoric together with long-standing suspicions undoubtedly caused much of the Gentile wariness and hostility that bordered on perceiving the Mormons as treasonous. Although the words of the Saints had little immediate effect, both North and South may have accumulated a backlog of distrust which those already dubious could feed upon. Critical, carping, self-righteous, and heavy-handed as the Mormon statements were, they can hardly be construed as treasonous, though in the heat of the times it is easy to see how the label of treason came to be bandied about.

By May of 1861, the war to the east had by no means reached its fury, but, following Fort Sumter and Lincoln's call for volunteers, the middle southern states of North Carolina, Arkansas, Tennessee, and Virginia had seceded. Brigham Young is reported in the Office Journal of May 1 as seeming "pleased with the news which showed more and more secession, and each party was preparing for war, thus giving the Kingdom of God an opportunity of being established upon the Earth."[44] On May 11, "The President [Young] remarked upon the subject of secession that it resolved itself into a few words, that the sentiment of the South was that if the North would not deliver up our fugitive slaves we will leave the family."[45] In late May the *Deseret News* proclaimed, with evident pleasure: ". . . while peace reigns in Utah, civil war, with all its horrors prevails among those who earnestly desired to see the soil of these valleys crimsoned with the blood of the Saints."[46]

But the most important action of May, 1861, was the quiet departure of Governor Cumming and his wife on May 17. As it was, Cumming's leaving seemed fairly hasty. On May 24, 1861, en route east, he wrote Acting Governor Francis [or Frank] Wootton from Fort Bridger that he regretted not seeing him before he left, and that the acting governor would find a schedule of public property and other papers Cumming had not been able to turn over on the eve of his departure.[47] As one historian put it, Cumming left, but "the thanks of a grateful community were sent after him for the faithful performance of his service towards them and to the General Government."[48] Secretary and now Acting Governor Wootton also sent in his resignation, but stayed on until new officials arrived.[49]

Traveler Richard Burton talked with Governor Cumming in 1860 and commented,

The scrupulous and conscientious impartiality which he had brought to the discharge of his difficult and delicate duties, and, more still, his resolution to treat the Saints like Gentiles and citizens, not as Digger Indians or felons, have won him scant favor from either party. The anti-Mormons use very hard language and declare him to be a Mormon in Christian disquise. The Mormons, though more moderate, can never, by their very organization, rest contented without the combination of the temporal with the spiritual power. The governor does not meet his predecessor, the ex-governor, Mr. Brigham Young, from prudential motives, except on public duty.[50]

It was officially reported that the governor left on a leave of absence, but it was presumed he did not expect or intend to return.[51] Nearly sixty years old and a staunch southerner, Cumming did not wait to be replaced by the new Republican administration but went to his home near Augusta, Georgia, where he lived in retirement until his death in 1873. The *Deseret News* had often written kindly of him and it seems that the Mormons had some respect for him, far more, to be sure, than for the next two governors. Acting Governor Wootton, the territorial secretary, hardly made a ripple in events during his tenure, for the Territory was obviously still very much under the control of Brigham Young, and there would soon be a new governor, at least in name, appointed by President Lincoln.

It was apparent that the Mormons' entreaties had failed to influence the new President to appoint a local governor, namely Brigham Young. And it really didn't matter at this time whether there was a territorial governor or not. Asked by editor and author T. B. H. Stenhouse how Acting Governor Wootton would get along in his new role, Cumming replied, "Get along? well enough, if he will do nothing. There is nothing to do. Alfred Cumming is Governor of the Territory, but Brigham Young is Governor *of the people*. By_____, I am not fool enough to think otherwise. Let Wootton learn that, and he will get along, and the sooner he knows that the better. This is a curious place."[52] Wootton, a Maryland lawyer, had received substantial recommendations for the post of secretary in the spring of 1860. A number of prominent citizens commended him to President Buchanan as did some thirty members of the Democratic State Convention held in Baltimore in March, a group of Maryland Democratic legislators, the Upper Marlboro County Bar, and Maryland Democratic senators and congressmen. Wootton had been active in support of Buchanan in 1856, and had lived some time in the West.[53]

By mid-1861, the Latter-day Saints and Utah were still a bit uncertain, but were going their own way without the presence of the army, and were interpreting events from their own theological viewpoint. There is no evidence at this time or later of any overt or covert agitation by the new Confederate States of America to entice Utah, though they must have been aware of the Mormon displeasure with many actions of the federal Union.

As was customary, Utah citizens made quite a show of celebrating the Fourth of July in an attempt to demonstrate their heartfelt loyalty to the Declaration of Independence and the Constitution. There were the usual parades and speeches suitable to the occasion. At the Bowery John Taylor said,

In regard to the present strife, it is a warfare among brothers. . . . No parties in the United States have suffered more frequently and more grievously than we have in the violation of our national compact. . . . Those who should have been our fathers and protectors, have thirsted for our blood and made an unconstitutional use of the power vested in their hands to exterminate us from the earth. Still we are loyal, unwavering, unflinching in our integrity; we have not swerved nor faltered in the path of duty. Shall we join the North to fight the South? No! Shall we join the South against the North? As emphatically, No! Why? . . . We have no hand in the matter. . . . We know no North, no South, no East, no West; we abide strictly and positively by the Constitution . . . the Constitution of the United States has ever been respected and honored by us. We consider it one of the best national instruments ever framed. Nay, further, Joseph Smith in his day said it was given by inspiration of God.[54]

At the same celebration Mormon Elder G. A. Smith asserted: "We are at the present time the only people in the United States that are willing to be governed by the Constitution, and to grant to all men the same liberties that we ourselves enjoy. . . . To be sure, there are a great many who pretend to honour the Constitution; but they are determined in the North and the South that they will fight each other, Constitution or no Constitution."[55]

NOTES

1. *Deseret News*, Feb. 27, 1861; also *Journal of Discourses Delivered by President Brigham Young, His Two Counsellors, the Twelve Apostles, and Others*, reported by G. D. Watt and J. V. Long (Liverpool: ed. and pub. by George Q. Cannon, 1964 photo-repr. ed.), vol. VIII, pp. 320–24 (hereafter cited as *Journal of Discourses*).
2. *Ibid.*
3. *Ibid.*
4. *Ibid.*
5. *Ibid.*
6. Richard F. Burton, *The City of the Saints, and Across the Rocky Mountains to California, 1860* (New York: Harper & Brothers, 1862), p. 224.
7. *Ibid.*
8. Burton, *City of the Saints*, pp. 227, 258; Bancroft, *Utah*, pp. 588–89.
9. Burton, *City of the Saints*, p. 261.
10. *Ibid.*, pp. 238–40.
11. Richard F. Burton, *The Look of the West, 1860: Across the Plains to California* (Lincoln: University of Nebraska Press, 1963), pp. 224–25, taken from Burton's earlier works. Tullidge, *History of Salt Lake City*, pp. 691–94. Also A. Howard Cutting, Journal of a Trip by Overland Route from Illinois to Sacramento, 1863, California File, Huntington Library, pp. 57–58.
12. Bancroft, *Utah*, pp. 578–90.
13. *Ibid.*, p. 589.
14. Burton, *The Look of the West, 1860*, p. 246.
15. *Ibid.*, p. 249.
16. Brigham Young Letters, Beinecke Library.
17. Brigham Young Office Journal.
18. *Ibid.*
19. *Ibid.*
20. *Ibid.*
21. *Ibid.*, Feb. 2, 1861.
22. *Ibid.*, Feb. 12, 1861.
23. *Journal of Discourses*, vol. VIII, p. 330.
24. *Ibid.*
25. Joseph Smith, "A Revelation and Prophecy: By the Prophet, Seer and Revelator," given December 25, 1832, in *Pearl of Great Price* (Liverpool: n.p., 1851).
26. *Ibid.*
27. *Ibid.*
28. Orson P. Whitney, *History of Utah* (Salt Lake City: Cannon, 1893), vol. II, p. 17.
29. Brigham Young Office Journal.
30. *Deseret News*, Mar. 6, Apr. 24, 1861.
31. Brigham Young Office Journal, Feb. 20, 1861.
32. *Journal of Discourses*, vol. VIII, p. 369.
33. *Deseret News*, July 10, 1861.

34. Preston Nibley, *Brigham Young, the Man and His Work* (Salt Lake City: Deseret News Press, 1936), p. 369.

35. Brigham Young Office Journal.

36. Brigham Young Letters, Mar. 28, 1861, Beinecke Library.

37. *History of Brigham Young, 1847–1867* (Berkeley, Cal.: MassCal Associates, 1964, 1966), p. 312.

38. Brigham Young Letters, Beinecke Library.

39. *Journal of Discourses*, vol. IX, pp. 3–5.

40. *Ibid.*, p. 7.

41. *Ibid.*, p. 55.

42. *Ibid.*, p. 36.

43. *Ibid.*, p. 234.

44. Brigham Young Office Journal, May 1, 1861.

45. *Ibid.*

46. *Deseret News*, May 22, 1861.

47. Governor's Papers, Utah State Archives, State Capitol, Salt Lake City.

48. Tullidge, *History of Salt Lake City*, p. 248.

49. *Ibid.*, p. 249.

50. Burton, *City of the Saints*, p. 216.

51. *History of Brigham Young*, p. 314.

52. T. B. H. Stenhouse, *The Rocky Mountain Saints* (New York: Appleton & Co., 1873), p. 445n.

53. Francis Wootton File, Appointment Files, Record Group 59, Department of State, National Archives, Washington, D.C.

54. Whitney, *History of Utah*, vol. II, pp. 28–29.

55. *Journal of Discourses*, vol. VIII, p. 360.

CHAPTER

III

Suspicions, and a New Governor

By JULY 9, 1861, it was reported that the Mormon president commented in his office: "Old 'Abe' the President of the U.S. has it in his mind to pitch into us when he had got through with the South. . . . Pres. Young was of opinion the sympathy of the people for the South was in case they should be whipped, and the northern party remain in power, he thought they wanted the war to go [so] that both parties might be used up."[1] He added on July 11, ". . . it would not do for the northern and southern party to fight too much at once."[2] Still later, on July 24, Young agreed that feelings of the government were still hostile to the Mormons "as they always have been . . . as there was in them a spirit to destroy everything."[3]

In the Bowery on July 28 the Mormon leader declared,

President Lincoln called out soldiers for three months and was going to wipe the blot of secession from the escutcheon of the American Republic. The three months are gone, and the labour is scarcely begun. Now they are beginning to enlist men for three years; soon they will want to enlist during the war; and then I was going to say that they will want them to enlist during the duration of hell. Do they know what they are doing? No; but they have begun to empty the earth, they cleanse the land, and prepare the way for the return of the Latter-day Saints to the centre Stake of Zion.[4]

Here is expressed another goal for the people of Utah: the even-tual return to the spiritual home of the Church in Missouri. Young continued,

The South say, "We could not bear the insults and affliction that has been heaped upon us by the North. We cannot help revolting from the rank Abolitionists that would destroy us and our negroes; we will not hold fellowship with the North any longer, but we will come out from them and be separate." The Abolitionists would set free the negroes at the expense of the lives of their masters; they would let the negroes loose to massacre every white person; that is the spirit of many of the Abolitionists I have conversed with. . . . Will it be over in six months or in three years? No; it will take years and years, and will never cease until the work is accomplished . . . I shall see the day when thousands will seek succour at the hands of this people.[5]

Continuing in his critical mood, Brigham Young is quoted as saying that "the leading men of the American Nation were in trouble and they do not know which way to turn." A few days later Young disparaged Lincoln: "Abraham was a pretty good man, but he acted as he would rather the Kingdom of God was out of the way; he was not the man to raise his voice in favor of Joseph Smith when his enemies were persecuting him, he with many others had assented to the deaths of innocent men, and through that he is subject to the influence of a wicked spirit."[6] This is perhaps unfair, but, although Lincoln was in Illinois at the time of the persecutions, it is not known that he protested them. On the other hand, could he have been expected to do so?

After hearing the news of First Bull Run or Manassas in Virginia in which the Union army had been badly whipped in late July, Young commented on August 27 "that the confusion of the people in the States was rapidly increasing, they seemed as if they had lost their sense." The brethren, quite naturally, endorsed these sentiments.[7]

While girding for the war that now looked to be a much more protracted one than at first expected, Washington had little time for the problems of remote areas such as Utah. But it is of importance that as early as June 27, 1861, Adjutant General Lorenzo Thomas wired the commander in Utah, Colonel Cooke, that "Any subsistence stores in your department which have not already been disposed of you will keep for the use of troops that will be moved into Utah from California."[8] Most of the supplies had been disposed of and the last troops left Fort Crittenden July 27. It would be well over a year before there were again federal forces from California in Utah. But the message showed what the thought was at this time in the Union officials' minds.

In fact, the Union was taking measures to protect the Overland Trail, though they would not be immediately effective. On July 24, 1861, Secretary of War Simon Cameron wrote Governor John G. Downey of California: "The War Department accepts for three years one regiment of infantry and five companies cavalry to guard the Overland Mail Route from Carson Valley to Salt Lake" and eastward.[9] Adjutant General Thomas the same day ordered Brigadier General Edwin Vose Sumner, who had succeeded Albert Sidney Johnston in command of the Department of the Pacific, to muster these troops into service.[10] However, the troops thus raised were diverted elsewhere in the West, as were later levies. It was not until mid-1862 that troops were found for the Overland Trail.

In October, 1861, General Sumner was recalled for duty in the East, and the command of the department devolved upon veteran Colonel George Wright, who became much involved in the affairs of Utah Territory during the war.[11] George Wright was around sixty years of age at this time, having been born in Vermont in 1801 or 1803. Graduating from West Point in 1822, he had a long and distinguished record in the Seminole Indian War, the Mexican War, and various struggles with the Indians in the West. He had received several brevet ranks for his gallantry, and had spent much time on the Pacific Coast. Upon his appointment to the Pacific Department Command from the Department of Oregon, Wright was made brigadier general of volunteers. He is generally credited with doing an outstanding job in the Department of the Pacific, shorthanded though he was. Wright served in that post until mid-1864, when he became commander of the Department of California. At the end of the Civil War he was transferred to the Department of Columbia, but drowned in the sinking of the steamer *Brother Jonathan* off northern California on July 30, 1865. Serving far from the major battlefields, Wright can be said to be one of the neglected military leaders of the Civil War.[12]

In line with the usual pattern of patronage, Lincoln did name a new set of territorial officers for Utah, none of them Mormons or from Utah as had been requested. John W. Dawson of Indiana was named governor, replacing Cumming. Frank Fuller was named secretary, and James Duane Doty, superintendent of Indian affairs, with S. R. Fox as surveyor-general. John Fitch Kinney continued as judge and chief justice, with new associate justices R. P. Flenniken and H. R. Crosby. The governor received his appointment October 3, 1861, and Secretary Fuller preceded him to Salt Lake City and succeeded Wootton as acting governor.

John W. Dawson, the new governor, had been a minor Indiana newspaper editor and politician, moving from party to party in the pre-war years. He was born in Cambridge City, Indiana, in 1820. His grandfather had been a slaveholder and his father was originally from the South. In 1838 he went to Fort Wayne, Indiana. He attended school, was an office clerk, later studied at Wabash College and Transylvania College, read law with his brother-in-law, and eventually opened his own law practice. He leased and soon owned the Whig-affiliated Fort Wayne *Times and Press*, beginning in 1853. While conservative on the slavery issue and anti-abolitionist, Dawson was strongly for temperance, for free public schools, and must be considered anti-Catholic, for his paper developed a noticeable Know-Nothing overtone. In 1854 he was the unsuccessful candidate for the legislature on a People's Party ticket. In 1855 he was a delegate to the national Know-Nothing Convention in Cincinnati. Dawson was also an unsuccessful candidate for Indiana secretary of state in 1856 for the People's Party or Fusion ticket, made up of Republicans and American or Know-Nothing party men. Later he was nominated by the Democrats for Congress and was read out of the Republican party at a district convention in 1858. However, as editor of the Fort Wayne paper, he supported Lincoln in 1860.[13] So it can be seen that Dawson was a political chameleon, though that was not unusual in those days of unsettled political parties.

While clearly prejudiced, one Mormon historian wrote of Dawson, "He was the editor and publisher of a party newspaper at Fort Wayne, Indiana, a man of bad morals, and a meddler in politics, who gave the Republican managers in his state a great deal of trouble. The undoubted fact seems to be that he was sent out to Utah on the recommendation of Indiana politicians of high rank, who wanted to get rid of him, and who gave no attention whatever to the requirements of his office."[14] Dawson was recommended to Lincoln by Interior Secretary Caleb Blood Smith of Indiana and others. Smith wrote that Dawson was about thirty-five years of age and an Indiana editor. "He possesses remarkable energy and has an unexceptionable character. We are confident that he would discharge the duties of the office with ability and fidelity."[15]

At the same time, as usual, anti-Mormon sentiments were being aired. Judge Benjamin F. Hall of Denver, Colorado Territory, wrote to Secretary of State Seward on October 30, 1861, about alleged secessionists: "They number some 5,000 of the border ruffians of Kansas and the destroying angels of Brigham Young. I presume that they are the worst people on the face of the earth to govern."[16]

Acting Governor Francis Wootton wrote to Secretary Seward September 5, 1861, that he was

happy to report that "all is well," that the citizens of the Territory have in no instance evinced a disposition to avoid any of their legal or Constitutional obligations, or to interfere in any manner with the administration of the several federal officers in Utah, but on the contrary, so far as I am informed, have rendered them a willing and hearty obedience. I am induced to make this statement at this time because of rumors which I observe to be in general circulation through the various presses of the country to the effect that Brigham Young had declared Utah independent and that the property of the government at Fort Crittenden (late Camp Floyd) and other military stations of the Department of Utah have been violently seized and appropriated by the Mormons. Such reports based on the idle and mendacious representations of irresponsible parties, if unnoticed, may produce a false impression at Washington and lead to unnecessary troubles; therefore, I have deemed it my duty to give them an official contradiction.[17]

In late September new Territorial Delegate John Milton Bernhisel left Salt Lake City by stagecoach to take up the delegate's duties as the nonvoting representative of Utah Territory in the House of Representatives, replacing William Henry Hooper. Hooper had served in the Thirty-sixth Congress, from 1859 to 1861, but had not been reelected in 1860. Bernhisel, a Mormon, was born near Harrisburg, Pennsylvania, in 1799. He graduated from the medical department of the University of Pennsylvania and practiced medicine in New York City. From there he moved to Nauvoo, Illinois, in 1843, and then to Salt Lake City in 1848. He had served as territorial delegate from 1851 to 1859. He resumed the practice of medicine in Utah, but was elected to the Thirty-seventh Congress as Utah delegate in March of 1861, and served until 1863.[18] Dr. Bernhisel had spent most of his time in the East from 1848 until 1860 and had built up a wide variety of political contacts. It is a bit uncertain why he returned as delegate, but it seems clear that Brigham Young approved. Hooper later returned to Congress, so Bernhisel's reelection apparently did not mean that Hooper was shoved aside.[19] Both Hooper and Bernhisel had apparently been able delegates, representing and working for Utah and the Mormons. Their tasks were not easy.

In the West the usual summer Mormon emigration season was reaching its peak in September, with more and more converts coming into Utah. Delegate Hooper on September 28 received a letter from the former governor, Cumming, implying that he would like to be petitioned by the people to be governor again, but nothing could or would come of it.[20]

Brigham Young continued to be free in his observations on the war and the federal government, and it is probable that we have a record of only a portion of his copious and usually acerbic comments. In mid-September, referring again to the Confederate victory at Bull Run, he wrote that "he would be glad to hear that Genl. Beauregard had taken the President & Cabinet and confined them in the South."[21]

On hearing of the Union's August defeat at Wilson's Creek in Missouri, Young prognosticated in October: ". . . now the contending parties in the States were using Guns and Cannon, but in time they would become so bloodthirsty that they would be ready to tye [sic] their left hand behind and fight with knives until they killed each other."[22] By December 10, Young was said to be quite "warm" over his problems with the United States and "he had no disposition to respond to the calls of a government, that had so lately shown their bitter hostilities against us, not alone by sending an army, but by burning the remnant of their arms rather than we should possess them, he felt like contending for our rights, and we were as well prepared to meet a million of the United States soldiers as 10,000, he believed now that an army was on the way to us."[23] No army was yet on the way, but the importance of the stand of Utah became increasingly vital to the Union in the fall of 1861.

The telegraph was a tremendous improvement in communications over the short-lived Pony Express, which had first appeared in Salt Lake City in early April, 1860.[24] Of immense support to the war effort of the North and to the advancement of national communications, and of especial interest to the leaders and people of Utah, was the completion of the transcontinental telegraph to Salt Lake City on October 17, 1861. Soon it would stretch clear to the West coast, a momentous event which profoundly altered the situation in the West and in Utah Territory. Acting Governor Fuller on October 18 wired President Lincoln: "Utah, whose citizens strenuously resist all imputations of disloyalty, congratulates the President upon the completion of an enterprise which spans a continent, unites two oceans, and connects with nerve iron the remote extremities of the body politic with the great government heart. May the whole system speedily thrill with the quickened pulsations of that heart, as the parracide hand is palsied, treason is punished, and the entire sisterhood of states joins hands in glad reunion around the national fireside."[25] Lincoln replied to Fuller on October 20, "The completion of the Telegraph to Great Salt Lake City is auspicious of the Stability & Union of the Republic."[26]

While these formal official statements went forth, Brigham Young sent an even more important message on October 18 to J. H. Wade, President of the Pacific Telegraph Company, in Cleveland, with the usual congratulations. But he added prophetic words: "Utah has not seceded, but is firm for the Constitution and laws of our once happy country, and is warmly interested in such useful enterprises as the one so far completed."[27] Wade replied to the Mormon leader on October 19 thanking him for the telegram which "should express so unmistakably the patriotism and Union-loving sentiments of yourself and your people. I join with you in the hope that this enterprise may . . . tend to annihilate prejudice, cultivate brotherly love, facilitate commerce and strengthen the bonds of our once and again to be happy Union."[28] A few days later Young sent the first telegram from Salt Lake City to San Francisco. The *Deseret News* called the telegraph "one of the greatest and grandest institutions of recent construction."[29] It was another sign of technical progress that was eroding Utah's isolation and making the Territory and its people more and more a part of the nation. The commercial opportunities were obvious, but Brigham Young immediately made frequent and extensive use of the telegraph both to receive information and give "advice" to Church leaders and even to shorten the time of communication with his European stations. Young's message to Wade as to loyalty was widely repeated and as early as October 19 was sent on to Washington.[30]

The telegraph gave Young a much more immediate view of what was going on in the war. On November 11 he wrote to John Van Cott, a Mormon missionary then in Copenhagen, Denmark, saying, "From latest telegram . . . though no important battles have taken place since the Bull Run affair, we can discern that mutual waste and destruction are going on at a rapidly increasing rate." He also wrote a good deal about building plans, the new theater, and raising cotton in "Dixie," that is, southern Utah.[31] In a similar vein, he wrote to Territorial Delegate Bernhisel, now in Washington, on November 12:

From other items in the . . . telegram we perceive that the torch of civil war is being lit up in new and widely distant points in our land, and that waste and destruction are increasingly rife in Virginia, South Carolina, Kentucky and Missouri, while at home we continue to enjoy the great blessings of peace, and uninterrupted procession of plans and labors tending to ameliorate and improve the condition of our fellow beings. The wise can appreciate the contrast and understand much of the cause while the simple pass on.[32]

Young was much concerned with immigration from abroad and with missionary work. He had his hand in almost every activity. His comments on the war were usually made to contrast with those extolling the much superior conditions in Utah. To Church President George Cannon in Liverpool, England, November 15, the Mormon leader mentioned an interruption in the telegraph around Fort Bridger, but went on to say: "While strife and bloodshed are wasting the States, we continue to enjoy the rich blessings of peace, in whose various occupations, according to localities and season, the people are most industriously occupied."[33] And on November 27, Young wrote to Cannon and others, "On our part we are happy being privileged to inform you that Utah continues

to be greatly blest with peace and continued prosperity, which the
great majority of the population are using to profit by to a degree
that will keep free the channel through which flow the rich blessings of Heaven. . . . We have several times had in print here in
the afternoon news of events transpired in Washington in the
forenoon."[34]

Much of Young's correspondence in December of 1861 per-
tained to the adoption of a state constitution aimed at admission
to the Union, which had been the major aim of Utah and the Mormon Church for some time. While the statehood movement was
taking on a fresh impetus, Dawson, the new territorial governor,
arrived on December 7.[35] On December 10, 1861, Governor Dawson presented his message to the territorial legislature. He spoke
of "the peculiar people of Utah," and was veiledly critical of the
Mormons. Very strongly pro-Union, Dawson asked,

Men of Utah! are you ready to join that host? . . . Why need I ask you
where you stand on this great question? Here, in this peaceful valley,
which you, by wonderful perseverance and industry, have reclaimed from
a state of nature, and made its sterile plains blossom as the rose, as few
people on earth could, and for which you are entitled to the thanks of
the nation—here, far removed from the scenes of conflict, where your
brethren and fellow citizens are ruthlessly shedding each other's blood,
you can not but look with deep, earnest interest upon the struggle and its
final result. United, as you are, in the bonds of a peculiar faith and social
life, which has, in a measure, separated you, as a peculiar people, from
your American brethren, you are yet bound to them by ties of kindred,
language, and country, and the recognition and worship of the same Divine Father and Lord and Savior Jesus Christ. You are a people of the
United States, and I was rejoiced to hear how you stand affected toward
the Federal Government—the Union and the Constitution.[36]

Governor Dawson also urged payment of the federal taxes of
$26,982 owed by the Territory. The tax was levied on real prop-
erty and improvements, with two-thirds to be collected in gold
and silver coin, though there was little coinage in Utah. All federal-
ly owned property was exempted. Yet since Indian title had not yet
been settled in Utah, this exemption included all land in the Territory. Thus there was technically nothing to tax. The legislature assumed the territorial tax quota and levied a one-percent tax on all
occupied land. The legislature had asked Congress to rescind

Utah's quota but that request was denied and the tax was later paid.[37]

It was not the most politic gubernatorial address, but in a few days it mattered not what Dawson had said. The legislature had begun its meeting December 9 and a bill was introduced calling for a convention of delegates to form a constitution and state government.[38] The act called for letting the convention ask the general government to admit Utah as a state.[39] The convention bill easily passed both houses, but Governor Dawson saw fit to veto it.[40] His excuse, if that is what it was, was that there was too little time between the passage of the act and the voting for or against a state convention on January 6, 1862. He also said there was too little time for the act to be submitted to Congress prior to election of delegates. But the territorial legislators and the public seemed to feel it was not necessary to submit the convention proposal to Congress. The *Deseret News* reprinted Dawson's veto message without editorial comment.[41]

On December 12, 1861, Delegate Bernhisel wrote Brigham Young a long letter. It is significant that he wrote to Young rather than to the territorial officials. Bernhisel had called on President Lincoln and found a number of others waiting. However, Bernhisel said Lincoln received him first, "very kindly and apparently very cordially, and seemed to recognize me . . . and he asked among other things whether we were getting on reasonably well in Utah. I answered in the affirmative, and remarked that in the language of ex-Governor Young's dispatches, we were firm for the Constitution and the Union. The President is affable and agreeable and has the appearance and reputation of being an honest man, and is popular with all parties except the secessionists."[42] This first visit was December 6 and Bernhisel again saw the President on December 11 about appointments. On December 10 he had an interview with Attorney General Edward Bates in regard to appointments:

. . . he was exceedingly kind and courteous. I stated to him among other things that the people of Utah would be gratified to have all the offices filled by citizens of that Territory, but he said that could not be. I am happy in being able to inform you that the feeling exhibited toward us as a people by the President, the head of departments so far as I have seen them, and other officers and employees of the Government, Members of

Congress and citizens throughout the country generally, was never before so kindly as at present, and nothing in my judgment has contributed so much to bring about this state of feeling as your excellent dispatch, saying that Utah had not seceded, but was firm for the Constitution and the Union. . . . If however our enemies, or the scribes and correspondents of the press, could find any just ground for exciting suspicion of disloyalty against us, it would revive all former prejudices against us, and we should never be able to gain admission into the Union as a State, nor obtain any favors from the President or Congress. I would therefore respectfully suggest that it will be the interest, and I presume it is the inclination of the citizens of our remote and sequestered Territory to pay the direct and income tax promptly and cheerfully.[43]

Bernhisel had written to his wife that he found Lincoln to be "affable and agreeable." He believed Lincoln warmest in nature of all the five presidents he had visited. In fact, Bernhisel felt he received a friendly reception.[44]

But the cause of more excitement in December of 1861 was what might be called the "Governor Dawson affair." The newly appointed territorial governor had arrived from the East on December 7 and he suddenly left Salt Lake City on the last day of the year, heading for his Indiana home. The first night out he was set upon and badly beaten. These are the plain facts, but the circumstances of the whole episode are cloudy and the stories vary. The event itself is perhaps not of paramount importance but, in light of the touchy relations between the federal government and the Mormons, and the image that Utah and the Saints often had in the East, it takes on increased significance. A month later the two associate justices also departed, leaving Chief Justice Kinney.[45]

The *Deseret News* on the first day of 1862 reported that the governor left "under circumstances somewhat *novel and puzzling*." In a news story full of innuendo and sarcasm the paper continued,

For the last eight or ten days previous to his leaving, he was confined to his room, and reported to have been *very sick*, and, what was worse, in a state of mental derangement, or in other words, distressingly insane. This report of his physician, not a very popular man in this community, was at first disbelieved, but it was subsequently ascertained to be verily true, and his affliction of a very serious character, so much so that he imagined that he had committed a heinous offence, no less than offering a gross insult to a respectable lady of this city, to whom he requested his physician to offer a large sum of hush money, &c., &c. When the fact of the governor's insanity was fully established many were the conjectures as to the cause which produced the aberration of mind under which he was laboring. Some were of the opinion that it was hereditary and that his ancestors in their lifetime had been similarly afflicted; others believed that his journey across the plains and the incidents thereof had affected his brain. There were some who thought that the labor of producing such a lengthy and profound message as the one he had in the Legislative Assembly . . . had been too much for his feeble mind; several opined that the state of the atmosphere in this high altitude had produced unexpected results upon the Hoosier who had probably never before inhaled a breath of pure air, while by far the greatest number to whom the awful circumstances attending his condition were made known unreservedly stated that, in their opinion, when all the facts in relation to the matter were made known it would fully be made to appear that the reason was a good cause for his assertions that he had made criminal approaches to a lady, and thus his insanity was attributable alone to a circumstance of that kind.[46]

Thomas B. H. Stenhouse, in his famous *Rocky Mountain Saints*, has a different story. Stenhouse was a prominent Mormon and editor at this time who later broke with the Church. He wrote that Dawson "was almost immediately a victim of misplaced confidence, and fell into a snare laid for his feet by some of his own brother-officials." Stenhouse does not blame the Mormons but federal officials: "Governor Dawson had been betrayed into an offense, and his punishment was heavy."[47] Stenhouse does not elaborate on his statements which really amount to charges of misconduct.

Historian Orson F. Whitney stated flatly that "it is a fact that Governor Dawson made indecent proposals to a respectable lady of Salt Lake City, and fearing chastisement at the hands of relatives or friends, hastily departed."[48]

Another historian, George A. Smith, who prepared some notes for the famous historian H. H. Bancroft in mid-1862, wrote of the various governors:

The administration of Acting Governor F. H. Wootton, of Maryland, was marked by no event of importance, saving only that when he left, bad liquor fell in price. Secretary and Acting Governor Frank Fuller's (of Maine) administration was remarkable for a change in favor of industry and temperance, and respect by the Executive for the Territorial laws.

The nineteen days of Governor John W. Dawson's (of Indiana) administration were remarkable simply for the difficulty experienced by the Governor in hunting a seamstress.[49]

Acting Governor Frank Fuller reported to the Utah Executive Department on January 4, 1862, that Dawson had said in a note on the day of his departure: "My health is such that my return to Indiana for the time being is imperatively demanded; hence, I start this day." Fuller went on to report: "Governor Dawson announced to me on the day of his arrival his intention to return to Indiana at the close of the Legislative session, but I am not aware that any reason was assigned by him for his departure at an earlier day, other than the one above given."[50] Mormon sources reported that "Gov. Dawson has threatened to shoot Stenhouse if he published anything about his wishes to sleep with Tom Williams' wife when she raised the fire shovel on him, and his offer to compromise for $3000 for her not to tell. She has made affidavit and seen Pres. Young."[51]

At any rate, whether the Mormons or others tried to be rid of Dawson or not, or whether he was foolishly indiscreet, the Church certainly was not happy with the aftermath. At Hank's Mail Station, the first night out of Salt Lake City, Dawson was attacked by what at the minimum was described as a "gang of rowdies."[52] Dawson was robbed, kicked and beaten quite seriously. One of the alleged assailants was Wood Reynolds, said to have been related to the lady reputedly involved. The whole band seems to have been of a wild, if not criminal, element. One of the supposed culprits, Lot Huntington, was shot by a deputy sheriff in January, 1862, while attempting to escape. John P. Smith and Moroni Clawson were killed by police in Salt Lake City while similarly occupied. Others were tried and punished. Reportedly the men killed had committed other robberies and "their tragic taking off was not regretted by the general community."[53]

According to Stenhouse, the police said that the prisoners who were killed had tried to escape and that they had shot them down. "It was believed that the prisoners were walking in front of the officers when the latter quietly put their revolvers to the back of their heads and 'stopped them.'" Editor Stenhouse felt that the Mormon authorities "were dreadfully annoyed by this attack upon Governor Dawson, for they had a greater desire to disgrace the Government in his person than to see him 'whipped.'"[54]

The *Deseret News* called the attack a "Disgraceful Outrage" and printed a statement by Dawson written on January 7, 1862. Dawson addressed it from Bear River Station to the paper. It seems that some of the guards with him were involved, according to Dawson.

Wood Reynolds the driver, accosted me insolently, when I at once jumped out and started for the house. Between the coach and the house he struck me, and on reaching the house Jason Luce and Reynolds, assisted by others, began and continued a most serious violence to me, wounding my head badly in many places, kicking me in the loins and right breast until I was exhausted, when they desisted, and staid till morning, carrying on their orgies for many hours in the night. Now, Sir! these desperadoes, having thus cast another stain on the city, as they have heretofore often done, will tell many stories about my giving them provocation that night.

Dawson named several of his attackers, "the traitors all of whom it should be the unremitting duty of the people of Salt Lake City to bring to speedy trial and condign punishment."[55]

Dawson had more to say about the case. He wrote to President Lincoln from Fort Bridger, January 13, 1862: "On leaving Great Salt Lake City on the 31st ult. en route for home & Washington I was followed by a band of danites." Dawson here means the alleged secret band of Mormons who were accused, without proof, of being a sort of secret police empowered to beat up, to drive out of Utah, and even to murder, enemies of the Church. There is no evidence that the assaulters of Dawson were Danites. The governor went on at length, complaining that he had been "viciously assaulted & beaten" and that the reason was his veto of the measure calling a state convention. Dawson had justified his veto on grounds that there was insufficient time for Congress to act on the calling of a convention or for the people to canvass the matter. But the governor added that "a further & a better reason" for the veto was "that the evident purpose of the convention was to put in operation a state government & if not admitted into the Union to completely oust Federal authority." He termed Mormon "loyalty" mythical and claimed there was much disloyal talk on the streets and that it was preached every Sunday in the Tabernacle. "The whole purpose of these people is to gain admission into the Union on an equal basis & then the ulcer polygamy will have a sovereign protection. . . . The horrid crimes that have been committed in this territory & which have gone unpunished, have no parallel among civilized nations."[56]

Characteristically, Brigham Young had much to say on all aspects of the Dawson case. On December 10 the Church president had written to Mormon official Wilford Woodruff regarding the governor's message to the legislature:

If I were the President or Speaker of the Legislature I would not refer the message to any committee or say one word about it, and trust there will not be anything said. They want us to pay taxes and then they will want us to send a thousand men to the war. What will they do about the taxes? The people have not the money. They would have to take wheat, lumber, and the like. They will not collect taxes here, neither will they get 1,000 men to join the army. They would spend $1,000,000 in sending an army here to collect $30,000. They have sought our destruction all the day long. Why do they not pay their own debts? They destroyed their arms and ammunition at Camp Floyd so that we should not get any, when the Government is owing Utah its quota of arms, etc. Abe Lincoln has sent these men to prepare the way for an army. An order has been sent to California to raise an army to come to Utah. . . . I pray daily that the Lord will take the reins of Government out of the hands of wicked rulers and give it to wise, good men. The Governor quotes my saying about the Constitution. I do now, and always have, supported the Constitution, but I am not in league with cursed scoundrels as Abe Lincoln and his minions who have sought our destruction from the beginning. Lincoln has ordered an army from California, for the order has passed over the wires. A Senator from California said in Washington a short time since that the "Mormons" were in the way and must be removed. Lincoln feels that he will try to destroy us, as Buchanan was unable to do.[57]

This was perhaps Brigham Young's strongest known anti-Lincoln statement during the presidency. And this view of Dawson was stated before his departure and beating.

Explaining Dawson's case to Delegate Bernhisel in Washington, Young wrote how the governor declined to sign the act to provide for electing delegates to the statehood convention. But the election would be held and the convention would meet anyway. Young went on:

On the 21st inst. Gov. Dawson called upon Widow Thomas Williams and on the 28th inst. a Dr. Chambers, who came here this season hailing from Minnesota, made a call upon her. A copy of Mrs. Williams' affidavit is herewith inclosed which enables you to readily judge for yourself of the fitness of Mr. Dawson for the office to which President Lincoln appointed him. How long does the government intend to persist in foisting such characters upon us, when they at least should appoint from residents of our selection, or better still, permit us to elect our own officers, or, still more just, admit us at once into the Union, especially when so pressed for funds with which to keep the governmental machinery in motion. So soon as the convention have completed their labors, and they are accepted and ratified, if need be, by the people, it is our purpose to no more endure the imposition of such men as . . . Governor Dawson, and others. This information you are at liberty to impart to whom and when you please. I wish you to inform the Government that it is our right to be admitted as a State, and that, if they do not admit us, they do not know their friends.[58]

Thus Young was instructing Bernhisel, as he continually did, on the policy of Utah, even though Young was not officially elected and Bernhisel had been elected by the people. Young continued in this important policy statement: "I also wish you, if the question arises whether we will furnish troops beyond our borders for the war, to tell them no, but that, if necessary, we are ready to furnish a home guard for the protection of the telegraph and mail lines and overland travel within our boundaries, upon such terms as other volunteer companies employed by the Government."[59] As to Dawson and others:

What course, if any, they will take in relation to us, upon their arrival in the States you will of course be acquainted with before we are informed; but we doubt not your ability to meet and head off any evil influence of theirs' [sic] readily. . . . You may now wish to know what you are to do, in case we are not admitted as a State. Stay in Congress and represent us as a Territory, or a State, just as they may choose to call us, for at present it is designed to proceed, at the time before signified, and elect two Senators and elect you our representative.[60]

Young apparently took the Dawson case very seriously and wished to set the policy and give explanation on behalf of the Mormons. To Elder Dwight Eveleth in San Francisco on the first day of the year 1862 he reiterated the case and added, "We have been time after time imposed upon by miserable specimens of Government appointees, but no one of them had so speedily and foolishly exposed his inward corruptions and so suddenly fled facing the legitimate result of his acts." [61] A few days later, he again commented to Bernhisel relative to the assault on Dawson:

Governor Dawson left for the east by stage on the afternoon of the 31st ult. accompanied by several desperadoes, asserted by some to have been hired by him as an escort, who it is reported, with the stage driver, assaulted the Governor at the mail station between the Big and Little mountains, and struck and kicked him quite severely. . . . The motives of the assailants for so brutal and cowardly an assault are unknown to me, unless one of them were activated by revenge for the governors insult to Mrs. Williams, one of whose daughters it is said he is courting. [62]

The Mormon leader repeated the general story in a letter to George Cannon in Liverpool on January 7, but does not mention the assault. He said Dawson declined "for sundry frivolous reasons, to sign a bill passed by the Assembly to provide for holding a Convention, &c., preparatory to the admission of Utah as a state." [63]

Still later, on January 14, Young again wrote Bernhisel that the guilty should be punished for their attack on Dawson, but,

It is not known how the governor will represent this matter in the east . . . but we have since heard of his uttering certain threats, much musings about revenge, &c. I regret as much as any person can possibly do, the existence in our midst of such desperate men, nor am I alone in this, the whole community deplores it, and despises their actions, but what can we do suppose we arrest them, try them in our courts for their offences, convict them, and they are incarcerated in the Penitentiary or otherwise undergoing the just punishment of their crimes? Some United States Judge is sure to liberate them by virtue of a writ of Habeas Corpus. . . . Thus all our efforts to legally rid ourselves of such characters have been abortive. The Government probably expended some fifty million of Dollars to send an army here the scum of which is still floating in our midst in the shape of bands of thieves and vagabonds, a moral pestilence, a terror alike to the citizen and the sojourner, the Federal Government alone is responsible for this order of things it must not complain if the "representatives of Federal authority" are among the sufferers. [64]

Thus Young at year's end sought to get out his version of the Governor Dawson incident and spike, if possible, any criticism from Dawson, his friends, or the enemies of the Church. In fact, the whole matter does not seem to have caused much of a ripple, if any, in wartime Washington. But undoubtedly Young felt the occurrence might injure Utah's chances for statehood.

As a matter of fact, Dawson's appointment had never been confirmed by the U.S. Senate.[65] It was said, probably correctly, that the Senate's refusal to confirm conveniently relieved Lincoln of an embarrassing problem.[66]

The Indians in Utah during 1860 and for the most part of 1861 had been fairly quiet, at least when compared with previous years. There had been some of the usual depredations and rumors of others, and over all hung a fear of more. Governor Cumming, who had departed in mid-1861, wrote in February, 1860, to then–Secretary of State Lewis Cass that "The Indians of this territory are numerous—well armed—and somewhat warlike. The withdrawal of the entire army from this territory seems to me injudicious and unjust both to the resident population as well as to the emmigration [sic] through the country. I would, therefore, suggest that about 500 (five-hundred) soldiers should be retained here, and be established at such points as are deemed desirable by the officer in command."[67]

The superintendent of Indian affairs for the Utah Superintendency at the time, Benjamin Davis, wrote to Washington and to the commissioner of Indian affairs on January 20, 1861:

It has become customary with many tribes to divide off into small bands and create a number of petty sub-chiefs. Each band roves *ad libitum* and thefts and murders and other offences are committed with impunity, because of the impossibility of detection. This has been caused by the failure of the Head Chief, where there is one, to exercise the necessary authority. This failure to do this is founded on the corrupting associations of the whites with the Indians. Each Indian has contracted the notion that he is good as his chief—hence no subordination. If the chiefs undertake to punish, whites interfere and thus the influence of the chief is destroyed—the offending party declares himself a chief and heads off a few others which constitutes his "band." To break this up, restore the power of the chief, and reestablish their organization is the policy I have inaugurated. . . . The citizens of this Territory have for many years been in the habit of carrying on an unrestricted traffic with the Indians and by this means everything of value given to them has been very soon afterward abstracted from them.[68]

There were reports of Indians becoming more hostile in the Ruby Valley and Deep Creek areas in western Utah and on the mail line in August of 1861; Agent William Rogers reported to the Utah superintendent August 18 that "I have had reliable information that if something is not done . . . they intend wiping out the stations and stock . . ." on the trails.[69] In the fall of 1861 James Duane Doty succeeded Davis as Utah superintendent of Indian affairs.

Although he had not yet arrived in Utah Territory, the newly appointed governor, Dawson, had written, while in Washington, to Interior Secretary Caleb Blood Smith on October 26, showing his strongly preconceived notions of the Mormons:

The Indians are substantially under the influence of the Mormons who is known have no homogeneity in common with other citizens of the United States, whose domestic polity is not in consonance with the Federal government, its constitution & laws—! In fact though they are professedly loyal to the constitution and obedient to the laws of the United States, they nevertheless, from the nature of their domestic institutions & from past causes of embittered feeling between them & the gentiles . . . are inclined to independence which may approximate rebellion should federal authority & arms prove in any considerable degree ineffectual during the existing war in maintaining our national colors beyond disputed boundaries.[70]

There were other indications of a possible increase in Indian troubles in the fall of 1861. An official of the Overland Mail Company wrote Indian Commissioner William P. Dole that, according to his reports, "Indians on our line West, within Utah Territory need provisions and will break up our line if not fed."[71] The army had already recognized the need of protecting the line, but had been unable to find troops sufficient for the task.

NOTES

1. Brigham Young Office Journal.
2. *Ibid.*
3. *Ibid.*
4. *Journal of Discourses*, vol. IX, p. 142.
5. *Ibid.*
6. Brigham Young Office Journal, Aug. 13, 21, 1861.
7. *Ibid.*, Aug. 27, 1861.
8. *War of the Rebellion, Official Records of the Union and Confederate Armies*

(Washington, D.C.: Government Printing Office, 1880–1900), ser. I, vol. L, pt. 1, p. 523 (hereafter cited as *O.R.*, and series I intended unless otherwise indicated).

9. *Ibid.*, p. 543.

10. *Ibid.*

11. Richard H. Orton, *Records of California Men in the War of the Rebellion, 1861 to 1867* (Sacramento, Cal.: State Printing Office, 1890), p. 19.

12. Aurora Hunt, *The Army of the Pacific* (Glendale, Cal.: Arthur H. Clark Co., 1951), p. 28; Ezra J. Warner, *Generals in Blue* (Baton Rouge: Louisiana State University Press, 1964), pp. 574–75; Francis B. Heitman, *Historical Register and Dictionary of the United States Army* (Washington, D.C.: Government Printing Office, 1903), vol. I, p. 1062.

13. Dawson, John W., "Charcoal Sketches of Old Times in Fort Wayne," ed. Alene Godfrey (Fort Wayne, Ind.: prepared by Staff of the Public Library of Fort Wayne and Allen County, 1958, rcpr. from *Old Fort News*, Jan.–Mar., 1959, pub. by Allen County–Fort Wayne Historical Society); Carl Fremont Brand, "History of the Know Nothing Party in Indiana," *Indiana Magazine of History*, 18 (June, Sept., 1922), 204, 273–74, 281, 284; B. J. Griswold, *The Pictorial History of Fort Wayne, Indiana* (Chicago: Robert O. Law Co., 1917), p. 341; J. Randolph Kirby, "Fort Wayne Common School Crusaders: The First Year for Free Schooling, April, 1853–March, 1854," *Old Fort News* (Fort Wayne, Ind.), 42 (Jan., 1979), 1–31; Charles Zimmerman, "The Origin and Rise of the Republican Party in Indiana from 1854 to 1860," *Indiana Magazine of History*, 13 (Sept., Dec., 1917), 260, 369; Harry J. Carman and Reinhard H. Luthin, *Lincoln and the Patronage* (New York: Columbia University Press, 1943), p. 108; Emma Lou Thornbrough, *Indiana in the Civil War Era, 1850–1860* (Indianapolis: Indiana Historical Bureau and Indiana Historical Society, 1965), 676–77; Rex M. Potterf, "John W. Dawson, Herodotus of Fort Wayne," *Old Fort News*, 32 (Summer, 1969); Mark E. Neely, Jr., "President Lincoln, Polygamy, and the Civil War: The Case of Dawson and Deseret," *Lincoln Lore* (Lincoln National Life Foundation, Fort Wayne, Ind.), Feb., Mar., 1975, nos. 1644–45.

14. William A. Linn, *The Story of the Mormons* (New York: Macmillan, 1902), p. 537.

15. Letters of Application and Recommendation during the Administrations of Abraham Lincoln and Andrew Johnson, 1861–1869, U.S. Department of State, Record Group 59, National Archives, Washington, D.C.; also microfilm M650, National Archives and Records Center, Denver, Colo.

16. *O.R.*, ser. III, vol. I, pp. 636–37.

17. Utah Territory, 1860–1873, Utah Territorial Papers, U.S. Department of State, Record Group 59, National Archives, Washington, D.C.; also microfilm, National Archives and Records Center, Denver, Colo.; Larson, "Utah and the Civil War," p. 57.

18. *Biographical Directory of the American Congress, 1774–1961*, p. 548.

19. Gwynn Barrett, "John M. Bernhisel, Mormon Elder in Congress," (Ph.D. diss., Brigham Young University, Provo, Utah, 1968; copy in Church Archives), pp. 158–60.

20. *History of Brigham Young*, p. 316.

21. Brigham Young Office Journal, Sept. 16, 1861.

22. *Ibid.*, Oct. 22, 1861.

23. *Ibid.*

24. Andrew Jenson, *Church Chronology, a Record of Important Events* (Salt Lake City: Deseret News Press, 1899), p. 63.

25. Lincoln, *Collected Works*, vol. IV, p. 558.

26. *Ibid.*

27. Whitney, *History of Utah*, vol. II, p. 30.

28. *Ibid.*, p. 31.

29. *Ibid.*, pp. 31–32.

30. O.R., vol. L, pt. 1, p. 666, Anson Stager to Thomas A. Scott of the War Department, Oct. 19, 1861.

31. Brigham Young Letter Books, Church Archives.

32. *Ibid.*

33. *Ibid.*

34. *Ibid.*

35. Jenson, *Church Chronology*, p. 66.

36. *Deseret News*, Dec. 18, 1861.

37. Larson, "Utah and the Civil War," p. 60.

38. *History of Brigham Young*, pp. 323–24.

39. *Ibid.*

40. *Deseret News*, Dec. 25, 1861.

41. *Ibid.*

42. John M. Bernhisel Papers, Church Archives, Dec. 12, 1861.

43. *Ibid.*

44. Barrett, *John M. Bernhisel*, pp. 160–61.

45. Bancroft, *Utah*, p. 605.

46. *Deseret News*, Jan. 1, 1862.

47. Stenhouse, *Rocky Mountain Saints*, p. 502.

48. Whitney, *History of Utah*, vol. II, p. 38.

49. Journal History, 1861–62, notes of George A. Smith, including list of governors, mid-1862.

50. Journal History, Jan. 4, 1862, "History of Brigham Young," p. 325.

51. Journal History, from Documentary History, p. 576, late 1861 or early 1862.

52. Whitney, *History of Utah*, vol. II, p. 38.

53. *Ibid.*

54. Stenhouse, *Rocky Mountain Saints*, p. 592; also George A. Smith to Bernhisel, Journal History, Jan. 18, 1862.

55. *Deseret News*, Jan. 22, 1862.

56. Brigham Young Papers, Church Archives; also in Robert Todd Lincoln Papers (contained in Abraham Lincoln Papers), Library of Congress; Mrs. C. V. Waite, *The Mormon Prophet and His Harem: An Authentic History of Brigham Young, His Numerous Wives and Children* (Cambridge, Mass.: Riverside Press, 3rd ed., 1867), p. 76.

57. Journal History, Dec. 10, 1861.

58. Brigham Young Letter Books, Young to Bernhisel, Dec. 30, 1861, Church Archives.
59. *Ibid.*
60. *Ibid.*
61. *Ibid.*, Jan. 1, 1862, Young to Dwight Eveleth.
62. *Ibid.*, Jan. 4, 1862, Young to Bernhisel.
63. *Ibid.*, Jan. 7, 1862, Young to George Cannon.
64. *Ibid.*, Jan. 14, 1862, Young to Bernhisel.
65. Earl S. Pomeroy, *The Territories and the United States, 1860–1890*, Studies in Colonial Administration (Philadelphia: Oxford University Press, 1947), p. 115.
66. Vincent G. Tegeder, "Lincoln and the Territorial Patronage: The Ascendancy of the Radicals in the West," *Mississippi Valley Historical Review*, 35 (June, 1948), 87; Roberts, *Comprehensive History*, vol. V, p. 14.
67. Utah Territorial Papers, U.S. Department of State, Record Group 59, National Archives.
68. Letters Received, U.S. Department of the Interior, Office of Indian Affairs, Record Group 75, National Archives, Washington, D.C.; also in National Archives and Records Center, Denver, Colo.
69. *Ibid.*
70. *Ibid.*
71. *Ibid.*, Overland Mail Company Treasurer A. J. Center to Dole, Nov. 19, 1861, from New York.

CHAPTER

IV

Statehood and Polygamy

THE YEAR 1862 OPENED on a note of discouragement and anxiety for the United States. The Civil War had not ended in 1861 as many optimists had expected. Federal armies were not yet even moving into the outer reaches of the Confederacy, except in a few areas; there had been battlefield defeats, accusations of a lack of generalship, and dissatisfaction with the Lincoln administration. Therefore, what happened in Utah and with the Mormons was far from the headlines. The President, administration, the people, had much more worrisome issues to occupy them. But in Utah the local issues were naturally paramount. There was excitement and disputation over Governor Dawson's sudden departure and the attack upon him. The Mormons were still ardently interested in obtaining statehood, apprehensive over their relations with the federal government, and intent on making known their version of their position in the war-torn Union. The problem, of course, was that so few were listening, outside of Utah.

On January 3 Delegate Bernhisel in Washington wrote, perhaps over-optimistically, to Brigham Young that he had been "courteously received" by the President and Cabinet at the annual New Year's visits.

On my arrival here the old members of Congress and officers of the Government as well as citizens and visitors at the Capitol, seemed very glad to see me. I mention these little matters as indications of the feeling at present existing toward our Territory, indeed, we as a people were never before so popular as we are at present, and this popularity is mainly if not entirely owing to your telegraphic dispatch saying that Utah had not seceded, but was firm for the Constitution and the Union. Governor Seward is supposed to be the controlling spirit of the administration.[1]

On January 10 Bernhisel, in a note marked "confidential," wrote: "It is thought that the Senate will reject the nomination of the present Chief Magistrate of Utah [Dawson], in that event I shall press your name for the appointment."[2] As pointed out, the Senate never did confirm Dawson, who had already left the Territory and who obviously would have to be replaced. Bernhisel reported the news and painted a discouraging picture of the Union: "It is thought there is an able, energetic, and efficient hand needed to control and direct affairs."[3] This was not an unusual assessment of Lincoln and the government war effort at this time.

Meanwhile, Young wrote to Bernhisel on January 4: "If the Government know who their friends are, and what their true interests in regard to Utah are, they will at once, upon the presentation of our memorial and constitution, admit us as one of the family of states."[4] In his letter of January 7 to George Cannon in Liverpool he had told of the Dawson incident and the meetings to form a constitution and added, repetitiously, "If Congress understand their true interests relative to us and know who their friends are, they will act promptly and favorably upon our petition for admission."[5]

Continuing his well-known attitude toward outsiders as territorial officials, Young remarked in his conversations that "most men assigned to any position by the Federal Government do not feel they are subject to the laws of their government, but feel their word is law, and outrage the laws of the Constitution, feeling they are agents of Federal power they consider they have a right to tyrannize and oppress any people they are sent among this is the reason why Government officials have so conducted themselves here."[6]

Young often praised Bernhisel for his able and adroit efforts in Washington in behalf of the Mormons and Utah.[7] He told Bernhisel of the meetings to elect delegates to the state constitutional convention and said, "Great enthusiasm and unanimity prevailed. Surely Congress will not be so blind to the true interest of the nation and so entirely regardless of the feelings of our citizens as to treat with neglect and dis-respect their wishes when so unmistakably made known in this public and unanimous manner."[8]

Bernhisel in turn wrote to the anxious Mormon leader on January 17 that he understood that the Senate Committee on the Judiciary would report unanimously against Dawson's nomination. So he called again on the President, urging the nomination of Brigham Young. He showed Lincoln the recommendations of Chief Justice Kinney and other officials. He said he told the President that "the people of Utah would prefer Ex-Governor Young to any other man living. His reply was, 'I suppose that is so, and if the nomination be rejected, I will consider your application with others, for definite judgment in regard to it.'" Bernhisel told Young that the constitution and memorial asking admission of Utah into the Union were presented to the House of Representatives and referred to the Committee on Territories, and by that committee to a subcommittee. "I have no means of knowing what that report will be, but the indications are that it will be unfavorable. . . ."[9]

On January 24 Bernhisel gave Young even more details of the Dawson affair and its aftermath in Washington. He wrote that he understood the nomination of Dawson had been buried in the Senate. Bernhisel, armed with affidavits and other material, had seen the President, who read the documents. Bernhisel quoted the President as saying: "'I have no recollection how I came to make the appointment. I have been trying to recollect, but have less recollection about it than any important appointment that I have made.'" Bernhisel continued, interestingly, "The President appears to take matters and things very easy; neither the war nor anything else seems to trouble him. The Dawson affair has created but little sensation here. The committee on Territories to whom were referred our memorial and constitution have not yet reported, and it is more than probable from present indications that they will make an adverse report. . . . One of the greatest objections to the admission of Utah, will be the paucity of our population, though I stated that it was much larger than the Census represents it."[10]

Something of Brigham Young's continuing suspicions may be found in his comments early in 1862 when he reportedly stated to Judge Kinney, as recorded in the Office Journal, "that before the States made war upon us they could consider that probably the Mormons would burn everything up, cut down the telegraph lines, and that they might hinder them from doing so, and if they did, it might be worse for them this time than it was last. The judge acquiesced. . . ."[11] There seems no foundation for the fear that the Union would make "war" upon the Mormons, unless, of course, they became involved in the Confederacy, which was extremely unlikely.

In a major and most revealing address in the Tabernacle in Salt Lake City on January 19, 1862, entitled "Evil Deeds and Evil Doers," Brigham Young mentioned First Bull Run again, calling it "Booby Run." And then he got into the meat of things: "I cannot be intimidated by saying that there is trouble ahead for us from the Government of the United States, so long as righteousness shall prevail among the people of God, even if they should be so unwise as to again attempt to oppress us." Utah was about to organize a state government and petition for admission into the Union: "This we do to please ourselves and our God." He then warned, "And if armies are again sent here, they will find the road up Jordan a hard road to travel. As for us, we will honour and preserve inviolate the Constitution of our country, as we ever have."[12]

He again accused James Buchanan of committing treason by levying war against Utah, and by sending an army. He added,

. . . if they again make war upon us, I know not what the Lord may do. . . . I am for scourging out the ungodly and all who work indignity among this people. Those who are against the Kingdom of God must suffer. . . . I can tell all the world that we mean to sustain the Constitution of the United States and all righteous laws. We are not by any means treasoners, secessionists, or abolitionists. We are neither negro-drivers nor negro-worshippers. We belong to the family of heaven, and we intend to walk over every unrighteous and unholy principle, and view everybody and everything as it is before God, and put everything in its place. . . . So we will adjust ourselves according to the lawful doings of the nation, and will not secede from our Government; neither will we be traitors to Jesus Christ, through ungodly rulers, but will take the privilege to chasten them and guide them into the paths of right, if they will be led herein.[13]

Continually holding forth on the war in the East, Brigham Young quipped on January 21, when he heard of the capture of the Confederate emissaries to Britain and France in the *Trent* affair, that he "would have punished them, they were leading ring leaders of the South rebellion."[14] Mason and Slidell were by no means the "ring leaders" of rebellion, but they were important Confederate figures, and the fracas over their detention reached even into the far West.

Upon the departure of Dawson, Secretary Fuller temporarily resumed the post of acting governor and approved a memorial to Congress seeking admission of Utah into the federal Union.[15] The County Court House in Salt Lake City had been the scene on January 20 of the constitutional convention, of which Daniel H. Wells was president. The work had not taken long: on January 22 the convention adopted the Constitution of the State of Deseret, and memorialized Congress for admission. An election under the new constitution was set for early March. The convention nominated candidates, unopposed. As expected, they were Brigham Young for governor, Heber C. Kimball for lieutenant governor, and John M. Bernhisel as representative to Washington for the new state. On March 3 the people unanimously adopted the constitution and slate of officers, reportedly without a dissenting vote.[16]

The state legislature was elected at the same time, and convened April 14 as the General Assembly. Everything moved with considerable speed and very little opposition. Even the failure of admission as a state in 1862 would not do away with this "ghost government" which continued to exist for several years after the Civil War, until 1870. In early 1863 Brigham Young was quoted as saying that the state governmental machinery was kept ready to function when admission did come.[17] The *Deseret News* had shown the sentiments of the populace when it reported on a meeting in Salt Lake City on January 6, 1862: "There was not a dissenting voice to the proposition to call a convention, to adopt a Constitution and form a State government, and then, should it be ratified by the people, to ask Congress respectfully but firmly for admission into the Federal family on an equal footing with the original states."

The *Deseret News* and the Mormon leaders kept up a steady stream of printed and spoken rhetoric regarding statehood. The newspaper editorialized:

The people inhabiting these mountain valleys, who sought refuge here from the ruthless hand of oppression, have borne patiently the impositions that have been practiced upon them under the operations of the

Territorial form of government provided by Congress, as administered by men of corrupt minds, from those holding the appointing power down to the least recipient of executive patronage—honorable exceptions not included—till they deem it unfitting and impolitic to submit to such things any longer; but they do not wish to secede from the constitution of the United States, and only claim that the rights and privileges accorded by that system of fundamental rules shall be extended to them. They, in short, wish to elect their own rulers, pay the expenses of their government, and do every other act which sovereign people have a right to do, and not inhibited by the constitution they so much revere. That is all they ask, and all they wish; and if extended to them, as it doubtless will be, they will rejoice exceedingly, and be glad that the day of deliverance has come. The holding of the convention and the adoption of a constitution for the future government of the people of Utah will be an important epoch in their history, as the result whatever it may be, cannot fail to produce a material change in their circumstances and condition for the better.[18]

The state convention ended January 23 and the *Deseret News* put it properly:

There was a determination of purpose manifest by the delegates, collectively and individually, to carry out the designs and wishes of the people in the institution of a State Government . . . and, that in the event of the request for admission into the family of States should be refused, they feared not the consequences of throwing off the Federal yoke and assuming the right of self-government, of which they have so long been deprived. . . . However, it is a matter of but little consequence to the people of Utah, whether Congress does, or does not, accord to them their constitutional rights, as they assume and maintain them peaceably, unless force be interposed to prevent, in which case they will do, as heretofore, as best they can and abide the result.[19]

The editorial amounted to a threat, but there is little evidence that Utah, if rejected for statehood, would ever seriously have considered going on its own. Chief Justice Kinney, probably the most acceptable non-Mormon federal official, in an address supported the statehood move: "Is Utah for ever doomed to remain in collonial [*sic*] vassalage barred of her Constitutional rights, denied the precious boon of 'self-government,' rendered doubly dear to citizens in consequence of the strangers appointed to rule over them?"[20]

It wasn't until January 30 that Brigham Young answered Bernhisel about the friendly New Year's Day reception of the Utah delegate. He felt it flattering, especially the attentions of Secretary of State Seward. Young asked, "... don't you think, and will not President Lincoln, Secretary Seward, and other Cabinet officers, and the Members of Congress readily conclude that it it is but just and Constitutionally right and far the best policy to at once admit Utah into the family of States, and correspondingly act in accordance with so correct a conclusion?"[21]

The letters, which were, in fact, instructions from Young to Bernhisel, were frequent, particularly at this time, even though Young still held no official position in the Territory. Young on February 5 told the delegate about the constitutional convention:

... there was not a particle of authority given Congress by the Constitution to organize Territorial government. . . . Such being the real fact on that point, what good reason can Congress urge against our admission to the family of States, our Constitution being strictly republican in form, and we having long ago proved our capability to sustain self government. Aside from the justness of our being relieved from our illegal colonial position, which we have borne so long and patiently, it most certainly is to their pecuniary interest to admit us, a view of so slight moment at present. You can inform the President that he need not appoint a Governor, Judges, etc., for Utah, or if he appoints them, that he can pay them their salaries there, and advise them to remain at home, for we have no use for them here.[22]

Young undoubtedly was aware that the main obstacle to public acceptance of statehood for Utah outside the Territory was the polygamy issue, but at that moment he chose to ignore it.

Young was also speaking out publicly on what he believed were the rights of Utah. In an address entitled "Constitutional Powers of the Congress in the United States," in the Tabernacle on March 9, Young said:

We are greatly blessed, greatly favored and greatly exalted, while our enemies, who sought to destroy us, are being humbled. We want our political rights, and they are here within our reach. . . . The people are here, and they possess rights. . . . It is our right to frame our own laws, and to elect our own officers to administer them. . . . The enemies of God and truth do not love us any better this year than they did last year, nor will their love for us increase in the year that is to come. . . . The valleys of Utah are the safest places in the world. There is no place upon this globe where a people can with more safety assert their rights before the heavens and in fact of all men. . . . We will cling to the Constitution of our country, and to the Government that reveres that sacred charter of freemen's rights; and, if necessary, pour out our best blood for the defence of every good and righteous principle.[23]

As the Mormons watched the heightening flames of Civil War, Young warned the people that it would be increasingly difficult to obtain manufactured goods from the East. In an address of February 2 he said, "At no distant period, merchandise in imported goods will cease in their territory, and the fabrics we wear will be manufactured by ourselves—imported fabrics will not be here." He urged the people to prepare to grow and manufacture what they would consume.[24] The situation never became that serious, for the Mormons had always produced much of what they used.

In answer to the concerns of many as to protection of the Overland Trail and the new telegraph line, Brigham Young wrote to H. W. Carpentier, President of the California State Telegraph Company in San Francisco, on February 14 that "Utah, without doubt, will, as early as practicable, take steps to protect the rights of the Overland Telegraph Co. within her borders."[25]

Keeping his foreign stations posted, Young told W. C. Haines in London on February 25 that "The South at this time is being worsted. The sympathies of our brethren are divided some for the Union and some for the South, but the South gets the greatest share. The wise among us read the programme of the war in the revelations of Joseph and the escapes and reverses of our common foe never leads us to the conclusion that peace will again be restored among the enemies of truth and workers of unrighteousness whether belonging to the North or South." Young went on to say that more respect was being paid "to the Mormon who hails from Utah."[26] As to the South being worsted, Young probably is referring to the Union victories at Forts Donelson and Henry in Tennessee in February, where the federal troops forced important breakthroughs in Confederate defenses. But sympathy with the South, per se, is hard to find. That there was and would continue to be anti-Union feeling was undoubtedly true. However, the third choice of sentiment among the people which seemed to predominate was pro-Mormonism.

On February 25, Young predicted to Bernhisel the election in

Utah of the pro-admission ticket and the unanimous confirmation of the constitution. Since there were no opposing candidates or questioned issues, the outcome was hardly in question.[27] The Mormon leader also told Bernhisel that the stumbling block of too small a population for admission was spurious. Secretary of State Seward's speech in favor of admission of Kansas was used in favor of Utah by Young. Seward had claimed that capability to sustain a republican form of government was the only criterion for admission, rather than population. Young felt Utah had proven its responsibility. He added: "The party in power, whose leader [Seward] . . . was in the Senate and whose Secretary of State he now is, most certainly should not swerve from so fair and just a position and endeavor to keep a large portion of their fellows in Territorial pupilage on the irrelevant question of population, especially when mere numbers have been often and correctly disregarded, and more especially when our population is already so large and increasing so rapidly."[28]

Young wrote to Church leaders and others on a wide variety of subjects and showed his concern over many issues. He reiterated his Indian policy, which had proven reasonably successful, for the Mormons at least, when he wrote to local Mormon official Orson Hyde at Springtown in Sanpete County, Utah, on March 8 that Indians in the area were "a poor miserable race!" and for that reason and others, "prudence counsels that they be dealt with on our part in the mildest, most forbearing and liberal manner that the circumstances and relative conditions of both parties will permit." As to the war, he told Hyde that "indications were that the South was becoming more united and in earnest, while the Radicals of the North were crowding extreme measures in Congress as to foreshadow early and wide dissensions in their ranks." He also commented on emigration, missionary work, the new constitution, and the Salt Lake City theater, one of his favorite projects.[29]

He again outlined Indian policy in a letter of March 15 to Bishop Thomas J. Thurston of Weber Valley in Morgan County: "All our experience proves that it is much cheaper, and it is certainly far better and more consistent with our professions, to conciliate the Indians in and around the settlement than, for a trifling amount, to excite their animosity and thereby incur the risk of loss of property and perhaps of lives."[30] As in so many policies,

Young took the pragmatic and logical approach which would benefit the Mormons rather than always making decisions on a higher philosophical plane.

To two elders who had gone east, Young wrote on March 11 that although the weather was bad on election day there had been quite an enthusiastic turnout and he had not yet heard of a single vote against the constitution.[31]

On March 18, Young, critical as usual of the federal government, is reported to have discussed with Heber C. Kimball "the wicked course the American Nation has taken with this people" and he complained that the government was "running into despotism. . . . The President observed that Abraham Lincoln was a sagacious man, but believed he was wicked."[32] It is difficult to know how exact these quotations from the Brigham Young Office Journal are, but there is no doubt that Young's view of Lincoln was not as idealistic in 1862 as the Mormon position was later to become.

As the spring brought news of Union successes on the Mississippi River and to a lesser extent in Virginia, Young wrote to Bernhisel: "Doubtless the Members of Congress feel highly elated by the recent successes, which is but natural; still by the time our Senators reach Washington with our new Constitution, &c., affairs may be in such condition as to cause quite a majority in both Houses to vote for our admission . . . when we have taken the proper and Constitutional steps for admission the Lord will rule their actions for the best interests of his cause and people on the earth, whichever way that may be, wherefore borrow no trouble to the case, for all will be well."[33]

In commenting on Confederate leadership, Young reportedly said on March 28 that if Jefferson Davis "had adopted the Guerrilla mode of fighting he would have been more successful."[34]

Bernhisel in Washington had been busy all winter and spring on behalf of Utah, or really on behalf of Young and the Mormons, though the three were nearly synonymous at this time. Bernhisel was involved in railroad and land matters, Indian problems, appropriations for the Territory, postal service, and other subjects. He obviously regretted having to write Young on February 21, "I am sorry to add that from all I have been able to ascertain from Members of Congress, that there is not the least prospect of our being admitted for a few years yet and until our population is much larger."[35]

By February 28 he concluded Secretary of State Seward would not favor admission, despite his view sanctioning the admission of Kansas. "Though I do not hear the slightest objection to our Constitution from any member of the Committee on Territories to which our Memorial and Constitution was referred, yet that committee voted unanimously against the admission of Utah, and I regret to add, that I do not know a single member either of the Senate or of the House who will vote for the admission of our Territory into the Union as a State."[36] This was even a colder reception than Bernhisel had expected. On March 7 the delegate informed Young that "one reason assigned by the Committee for rejecting our application for admission was that it was inexpedient at present to admit any Territory into the Union as a State."[37]

Bernhisel was even more pessimistic on March 21:

I am sorry to be obliged to state that the prospects of the admission of Utah into the Union are very discouraging, or rather that there are no prospects at all of this desirable event. Although Governor Seward delivered in the Senate the flaming speech to which you refer in favor of the admission of Kansas, yet he would not say a word in favor of the admission of our Territory. The House Committee on Territories to whom our Constitution was referred did not make the slightest objection to it, that I heard or that I am aware of, yet they unanimously rejected our application for admission. One reason for their action was, the bitter and deep rooted prejudice aginst the 'peculiar institution' and against us as a people which is everywhere showing its cloven foot. And another was the smallness of our population. If our population were equal to the present ratio of representation, which is one hundred and twenty six thousand nine hundred and three, we might claim it as a right, but I regret to say, that until our population is in that neighborhood, we have scarcely the shadow of a chance of admission. I am sorry to be obliged to write you such unwelcome news, but I feel it to be my duty to inform you of the true condition of affairs here.[38]

Bernhisel was undoubtedly perceptive here. The institution of polygamy was certainly the biggest roadblock to admission. The population restriction was largely an excuse, for, if the population had been sufficient, Congress could hardly have turned Utah down. There was no doubt that the 1862 fight for admission had failed.

Bernhisel was running into other problems. He explained to Brigham Young on April 4 that the House Committee on Territories desired to annex a considerable portion of western Utah to Nevada. He assigned the reason, quoting the committee chairman, to make Nevada as large as Utah. But Bernhisel felt the true reason was that the new annexation to Nevada would include gold mines in the Humboldt Mountains.[39] Bernhisel had an additional difficulty. He wrote Young on April 18 that some of their enemies were trying to get Brigham Young's Indian accounts refused by Congress. These were monies spent by Young when he had held the post of Indian agent in Utah along with all his other duties. Bernhisel was working to prevent this refusal.[40]

It had been a snowy, stormy, wet winter and spring in Utah. Yet this did not prevent large turnouts for the uncontested elections, conventions, meetings, and for the April gathering of the new proposed "state" legislature. Prior to the convening of this deliberative body, Brigham Young in the Tabernacle on April 8 once more outlined his policy:

I wish to inform all the inhabitants of the Territory of Utah, Jew and Gentile, bond and free, male and female, black and white, red, copper-colored and yellow, that, in organizing a State Government we shall not infringe in the least upon the Constitution of our country, upon any principle contained in the Declaration of Independence, nor upon any constitutional law that has been enacted by the Congress of the United States. Will this step bring upon us the disapprobation of the Government of the United States? That is not for me to say; it will be as God may direct. . . . It is well known that the Congress of the United States has no power granted in the Constitution to organize a Territorial Government, and every power that is not named in the Constitution for Congress to act upon is reserved to the people. But Congress assumes power that does not belong to it, and if it continues to do so, soon the last vestige of the free, independent, Republican and Democratic Government we have enjoyed will be merged into a military despotism, if there is anything left. Our Government is at present engaged in an expensive war. It has been supposed that the South would soon be subjugated, that they would yield the point and submit. They will not, and the war has scarcely commenced. The slave States do not as yet appear to be whipped or conquered. Both North and South are in the hands of the Lord, and so are we.[41]

The new legislature, with federal approval or not, met on April 14, 1862, in Salt Lake City in a joint session. "Governor" Brigham Young reiterated many of the same old themes. He held that the citizens of a territory, despite numbers, should have a voice in the Representative branch of the government, and be allowed to vote for the governor or chief magistrate, and, if possible, all the territorial officers. He said that when the people properly express their wish to become a state they should be welcomed. California was used as an example. Young concluded: "I wish it distinctly understood that I object to any action being taken in this or any other matter, except on the ground of right and justice, and in no wise as an evidence of our loyalty, for it has ofttimes been severely tested, and has on every occasion emerged from the test with unsullied purity. We are not here as aliens from our government, but we are tried and firm supporters of the Constitution and every constitutional right."[42] On April 16 other state officers were elected by the legislature. William H. Hooper (territorial delegate before Bernhisel) and George Q. Cannon were chosen senators. The secretary of state was Daniel H. Wells. Bishop Cannon was in Europe at the time on Church business and was to join Hooper in Washington. Utah's territorial delegate, Bernhisel, was already in Washington and was to be the new representative of the state of Deseret.[43]

The memorial to Congress of April 17 from the General Assembly of the proposed state of Deseret read in part:

[We] respectfully state that our peculiarly isolated position, the well proven inadequacy of a Territorial organization to meet the wants of a rapidly increasing population now numbering from eighty to a hundred thousand, a disposition to lessen Government expenditures when they are of necessity so great, and an earnest desire to enjoy those inherent, inalienable, and Constitutional rights guaranteed to every American citizen have induced the citizens of Utah to unanimously and Constitutionally organize a State government, preparatory to their admission into the Union as the State of Deseret.[44]

The quest for statehood for Utah was now entangled in the move by Congress to ban the institution of polygamy, which was no doubt the major obstacle to statehood. The Mormons had a few friends in Congress, but they also had a good many enemies, who were far in the majority. Representative Justin S. Morrill of Vermont, originator of much important civil legislation, introduced on April 8, 1862, a bill in the House "to punish and prevent the practice of polygamy in the Territories of the United States, and for other purposes, and to disapprove certain acts of the Legislative Assembly of the Territory of Utah." This measure was referred to the Committee on Territories.[45] The bill was reported back to the House on April 28 with recommendation that it pass, which it did the same day with no recorded vote.[46] There was no debate. The Senate received the measure on April 29.[47] It was reported out from committee on May 9.[48] Delegate Bernhisel described the passage of the anti-polygamy bill in the House factually to Brigham Young on May 2, and of the final passage he wrote, "A few voices were heard in the negative on the democratic side of the Hall."[49]

On June 3 the Senate briefly debated the measure and it passed, thirty-seven to two. The two opposed were senators James A. McDougall and Milton S. Latham of California. McDougall opposed the bill although he deplored polygamy as a "vicious practice." But he felt the nation had enough trouble on its hands without invoking further discord. He felt this legislation would mean cutting of the transcontinental communication and it "certainly will invite great hostility, and interfere with the general interests of the country." Furthermore, and McDougall was correct here: "Its provisions will be either ignored or avoided."[50] Brought back to the House on June 5, amendments to the bill were concurred in on June 24.[51] The bill had never received the expected acrimonious debate; it was signed by the President on July 2, 1862.

The anti-polygamy measure stated that anyone practicing polygamy should be adjudged guilty of bigamy. Upon conviction such a person could be fined no more than $500 and imprisoned for not more than five years. The act disapproved and annulled all acts of the Utah Territorial Legislature relative to polygamy. A final section ruled that no corporation or association for religious or charitable purpose could hold more than $50,000 in real estate in any territory.[52] According to most authorities, the anti-polygamy act of 1862 was largely a dead letter in the law books as to enforcement. It was almost completely ignored by the Mormons and by law-enforcement agencies.[53]

The scene as far as statehood for Utah Territory went had shifted more and more to Washington. While the polygamy bill was before Congress, John M. Bernhisel, with consent as a territorial delegate, on June 9 laid before the House the constitution formed by the Utah convention and the memorial asking Congress to admit Utah into the Union.[54] The documents were sent to the Committee on Territories. Vice-President Hannibal Hamlin presented the same documents to the Senate and they were also referred to the Committee on Territories.

Bernhisel and Deseret "Senators-elect" Hooper and Cannon, who had come to Washington from Britain, were striving to secure statehood. The senators-elect were allowed the courtesy of the Senate floor.[55] Although it appears they did win some friends, as one historian put it, "The wall of prejudice was too thick to be penetrated . . . [Utah] was still deemed by many disloyal, unpatriotic, unworthy to be trusted with the privilege of governing herself."[56] Had the Mormons abandoned polygamy it is possible and even probable that Utah would have been admitted. There was also some concern over the fact that church and state were so closely tied in Utah, with considerable church domination.

Brigham Young gave his instructions to the new "senators" as early as April 25: "It will be well to bear in mind that the action of the General Assembly was not designed to infringe and has not in the least infringed upon our territorial organization . . . but merely went far enough to initiate a State organization as fair ground upon which to petition, and in readiness to so put in operation as soon as Congress answers our petition for admission." But, in actuality, Young had created a second government for Utah which, with his own powerful position and the Mormon Church, was essentially circumventing the inept territorial government.[57]

In the same letter Young stated that a new territorial governor to replace Dawson "will be received and treated with the courtesy due his position, so long as he demeans himself properly and as a good citizen." Young claimed no one had interfered with Acting Governor Fuller or Chief Justice Kinney.[58] Then, turning to the larger issue, Young wrote, "In all this, after patiently waiting for our political rights during long years past, we have at length only exercised this portion of our Constitutional rights as American citizens; and . . . still patiently postpone the full exercise of these rights until we hear the results of your efforts in Washington."[59] On June 5, Young wrote Hooper, "You fully understand our feelings in regard to admission, and it merely remains for you . . . to do the best you can under the circumstances, trusting in the Lord who ordereth the results; and when you have done this, of course, you are at liberty to start for home."[60] To Bernhisel, the same day, Young wrote that work on the temple was progressing favorably and the recent high water had done little damage. Thus, "the people continue peaceful, prosperous, and greatly blest."[61] To Elder Chauncey West in Liverpool, also on June 5, Young played down the Indian troubles, again saying: ". . . the hue and cry about hostile Indians between Ft. Bridger and Platte [River] Bridge has thus far resulted principally in smoke, as we felt assured at the time it would be."[62] But, actually, there was plenty of destructive smoke and fire.

Brigham Young continued to disseminate his message about Utah and the Mormons. To one A. Barber in Burlington, Iowa, on June 17 he wrote,

Profanity, drunkeness, gambling, &c., are more frowned upon and less indulged in here than in any community I know of, and nearly all practice the golden precept, "mind your own business," which makes the conduct of affairs and social intercourse very pleasant and we daily aim to increase the love for and practice of the aforesaid excellent precept. All desiring to come here for laudable and legitimate purposes are welcome, and all are respected and treated courteously, so long as they conduct themselves in accordance with wholesome laws, regulations, and customs. All the channels of business usual in a newly settled and isolated country like this are equally open to all, and new channels are continually opening for the energies, skills and capital of the young and enterprising, as also for the moderate calculations for winning a comfortable and honorable livelihood.[63]

The precept of minding one's own business was undoubtedly a worthy one, but Brigham Young himself and the Mormon Church seem to have had influence in almost every activity, project, and policy. It was Young and the Church that set the "wholesome laws, regulations, and customs."

Bernhisel had presented the prospective senators and other

Mormon leaders to the President "who," he wrote, "received us in a quite easy and friendly manner. In the course of the interview I spoke to his Excellency of our Constitution and memorial asking Congress to admit our Territory into the Union as a State. He simply remarked that he had heard of it from the Vice President, and then made some inquiries in regard to our population." [64]

By July 4 Bernhisel reported to Brigham Young that the Senate Committee on Territories seemed more favorably disposed to Utah than did the same committee of the House. He presented the new "senators" and Brigham Young, Jr., to Secretary of State Seward. Bernhisel wrote that "the Secretary was not inclined to say much in regard to" statehood. Bernhisel continued that Seward "made some inquiries relative to our population, and remarked that the subject of population was a subordinate question, for if the population of a Territory was not sufficient to entitle her to admission, that it was constantly increasing, and that she would soon have enough." Bernhisel tried to introduce his group to Secretary of War Edwin M. Stanton but did not manage it. Bernhisel thought that, of the seven members in the Senate Committee on Territories, Senators Benjamin Wade of Ohio and Samuel Pomeroy and James Henry Lane of Kansas, all Radical Republicans, favored admission, but there was difficulty in getting a quorum. [65]

On July 11 Bernhisel again wrote Young a frank letter describing his interview with Representative John Phelps of Missouri, who was critical of the Mormons: "In the course of the interview as I expected he would, he also brought up that horrid Mountain Meadows massacre. This atrocious affair has done us, and still continues to do us as a people incalculable injury, and will prove a serious obstacle to our admission into the Union as a sovereign and independent State, and the miscreants who were engaged in this cold blooded and diabolical deed, will have a fearful account to render in the judgment of the great day." [66]

By mid-summer of 1862 the prospects for statehood for Utah Territory any time soon had virtually disappeared. The memorials and the constitution died a very quiet death in the territorial committees of Congress.

In 1862, as in previous years, Utah put on a grand and spectacular Fourth of July celebration, followed on July 24 with observance of Pioneer Day. Among the dignitaries at the latter occasion in Salt Lake City was the newly arrived and newly appointed governor, Stephen S. Harding. Governor Harding was, like his predecessor, from Indiana, and had arrived in Salt Lake City on July 7. A few days later the two new territorial judges, Charles B. Waite and Thomas J. Drake, came in, joining Chief Justice Kinney. Fuller was still secretary, and James Duane Doty still superintendent of Indian affairs.

A lawyer and politician, Stephen S. Harding was born in Ontario County, New York, in 1808, but as a youth moved with his parents to Ripley County, Indiana. He received a typical scanty and rudimentary education in the near-wilderness schools, but at sixteen was himself teaching country school. By 1828 he was admitted to the bar after studying law in Brookville, Indiana. He then opened an office in Richmond. After a brief time in New Orleans, Louisiana, where he saw slavery at first hand, he returned to Indiana in 1829 and located at Versailles, where his law practice prospered. He was a Whig until 1840, but was known as a zealous and extreme abolitionist. He had been nominated several times for governor and lieutenant governor of Indiana on the Liberal ticket, but was never elected.[67]

Harding had left the Whigs in 1840 because they were not strongly enough opposed to slavery. It was his view that the U.S. Constitution did not approve servitude but was in fact against slavery.[68] He was known not only as a lawyer and office seeker, but as a skillful orator in the style of the day.[69] As a young man, while on a trip east, he apparently had met Joseph Smith and was an overnight guest in his home. Harding rejected Smith's efforts to enlist him in Mormonism.[70] Widely read in the anti-slavery publications, he used these viewpoints in his speeches. He was said to have had a deep, resounding voice and a convincing manner.[71] And he was completely uncompromising in his abolitionist views. By 1856 Harding had joined the embryonic Republican party in Indiana and in 1860 was a member of the State Central Committee.[72] Indiana had an important role in the nomination of Lincoln.

Harding had powerful backing for the post of governor of Utah Territory. He had met Lincoln with Indiana Radicals Henry Smith Lane and George Washington Julian in December, 1861, and wrote that Lincoln had told him that if Dawson's appointment were not confirmed by the Senate, Harding would have it.[73] Harding's recommendations included such powerful support as a letter from Governor Oliver Perry Morton of Indiana. All of Harding's letters mention his loyalty to the Republican party, which meant mainly the Radical element. Lane and Julian also wrote in his behalf, as did various Indiana officials, congressmen, legislators, and others, many of them signing petitions in his favor. An Indiana Republican, they felt, deserved the post. Harding was "an honest man, a good lawyer and tried Republican" who had long supported "free principles."[74] Harding himself wrote fellow Radical Secretary of the Treasury Salmon P. Chase in his own behalf. Chase wrote to the President on March 21, endorsing Harding.[75]

On February 16, 1862, Harding himself wrote to Lincoln reminding him of the "promise" in December. Harding said that, despite Dawson's view to the contrary, he would not ask for any military force for protection against any violence from the hands of the people of Utah. Harding assured the President: "If I had not the public confidence that I can restore peace and harmony in that territory I would not deserve the position which my friends had asked for me. But having the fullest confidence in my ability as a pacificator and that I can greatly subserve the interest of my country, if the opportunity shall present itself, I will be doubly thankful to your Excellency, for that important trust."[76] Harding, of course, received the appointment. The new associate justices of Utah Territory named by Lincoln, Thomas J. Drake of Michigan and Charles B. Waite of Illinois, were supporters of Harding and the Radical Republicans.[77]

Both Brigham Young and the newly arrived governor orated at length in Salt Lake City on Pioneer Day. Brigham Young took the opportunity once more to expound on the patriotism of the Mormons: "If there is one portion of the people belonging to the Government of the United States who love, revere, and hold sacred the Constitution of that Government more than any other portion, it is the Latter-day Saints. . . . God did not design that we should entirely leave the Government of the United States, neither did we wish to. . . . We are now asking for admission as a State, and we intend to continue to ask, and 'bide our time,' and to live by and honor the Constitution of our country, whether others do so or not."[78]

Harding was cheered as he rose and said:

If I know my own heart, I come amongst you a messenger of peace and good will. I have no wrongs—either real or imaginary, to complain of, and no religious prejudices to overcome—[applause]. Believing, as I do, that the Constitution of the United States secures to every citizen the right to worship God according to the dictates of his own conscience; and, holding, further, that the Constitution itself is dependent for its support and maintenance on the preservation of that sacred right, it follows, as a corollary, that under no pretext whatever, will I consent to its violation in this particular, by any official act of mine, whilst Governor of this Territory—[tremendous applause].

Harding went on at some length on religious freedom. Then he turned to Utah itself:

On every hand I behold a miracle of labor. Fifteen years ago to-day, you and your Pioneers, by their heroism and devotion to a principle, consecrated this valley to a civilization wonderful "to the stranger within your gates," and in the developments of which a new era will be stamped not only upon the history of our own country, but on the world. You have indeed "caused the desert to blossom as the rose." . . . Wonderful progress! Wonderful people! . . . Honestly conform to the standard of your creed and faith, and though you may for a time be "cast down," you cannot be destroyed [great applause]. . . . This is the hour when your loyalty to our common country is most acceptable and grateful to the heart of every patriot. . . .[79]

With such words Harding was naturally warmly received by the citizens of Utah in the summer of 1862. He did appear to be more understanding of Mormon institutions and less an enemy in their eyes. But his attitude was soon to change.

The Mormon president remained conscious of the criticism of polygamy. In remarks in the Bowery on July 6 Young argued: "Monogamy, or restriction by law to one wife, is no part of the economy of heaven among men." The recent law to punish polygamy was a case of Congress undertaking "to dictate the Almighty in his revelations to his people. . . . Why do we believe in and practice polygamy? Because the Lord introduced it to his servants in a revelation given to Joseph Smith, and Lord's servants have always practiced it."[80] In the same address Young said Mormons had "never suffered anything in comparison to what the people in many of the states are now suffering. . . . The present Government of the United States is self-destroying as they are now proving."[81]

In another Bowery address that day Young kept up his criticism of the government of the United States.

We say that we live in a Republican Government, and we hold that we have the best national constitution in the world; but a wicked people will corrupt themselves and do wickedly under any government, and, in so doing, will sooner or later be destroyed. . . . The people in the States have violated the Constitution in closing their ears against the cries of the oppressed, and in consenting to shedding innocent blood, and now war, death and gloom are spread like a pall over the land, which state of things will sooner or later spread all over the world. The world is at war against the truth and against those who propagate it.[82]

Young also made known his views on the war itself. He wrote to Elder Eveleth in San Francisco on July 17:

You are correct in your statement that the war is not quite ended and singular as it may sound, it is further from being ended as the North wished it to than when it began. Of course, Congress has no Constitutional right to pass such an act as the one against polygamy, except for the District of Columbia, but the Constitution is an instrument of writing that of late seems to be very readily disregarded when interfering with partisan purposes. But you are safe in concluding that it, like all other projects of the same nature, will disappoint the expectations of those who strive to hinder the progress of truth.[83]

Then, to Captain Walter Gibson in the Hawaiian Islands on July 18 Young wrote, "By our latest dispatches it appears that the prospects of the North's conquering the South are much poorer than they have been at any time since the war began. These circumstances, contrasted with the relative numbers, wealth, and facilities of the two parties, plainly indicate an ordering of events that neither party in the least comprehends or recognizes."[84] By the latest war news he probably meant the unsuccessful attempt by Union General George B. McClellan to defeat Lee or capture Richmond on the Peninsula of Virginia.

Returning to the now quiescent effort toward statehood, Young wrote on August 6 to Senator-elect Cannon, back in Liverpool, "The non-action of Congress upon our petition creates no surprise in your constituents, nor the least feeling that you were one particle remiss in labor or duty." [85]

In an August 31 address in the Bowery Young spoke of a famous dispute between editor Horace Greeley and President Lincoln. According to Young, "Mr. Lincoln declared it was his intention to do everything in his power that he thought would save the Union. This was very just and correct in him, but has his course invariably tended to save the Union? Time will show. There is no man can see, unless he sees by the gift and power of revelation, that every move that has been made by the Government has been made to fulfil the sayings of Joseph Smith the Prophet, and all earth and hell cannot help it." He referred again to the prophecy of Joseph Smith on the dissolution of the Union and went on:

The wickedness of the wicked is onward and downward, while the righteousness of the righteous is onward and upward. Light and darkness, or in other words, right and wrong, are with us, and men choose darkness rather than light, wrong rather than right. This is their condemnation. They dispise the truth and those who will declare it. . . . We are determined to build up the Kingdom of God on the earth, to bring forth Zion, to promote the cause of righteousness on the earth, and to walk under foot sin and wickedness. There is an opposing party who are determined that the Kingdom of God shall not be built up, and who do all in their power to destroy it and its supporters. . . . Our course is onward to build up Zion, and the nation that has slain the Prophet of God and cast out his people will have to pay the debt. They will be broken in pieces like a potter's vessel; yes, worse, they will be ground to powder. [86]

NOTES

1. Bernhisel Papers.
2. *Ibid.*
3. *Ibid.*
4. Brigham Young Letter Books, Church Archives.
5. *Ibid.*
6. Brigham Young Office Journal, Jan 9, 1862.
7. Brigham Young Letter Books, Church Archives, Jan. 14, 1862.
8. *Ibid.*
9. Bernhisel Papers, Jan. 17, 1862.
10. *Ibid.*, Jan. 24, 1862.
11. Brigham Young Office Journal, Jan. 8, 1862.
12. *Journal of Discourses*, vol. IX, p. 157.

13. *Ibid.*
14. Brigham Young Office Journal.
15. Whitney, *History of Utah*, vol. II, p. 38.
16. *Ibid.*
17. *Deseret News*, Jan. 21, 1863.
18. *Ibid.*, Jan. 15, 1862.
19. *Ibid.*, Jan. 29, 1862.
20. *Ibid.*, Feb. 5, 1862.
21. Brigham Young Letter Books, Church Archives.
22. *Ibid.*
23. *Journal of Discourses*, vol. X, pp. 38–41.
24. Nibley, *Brigham Young*, p. 377.
25. Brigham Young Letter Books, Church Archives.
26. *Ibid.*
27. *Ibid.*
28. *Ibid.*, Feb. 25, 1862.
29. *Ibid.*
30. *Ibid.*
31. *Ibid.*
32. Brigham Young Office Journal. Unfortunately, the words following this comment on Lincoln are crossed out and unreadable.
33. Brigham Young Letter Books, Church Archives, Mar. 22, 1862.
34. Brigham Young Office Journal. Unfortunately, the Office Journal for the rest of 1862 and 1863 is no longer as full in expressing the views of Brigham Young, and is less personal, with more notations of appointments.
35. Bernhisel Papers.
36. *Ibid.*
37. *Ibid.*
38. *Ibid.*
39. *Ibid.*
40. *Ibid.*
41. *Journal of Discourses*, vol. X, pp. 32–33.
42. Whitney, *History of Utah*, vol. II, pp. 42–43.
43. *Ibid.*
44. Brigham Young Letter Books, Church Archives.
45. *Congressional Globe*, 37th Cong., 2nd sess., pt. 2, p. 1581.
46. *Ibid.*, pp. 1847–48.
47. *Ibid.*, p. 1854.
48. *Ibid.*, pt. 3, p. 2031.
49. Bernhisel Papers.
50. *Congressional Globe*, 37th Cong., 2nd sess., pt. 3, p. 2507.
51. *Ibid.*, pp. 2587, 2906.
52. *Ibid.*, Appendix, p. 385.
53. Whitney, *History of Utah*, vol. II, p. 70.
54. *Congressional Globe*, 37th Cong., 2nd sess., pt. 3, p. 2620.
55. Bernhisel Papers, June 12, 1862.

56. Whitney, *History of Utah*, vol. II, pp. 58–59.

57. Brigham Young Letter Books, Church Archives.

58. *Ibid.*

59. *Ibid.*

60. *Ibid.*

61. *Ibid.*

62. *Ibid.*

63. *Ibid.*

64. Bernhisel Papers, June 12, 1862.

65. *Ibid.*, July 4, 1862.

66. *Ibid.*, July 11, 1862.

67. *National Cyclopaedia of American Biography* (New York: James T. White & Co., 1900–1907), vol. XII, p. 515.

68. Thornbrough, *Indiana in the Civil War Era*, p. 25.

69. Etta Reeves French, "Stephen S. Harding: A Hoosier Abolitionist," *Indiana Magazine of History*, 27 (Sept., 1931), 207–9.

70. *Ibid.*, p. 210.

71. *Ibid.*, p. 212.

72. *Ibid.*, p. 227.

73. Stephen S. Harding to Lincoln, Feb. 16, 1862, Letters of Application and Recommendation, U.S. Dept. of State, Record Group 59, National Archives; see also Tegeder, "Lincoln and the Territorial Patronage," pp. 86–87.

74. Various letters in Letters of Application and Recommendation relative to Stephen S. Harding, Feb.–Apr., 1862.

75. *Ibid.*, Mar. 21, 1862.

76. *Ibid.*, Feb. 16, 1862.

77. Tegeder, "Lincoln and the Territorial Patronage," pp. 86–87.

78. *Deseret News*, July 30, 1862.

79. Tullidge, *History of Salt Lake City*, pp. 269–70.

80. *Deseret News*, Aug. 6, 1862; *Journal of Discourses*, vol. IX, p. 322.

81. *Journal of Discourses*, vol. IX, pp. 320–22.

82. *Ibid.*, pp. 322–23.

83. Brigham Young Letter Books, Church Archives.

84. *Ibid.*

85. *Ibid.*

86. *Journal of Discourses*, vol. IX, pp. 367–68.

CHAPTER

V

Indians, Militia, and Apostates

THE SPRING OF 1862 saw Utah's only direct military participation in the Civil War. It originated when Senator-elect Hooper was accompanied in April on his long trip east by the thirty-man mounted escort of Colonel Robert T. Burton and the Utah Militia. Although the militia was in fact a Mormon organization, in this case the troops were ordered out by Acting Governor Fuller. They were to guard the mail, stage, and wagon trails eastward as the Indians were reportedly becoming more hostile and had destroyed several mail stations between Fort Bridger and the North Platte, had burned coaches, stolen stock, and had killed stage drivers.[1] Fuller, Chief Justice Kinney and other leaders, some of whom were associated with the mail and telegraph lines, had asked the War Department to have Superintendent of Indian Affairs James Duane Doty raise and put in operation a regiment of volunteer rangers or cavalry from Utah Territory.[2] This obviously was intended to bypass the Mormon Militia and Brigham Young. Young, however, wired Washington on April 14, through Delegate Bernhisel, that he knew of the move by Fuller and others, but that, "So far as I know, the Indians in Utah are unusually quiet. . . . Besides the militia of Utah are ready and able as they ever have been, to take care of all the Indians within our borders, and are able and willing to protect the mail lines, if called upon so to do."[3]

Actually, Young joined Fuller in raising the Burton party. But, to lend a military air, Lieutenant General Daniel H. Wells of the

Nauvoo Legion Militia, Utah Territory, on April 25 issued his own orders in compliance with the request of Acting Governor Fuller that Colonel R. T. Burton be authorized to raise his force and proceed on the Overland Mail Route to guard the route, mails, passengers, and property. Mail coaches were to travel with the troops and Burton would remain on the line until troops from the East arrived or so long "as it may be necessary to quiet the Indians, who are said to be hostile, and the road considered safe from their depredations."[4]

Young had issued specific orders to Burton on April 24: "In traveling be constant and vigilant and keep together and allow no straggling from Camp either night or day. There must not be any drinking of spirituous liquors, neither swearing or abusive language of any kind, and treat every body with courtesy and prove there is no necessity of trouble with the Indians when white men act with propriety. If you can speak with Indians treat them kindly showing them that you are their friends and so far as you are able, investigate the cause and origin of the present difficulties."[5] Strange military orders, indeed!

On May 16 Burton reported from Deer Creek that they had seen no Indians and that the weather was the main problem. They had found deserted mail stations from Green River to Deer Creek, in what is now Wyoming, with stock and other property missing and probably stolen. At Ice Spring Station they found a locked mail of twenty-six sacks, many of which had been ripped open and scattered over the prairie. Burton complained that letters "had been opened and pillaged, showing conclusively that some renegade whites were connected with the robbery." Burton felt the depredations may have been the work of about thirty Snakes and Bannocks from the north. He said he learned that some of the "Indians" spoke plain English and one even spoke German.[6] Brigham Young wrote to Delegate Bernhisel on April 25 of his suspicions about the reported Indian forays to the east: ". . . whether the troubles were caused by Indians or whether some persons are taking measures to induce Government to send troops along the line to gratify private designs in money making, etc., is not yet clear, though I am inclined to the opinion that the last named is the cause or source of what little interruption has happened."[7]

But on April 28, 1862, the situation changed drastically. U.S.

Army Adjutant General Lorenzo Thomas, by order of the Secretary of War and the President, wrote to Brigham Young: "By express direction of the President of the United States you are hereby authorized to raise, arm, and equip one company of cavalry for ninety days' service." The company was to have officers and from fifty-six to seventy-two privates. It "will be employed to protect the property of the telegraph and overland mail companies in or about Independence Rock [now in Wyoming, on the Oregon Trail], where depredations have been committed, and will be continued in service only till the U.S. troops can reach the point where they are so much needed." The company therefore might be disbanded before the ninety days were up. "It will not be used for any offensive operations other than may grow out of the duty hereinbefore assigned to it." The officers would be mustered in by a civil officer of the U.S. Government at Salt Lake City and the men by company officers. They would receive only the allowances authorized by law.[8] The intriguing point about this request is that it did not go to the territorial government officers but to Brigham Young, a tacit recognition of who really controlled Utah. (Requests for troops normally went to the state or territorial officials.) This request arrived by telegraph on the same day it was sent (April 28).

Brigham Young immediately issued orders the same day to Lieutenant General Daniel H. Wells of the militia or "Nauvoo Legion." "In accordance with the express direction of the President of the United States, telegraphically communicated at even date from the War Department . . . authorizing me 'to raise, arm and equip one Company of Cavalry for ninety days service,' I hereby request you to forthwith muster said Company into the service of the United States."[9] As we have seen before, the militia was the *Mormon* militia, completely controlled by Young and the Church: there was no other.

Remarkably, by April 29 the company was raised and was being organized under the command of Captain Lot Smith. The *Deseret News* commented correctly: "The request came unexpectedly, but was responded to with that alacrity that has ever characterized Governor Young and the citizens of Deseret when their services have been required by the Government, either to fight the battles of their country or to protect its citizens."[10]

Adjutant General Lorenzo Thomas on April 24 gave some explanation of the request. The Secretary of War had directed on April 10 and 11 that protection be given the Overland Mail Route against Indians and other depredations. Soldiers should be sent from farther east to protect the trail, but until that could be done and the troops put in position, a company of mounted men should be raised in Utah. A regiment was not needed. Senator Milton S. Latham of California had suggested that Young be authorized to raise, arm, and equip such a force of 100 mounted men. This would be for three months and their duty would be to protect the mail and stage route. "From the personal interest Brigham Young is said to have in the telegraphic communication with Salt Lake and from his known influence over his own people, and over the Indian tribes around, this plan is supposed to offer the most expeditious and economical remedy to the obstructions to the mail route. The objection to this plan is that Brigham Young is not a functionary recognized by the United States Government, and a requisition for volunteers from Utah should be made upon the Governor of the Territory."[11]

Also on that active April 28 General Wells issued his orders. Pursuant to instructions from ex-Governor Brigham Young and in compliance with a requisition from the President, Major Lot Smith of the Battalion of Life Guards was directed to enlist voluntarily for ninety days a company of mounted men. There would be one captain, one first lieutenant, one second lieutenant, one quartermaster sergeant, one first sergeant, four sergeants, eight corporals, two musicians, two farriers, one saddler, one wagoner, and seventy-two privates. Major Smith held the command with rank of captain.[12]

Smith was ordered to patrol the road and render all necessary aid. The company was ordered by Wells not to camp near any of the mail stations "as to give trouble or inconvenience; but sufficiently adjacent to render prompt and ready aid when required." As with Burton, Captain Smith was enjoined to preserve strict sobriety in camp "and prevent the use of all profane language or disorderly conduct of any kind." Troops of the United States were expected to be on the road soon to relieve the company. Further, "It is desirable to cultivate as far as practicable friendly and peaceful relations with the Indians." Care was to be taken of the horses and mules on the expedition. Vigilance should be maintained against surprises and the "greatest economy must be used with ammunition; none should be heedlessly wasted."[13]

Young replied with pride to the adjutant general in Washington on May 1 that immediately on receipt of his telegram at 8:30 P.M. on April 28 he had requested General Daniel H. Wells to raise the company. Officers had been sworn in April 30, the enrolling attended to, and the company had gone into camp near Salt Lake City. Young said the whole force, with ten baggage and supply wagons, took up the line of march east May 1.[14] Ben Holladay of the famous stage line wired Young from New York May 2: "Many thanks for your prompt response to President Lincoln's request. As soon as the boys can give protection, the mails shall be resumed."[15] It was ironic that Daniel H. Wells, Robert T. Burton, and Lot Smith, now aiding and serving the United States, had led Mormon forces against federal troops in the so-called Mormon War a few short years before.

In an address in Salt Lake City on May 4, General Wells commented on the expeditions:

It is all right with regard to those expeditions going forth, and will result for the benefit of this people. The people of this kingdom are minute men, or should be, and they should be prepared to go as circumstances shall direct, and in this way we prove ourselves before God, that we are ready to do his will, and to do his bidding. The requisition was made by the proper authority at Washington, and was readily responded to, as has always been the case when a call has been made through the proper channel, and the compliance with this call will result in good. Our brethren will perform their duties and do honour to their country. It is our country; we are citizens of the American Government, and we have always done it whenever called upon, and we have shown ourselves ready to respond to our duty as good citizens, no matter what usage we have received in return. This proves a weapon in the hands of this people for their defense.[16]

Although in the end the militia expeditions did no real fighting and only a little chasing of Indians, they were there on the Overland Trail and did their job. The stages started east again, but not until June 5.

Brigham Young wrote regarding the expeditions to Bishop Eveleth in San Francisco on May 7: "The streams are so high and the snow in places so deep and soft in the mountains that the company makes slow progress as yet. . . . The signs of the times are favorable in Utah; and our God continues to signally bless his people both here and elsewhere."[17]

The expedition went on its way with the words and prayers of Brigham Young. It was a harsh venture as the weather was truly ghastly, with ten feet of new snow, impassable roads, washed-out bridges, floods, and rain. The company reached Independence Rock twenty days after leaving Salt Lake City. In reality, the Mormon troops were under the overall federal command of Brigadier General James Craig. After working from the North Platte westward to and out of Fort Bridger, the company returned to Salt Lake City and was disbanded August 14.[18]

Smith and Burton reported extensively. Major or Captain Lot Smith wrote Brigham Young from Pacific Springs on June 15 that he had seen General Craig. The general apparently was pleased with the Mormon response. Smith quoted Craig as saying that Utah was perfectly "loyal, and as far as he knew always had been. He also remarked, we were the most efficient troops he had for the present service. . . ."[19] Again, from Pacific Springs on June 27, Smith wrote to Young that he had received orders from Craig through Lieutenant Colonel William O. Collins to march back to Fort Bridger to guard the line from Green River to Salt Lake City. He said Collins and others were gentlemen and expressed themselves pleased with the Utah company. "Col. Collins is decidedly against killing Indians indiscriminately, and will not take any general measures, save on the defensive, until he can ascertain satisfactorily by whom the depredations have been committed, and then not resort to killing until he is satisfied that peaceable measures have failed."[20] Smith was obviously proud of Collins's compliments to the Utah company.

Secretary of War Stanton, on August 24, authorized General James Craig at Fort Laramie to raise 100 mounted men in the mountains and to reenlist the Utah troops for three months as Craig had requested. It was impossible to send Craig reinforcements at the time.[21] Nothing came of the reenlistment idea. General Craig reported to General-in-Chief Halleck from Fort Laramie on August 25 that the then governor of Utah, Stephen Harding, had wired that he had interviewed Brigham Young regarding the reenlistment of Mormon troops. Harding reported, "You need not expect anything for the present. Things are not right." Also, Craig felt that "rebel agents" had been at work among the Indians. Some of the emigrants to the Salmon River mines, he wrote, were from border slave states.[22]

From Fort Bridger, Smith and most of his command operated against Indians who had robbed a nearby ranch. They went high up into the Snake Country but did not find the culprits. One man drowned in the Snake River, the only fatality of the expedition. Smith's company got back to Salt Lake City August 9 and were mustered out August 14. The expenses of both expeditions were paid by the federal government.[23]

It appears that the Mormons were proud of their assistance to the Union and pleased with their own quick response. The expeditions had aided the hard-pressed Union army, and were the only direct operations by Mormons or Utah troops during the Civil War. In some ways the Lot Smith expedition was unusual. While not of transcendent importance, it was in actuality the only body of troops during the Civil War that was sponsored by a religious faith.[24] It was said that every night before retiring the Mormon soldiers held evening prayer. The day after their start on May 1 from Salt Lake City the company was met by Brigham Young and General Wells at Emigration Canyon east of the city. Young reportedly emphasized loyalty to the country and stated that they must defend the Union at all hazards.[25]

Young was quoted as saying,

I desire of the officers and privates of this company, that in this service they will conduct themselves as gentlemen, remembering their allegiance and loyalty to our government, and also not forgetting that they are members of the organization to which they belong, never indulging in intoxicants of any kind, and never associating with bad men or lewd women, always seeking to make peace with the Indians. Aim never to take the life of an Indian or white man, unless compelled to do so in the discharge of duty, or in defense of your own lives, or that of your comrades.

He wanted the troops to hold councils with the Indians in order to win their friendship. He added,

Although you are United States soldiers you are still members of the Church of Jesus Christ of Latter-day Saints, and while you have sworn allegiance to the constitution and government of our country, and we have vowed to preserve the Union, the best way to accomplish this high purpose is to shun all evil associations and remember your prayers, and try to establish peace with the Indians, and always give ready obedience to the orders of your commanding officers. If you will do this I promise you, as a servant of the Lord, that not one of you shall fall by the hand of an enemy.[26]

If this quotation is exact, it can be wondered that Young would make such rash prophetic assurances as to casualties. Possibly he was guessing that there would be no real action.

A number of diaries, reminiscences, and other first-hand accounts of the expeditions have been preserved. Major or Captain Smith kept a rather sketchy journal, which emphasized the very rudimentary roads, the deep snow, and the difficulties of travel: it was a severe May for weather in Utah and the future Wyoming.[27]

Private Joseph A. Fisher related: "As we crossed the plains going East we passed many mail stations—one every ten miles. All we encountered along the way, lay in heaps of blackened ashes, until we arrived at Independence Rock. Many of the Mail stations were still smouldering when we came upon them. Wagon-loads of United States mail were scattered and destroyed by the Indians. In one place the remains of a stage coach was still standing . . . sacks of mail were piled up as breastworks."[28]

As to the Indians in the western part of Deseret in the early summer of 1862, Superintendent James Doty is reported as saying, with much optimism, that they "were anxious to learn the arts of peace, and only await agricultural implements and decent men to teach them agricultural pursuits. . . . The Superintendent is no communistic dreamer, and entertains the idea that ploughs, hoes, spades and shovels, with good instruction and decent treatment will contribute vastly better to the well-being of the Indians, and the safety of the overland emigrants than the course heretofore pursued with the redskins."[29]

Military tactics were used again in 1862 by the Mormons, but this time for a different reason. Throughout the history of the Latter-day Saints there had been occasional apostates, Mormons who differed with Brigham Young and the main Mormon body. Some had just individually left the Church, others had set up splinter organizations of their own, of varying size and viability. In the Civil War years, and particularly in 1862, during the period of Utah's application for statehood, the main apostate group was the Morrisite movement. It had been causing dissension for a few years and finally the conflict came to a head. Nationally, and as far as the Civil War was concerned, the "Morrisite War," as it is called, was of no great significance. But in Mormon and Utah history it must be seen as a major event.

For a number of years a Welshman, Joseph Morris, had received what he called revelations and impressions from the Lord. As a Mormon, he began in the late 1850s to disagree with Brigham Young, and was opposed to polygamy. As Morris's "revelations" increased in number he apparently felt that Young did not have enough such enlightenments from the Deity. At first Young and the Church paid little attention to his apostasy. Eventually Morris and some of his followers on the Weber River took over Kington Fort, about thirty-five miles north of Salt Lake City, as the headquarters of their so-called Morrisite faith. Morris and his claim of revelations did attract some followers. Going beyond the standard Mormon creed, the Morrisite disciples consecrated all they possessed to a common fund. Christ was to come among them soon and then they would have no wants. The idea was that when anyone wanted his consecrated possessions, they could be applied for. By 1862 the faith was beginning to lose adherents and some of the dissenters had difficulty in getting their property back, or claimed that they had had more property than they actually put in. The Mormon Church began to sense that it should be paying more attention to Morris's group, which called itself the Church of Jesus Christ of Saints Most High. Morris himself brought increased notoriety to the group as he prophesied the second coming of Christ and gave a specific date when this was to occur—always a dangerous ploy for a religious leader.

In early 1862 the Morrisites arrested three dissenters who were trying to reclaim their property. Chief Justice Kinney in Salt Lake City issued a writ on May 22 for the release of the prisoners and the arrest of Morris and his main lieutenants. The Morrisites refused to receive the writ and Morris continued to announce his revelations. On June 10 Judge Kinney issued a second writ, demanding release of the prisoners with a writ of attachment citing Joseph Morris, John Banks, Richard Cook, John Parson, and Peter Klemgard for contempt of court. Kinney urged Acting Governor

Fuller to call out the militia as a posse to enforce the writs. There is considerable dispute as to whether Judge Kinney acted on his own or reacted to pressure brought by Young and the Mormons. Kinney denied the full responsibility and said Young approved of the action.

At any rate, some 200 men went to the Morrisite encampment. (Some estimates put the force at 250 men plus two artillery pieces, and others put the figures even higher.) The posse reached the bluffs south of Kington Fort early in the morning of June 13. They sent a message to Morris demanding compliance with the writ and his surrender. Deputy Marshal Robert T. Burton, who had led a body of the militia, was leader of the posse.

Morris and his group assembled in the Bowery in the open while Morris awaited a revelation. Impatient with the delay, Burton ordered two warning artillery shots fired. One did go overhead, but the other smashed into the encampment, killing two women and wounding a teen-aged girl. The Morrisites had no adequate defense, but they got their guns and did what they could. Firing became fairly sharp. On the afternoon of the third day of the siege the posse charged the so-called fort and demanded the surrender of the Morrisites in the Bowery. Two Mormons had been killed in the fighting.

That evening, June 15, a Sunday, Burton ordered about twenty men to enter the fort and again demanded surrender. The Morrisites reportedly began to throw down their arms. What happened next is highly conjectural. Joseph Morris said he wanted to make a speech and Burton ordered him to be quick about it. The Mormons claim Morris shouted that he would never surrender and tried to get away. Burton ordered him to stop, but he did not. Burton then shot Morris and two women who tried to interfere. Morrisite John Banks was fatally wounded. Morrisite accounts say that Burton shot Morris before he could speak, and then shot Banks. The women objected and, according to this version, they were also shot. Deaths in the encounter are usually put at ten Morrisites and two members of the Utah posse, with an undetermined number wounded. The remaining Morrisite men, about ninety in all, were taken to Salt Lake City for trial on charges of murdering the two posse members and resisting due process of law. Judge Kinney assessed bond and ordered trial for March of 1863, the next session of court. The bodies of Morris and Banks were displayed in the city hall.

Eventually seven of the Morrisites were convicted of second-degree murder and sentenced to from ten to fifteen years. The other sixty-six were fined $100 after being convicted of resisting arrest. The incident gave rise to charges on all sides. The new governor, Harding, offered full pardon to the Morrisites and remission of fines. This drew strong criticism from the Mormons, who had initially cheered Harding on his arrival. Non-Mormons accused Judge Kinney of being influenced by Brigham Young. Eventually both Harding and Kinney were removed, though the Morrisite uproar was only part of their difficulties. The future of the Morrisites was dim. Some left, escorted out of Utah by the federal troops of General Connor, some were employed at federal Camp Douglas, and others settled in Soda Springs, Idaho. Some of the descendents of the Morrisites still live in Deer Lodge Valley, Montana.[30]

NOTES

1. Whitney, *History of Utah*, vol. II, pp. 42–43.
2. Tullidge, *History of Salt Lake City*, p. 252.
3. Brigham Young Letter Books, Apr. 14, 1862, Church Archives.
4. *Deseret News*, Sept. 10, 1862; Fred B. Rogers, *Soldiers of the Overland* (San Francisco: Grabhorn Press, 1938), p. 17.
5. Brigham Young Letter Books, Church Archives.
6. *Deseret News*, May 21, 1862.
7. Brigham Young Letter Books, Church Archives.
8. O.R., ser. III, vol. II, p. 27.
9. Brigham Young Letter Books, Church Archives.
10. *Deseret News*, Apr. 30, 1862.
11. O.R., vol. L, pt. 1, pp. 1023–24, Apr. 24, 1862, "Report on Measures Taken to Make Secure the Overland Route to California."
12. Tullidge, *History of Salt Lake City*, p. 255.
13. *Ibid.*, pp. 255–56.
14. *Ibid.*, p. 256.
15. *Ibid.*
16. *Journal of Discourses*, vol. IX, "Responsibilities Resting upon the Saints, etc.," pp. 352–53.
17. Brigham Young Letter Books, Church Archives.
18. For a lengthy and somewhat romantic account of both expeditions, see: Margaret M. Fisher, *Utah and the Civil War, Being the Story of the Part Played by*

the People of Utah in That Great Conflict with Special Reference to the Lot Smith Expedition and the Robert T. Burton Expedition (Salt Lake City: Deseret Book Company, 1929).

19. Tullidge, History of Salt Lake City, p. 257.

20. Ibid.

21. O.R., ser. III, vol. II, p. 453.

22. O.R., vol. XIII, p. 596.

23. Whitney, History of Utah, vol. II, p. 47.

24. Margaret Fisher in Utah and the Civil War undoubtedly exaggerates the importance of this company, but does show the religious origins. For instance, it is quite excessive to state, as on p. 10, "This Expedition was the most hazardous ever performed in the West by United States troops in defense of their country."

25. Fisher, Utah and the Civil War, pp. 24–25.

26. Ibid., pp. 25–26.

27. Ibid., pp. 30–35.

28. Ibid., pp. 26–37.

29. Deseret News, June 11, 1862.

30. Nearly all volumes on Utah and the Mormons cover the "Morrisite War" with much disagreement. While the affair had considerable local importance, I do not feel it is necessary here to belabor the extensive and controversial details. For summaries see, for example, C. LeRoy Anderson and Larry J. Halford, "The Mormons and the Morrisite War," Montana, the Magazine of Western History, 24 (Autumn, 1974), 42–53, and Stenhouse, Rocky Mountain Saints, pp. 593–601.

CHAPTER

VI

Crossing the Jordan

"CALIFORNIA VOLUNTEERS FOR SALT LAKE," read the headline in the *Deseret News* of June 25, 1862. "The 3rd regiment California volunteers, Col. Connor, arrived at Stockton the last of May and formed an encampment at the race courses which had been named 'Camp Halleck.' The regiment was reported to be eight hundred strong when it left Benicia [Barracks]. . . . Much is said about the regiment which is supposed to be a very efficient force. . . . Its destination gives the corps great celebrity." Thus Utah was about to receive a new garrison of federal soldiers to guard and protect the transportation and communication lines. How much more would they be expected to do? This time they were volunteers from the West rather than regulars from the East. The Mormons of Utah had naturally been hopeful that the army had left permanently after the evacuation of Fort Crittenden in July of 1861. They had themselves tried to furnish guards for the Overland Trail, but now bluecoats from the outside were coming again. A number of officers of the army had been involved in the Mormon War, so neither the army nor the Mormons regarded the other very highly, although Albert Sidney Johnston and other officers who had participated in that "war" had gone south. But the military still had a jaundiced view of the Mormons.

As an example of the feeling in the army, Major James H. Carleton wrote to the Army of the Pacific Headquarters in San Francisco from a camp near Los Angeles, July 31, 1861. He had been in the San Bernardino area where there were many Mormons. In his letter he included a rather bitter denunciation of the Saints, writing of those in Utah as well as in California:

Nearly all Mormons are foreigners. Among these are Welsh, English, Norwegians, Swedes, some Germans, and a few French. They are evidently of the lowest and most ignorant grade of the people in the several countries from whence they have come. Mixed in with these are a few low, unprincipled Americans. The most intelligent and crafty of these, commencing with Brigham Young, are the directors and rulers of the whole mess . . . their government is solely a hierarchy, and notwithstanding, in theory, they are assumed to be a population obedient to the laws of our common country, practically they score and deride, and set at defiance all laws that interfere with their safety or interest, save those promulgated by the great council of the church.

The outspoken Carleton went on: ". . . it is easy to imagine what a sway, what a complete and absolute control the council and the prophet have over the minds and persons and possessions of every subordinate member of the church, both at home and abroad . . . there is a real power, a hand raised to strike from existence those who show the least sign of disobedience or of recusancy. That hand is secret and invisible." He claimed that the foreigner with no knowledge of America is taught "to abhor and contemn us. . . . What but crime, when assassin-like it can strike unseen? What but open sedition and treason among the whole people wherever it has gained strength?" This was written, of course, before troops had been sent to Salt Lake City.[1]

As we have seen, in July of 1861 then Secretary of War Simon Cameron wrote to Governor Downey of California that the War Department had accepted for three years' duty one regiment of infantry and five companies of cavalry to guard the Overland Mail Route from Carson Valley to Salt Lake and eastward. General Sumner was to muster in the men. Adjutant General Lorenzo Thomas on July 24 confirmed this to Brigadier General Edwin V. Sumner, commanding the vast Department of the Pacific from San Francisco.[2] But there was to be over a year's delay. Pressures to keep soldiers in California, the need for operations in the Southwest, the raising of volunteers, and winter weather all added to the slowness.

In October, 1861, George Wright took over command of the Department of the Pacific from Sumner. During 1861 and 1862 the enlistment of men continued in California and a number of conscientious and capable officers were given commands. One of these was Patrick Edward Connor, a man possessing a rather enigmatic personality. He left few personal letters, so far as we know, so that we must analyze his actions principally from his extensive official correspondence. That he was a proficient, fascinating, somewhat cantankerous character there is no doubt. He was strong-willed, devoted to his country, ambitious and tenacious. He was often suspicious—which may or may not be a fault. He was unquestionably a hard worker and a strong, though not overbearing, disciplinarian. Yet, when all this and more is said, Connor's personality remains somewhat nebulous and elusive.

Details of Connor's early life are sketchy. He was born on St. Patrick's Day in 1820 in County Kerry, Ireland, near the beautiful lakes of Killarney. Apparently the paternal name at the time was O'Connor. His parents brought him to New York City as a child. How much formal education the youngster had we do not know, although there may have been some. He enlisted in the Regular Army of the United States on November 28, 1839.[3]

Much of Connor's early army experience was in the Seminole War and in the then "West" at Fort Leavenworth, Kansas, and in Iowa. At Fort Des Moines he was honorably discharged as a private in late November, 1844, his term of enlistment having expired. He spent two years in New York before arriving in Texas in early 1846. He enlisted in the Texas Volunteers in May of that year under the call of General Zachary Taylor. At this time he listed his name as Connor, though at times records show O'Connor. It is not clear if he was in the Mexican War battles of Resaca de la Palma and Palo Alto, though some mention is made of such service. By this time Connor was a first lieutenant in the Texas Foot Riflemen. In July, 1846, he was mustered into U.S. service at Camargo, Mexico, as a first lieutenant in Captain Charles A. Seefield's independent company of Texas volunteers. His unit joined the Army of the Center under General John E. Wool and marched to Saltillo, Mexico.

Connor was promoted to captain in February, 1847, and his company was attached to Colonel William H. Bissel's Second Illinois Volunteers. On February 22 Connor took part in the battle of

Buena Vista. Apparently Connor and his men acquitted themselves well, for General Zachary Taylor officially reported "Captain Connor's company of Texas Volunteers, attached to the Second Illinois regiment, fought bravely, its captain being wounded and two subalterns killed." Connor's wounds did not cause him to leave the battle, though his company suffered severely. One story is that General Wool asked, " 'Captain Connor, where are your men?' The captain, pointing to the bodies of his men strewn upon the field, answered: 'General. There,' and pressed forward." [4]

Connor was honorably discharged near Monterrey, Mexico, May 24, 1847. He reportedly resigned because of rheumatism. It is not clear what he was doing during the next three years, but he headed west to arrive in California in January of 1850, lured by gold finds. He was involved in a disastrous boating accident near Crescent City, California, while on his way to the Trinity River area where gold had been found. Caught in a pounding surf in a small boat, five of his party of ten drowned. [5]

Connor then embarked upon mining, only to become one more member of the vast army of unsuccessful seekers after the elusive metal. He then engaged in cutting and shipping pilings, and served in a group of California Rangers seeking the notorious bandit Joaquin Murieta and his gang of desperados. They were successful in killing Murieta and some eleven of his men. By 1854 Connor was doing surveying, and in August of that year married another native of County Kerry, Johanna Connor of Redwood City, California. [6] The couple moved to Stockton, California, their home for the next few years. They had three children, two of whom died in infancy. Connor operated a ranch and a gravel pit, and also served in a number of local offices including those of postmaster and secretary of the State Fair. He held various posts in local military groups—the Stockton Blues, the Anniversary Guards, and the Second Brigade. In 1858 the versatile Connor set up the city waterworks. He next took a contract for building the foundation of the State Capitol, but he was unable to complete this because he entered the service. [7]

As the secession crisis mounted, a number of pro-secessionists were reported to be in and around Stockton, and it is alleged that Connor's strong Unionism and outspokenness made him the target of threats. [8] On August 14, 1861, Secretary of War Cameron told California's Governor Downey to organize, equip, and have mustered in as soon as possible four regiments of infantry and one of cavalry. This second call resulted in the formation of the Second Cavalry and the Second, Third, Fourth, and Fifth Regiments of Infantry. The Third Infantry was organized at Stockton and Benicia Barracks from September to the end of the year. A number of Stockton citizens joined up.[9] Connor, with his relatively extensive military experience, was named colonel. By November 16 he and his family had moved to Benicia Barracks, where much of the regiment was stationed. It appears that from the beginning Connor applied his idea of tight discipline.[10]

On March 28, 1862, Connor was ordered by General Wright to have his regiment put in readiness to move at an early day.[11] Connor moved to Camp Halleck at Stockton on May 26. General Wright wired the War Department on May 30 that, although he had received orders to prepare a command to protect the Overland Mail Route, he had received no instructions as to how far east it was intended that the troops would go. "At present there seems to be no danger apprehended on the mail route between here and Salt Lake. Unless otherwise instructed, I shall advance Colonel Connor to the neighborhood of Salt Lake."[12] General Wright reported to Washington on June 28 that he had reviewed and inspected the Third Infantry near that city. "The regiment," he said, "made a very fine appearance; the arms, clothing and equipments were in high order. The industry and untiring zeal and energy of Colonel Connor is manifest throughout. He has a regiment that the State may well be proud of."[13]

After more preparation, Connor, on July 12, reported to San Francisco Headquarters that his "Utah Column" had left Camp Halleck that morning for Salt Lake City. He had fifty teams and wagons of 23,000 pounds each, and around 850 men. By July 19 he was at El Dorado, California, near Placerville.[14] Connor's force had arrived at Fort Churchill in Nevada Territory by August 3. He reported to San Francisco:

The men are in excellent health and spirits and have stood the trip remarkably well. The animals are all in good order. . . . The roads were, with little exception, in good order, and I am myself much pleased with the result so far. I find since entering this Territory that there are many sympathizers with the Southern rebels along our entire route; but while they are loud-mouthed brawlers before our arrival, are very careful in the expressions of such sentiments during our stay at any point. Still, they are known and can be identified as open and avowed secessionists. I have not as yet taken any steps to check them by arrest and punishment, but await further instructions from headquarters. . . . From the information I have received there is an immense immigration on the route this season, and I fear I will find grass rather scarce, consequently I contemplate dividing my command at this point, to reunite at Ruby Valley.[15]

There is no way of analyzing the sentiments of Connor's alleged pro-secessionists, but throughout the war he seemed very quick to assign such labels. Certainly he did encounter those who were opposed to the army and even to the Union in one degree or another.

On August 6 at Fort Churchill, under orders No. 1, Connor assumed command of the Military District of Utah under the Department of the Pacific, which comprised the Territories of Utah and Nevada. In his orders Connor said,

Being credibly informed that there are in this district persons who, while claiming and receiving protection to life and property, are endeavoring to destroy and defame the principles and institutions of a Government under whose benign influence they have been so long protected, it is therefore most rigidly enjoined upon all commanders of posts, camps, and detachments to cause to be promptly arrested and closely confined until they have taken the oath of allegiance to the United States, all persons who from this date shall be guilty of uttering treasonable sentiments against the government, and upon a repetition of the offense to be again arrested and confined until the fact shall be communicated to these headquarters. Traitors shall not utter treasonable sentiments in this district with impunity, but must seek a more genial soil, or receive the punishment they so richly merit.[16]

At Fort Churchill Connor faced another problem. Part of the Second California Cavalry had come in to join his forces. But he reported August 11 that one captain of this outfit was under guard, "and the men and the majority of the officers in a state of insubordination. The command lost thirty men by desertion on the route. . . . Matters are all right now, and will remain so while they are under my immediate command."[17]

On August 15 Connor issued orders for the march east of about 700 men from Fort Churchill and by September 1 the main party was at Ruby Valley.[18] Connor now left his command and scouted

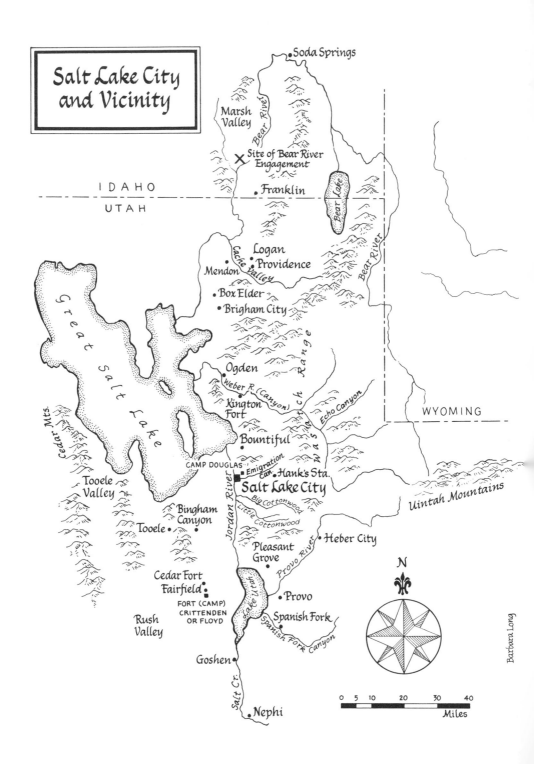

Salt Lake City and Vicinity

Soda Springs

Marsh Valley

Bear River

IDAHO

UTAH

X Site of Bear River Engagement

Franklin

Bear Lake

Bear River

Logan

Providence

Mendon

Cache Valley

Box Elder

Brigham City

Great Salt Lake

Wasatch Range

Ogden

Weber R. (Canyon)

Kington Fort

Echo Canyon

WYOMING

Cedar Mts.

Bountiful

CAMP DOUGLAS

Emigration Can.

Hank's Sta.

Salt Lake City

Tooele Valley

Jordan River

Big Cottonwood

Little Cottonwood

Uintah Mountains

Bingham Canyon

Tooele

Provo River

Heber City

Pleasant Grove

N

Cedar Fort

Fairfield

FORT (CAMP) CRITTENDEN OR FLOYD

Lake Utah

Provo

Spanish Fork

Rush Valley

Spanish Fork Canyon

Goshen

Salt Cr.

Nephi

0   5   10   20   30   40

Miles

Barbara Long

the route clear to Salt Lake City. Not only did he investigate the route over the emigrant trail but he had a sharp eye out for the kinds of people he was to be involved with.

His report to Army Headquarters at San Francisco of September 14 was his first major statement on the Mormons, but by no means his last or even his most critical, though it was vitriolic enough. "It will be impossible for me to describe what I saw and heard in Salt Lake, so as to make you realize the enormity of Mormonism; suffice it, that I found them a community of traitors, murderers, fanatics and whores. . . ." It is not clear just how he arrived at this conclusion. But Connor went on: "The people publicly rejoice at reverses to our arms, and thank God that the American Government is gone, as they term it, while their prophet and bishops preach treason from the pulpit. The Federal officers are entirely powerless, and talk in whispers for fear of being overheard by Brigham's spies. Brigham Young rules with despotic sway, and death by assassination is the penalty of disobedience to his commands. I have a difficult and dangerous task before me, and will endeavor to act with prudence and firmness." He then told of the condition of old Camp Floyd, now known as Fort Crittenden, and his plans for a new fort. "I have found another location, which I like better [than Fort Crittenden]. . . . It is on a plateau about three miles from Salt Lake City; in the vicinity of good timber and sawmills, and at a point where hay, grain, and other produce can be purchased cheaper than at Fort Crittenden. It is also a point which commands the city, and where 1,000 troops would be more efficient than 3,000 on the other side of the Jordan." Connor clearly meant that the new campsite would afford a better position from which to watch the city and its population. The Jordan is a small stream running to the west of Salt Lake City. The old fort was to the west of it.[19] Connor concluded: "If the general decides that I shall locate there, I intend to quietly intrench my position, and then say to the Saints of Utah, enough of your treason; but if it is intended that I shall merely protect the overland mail and permit the Mormons to act and utter treason, then I had as well locate at Crittenden. The Federal officers desire and beg that I will locate near the city. The Governor [Harding] especially is very urgent in the matter." Connor went on to express his uneasiness about the lateness of the season.[20]

Military authorities and others had generally expected that the army would reoccupy Fort Crittenden. In the fall of 1861, Acting Governor Wootton had advised Secretary of State Seward against placing federal troops in Salt Lake City.[21]

General Wright in San Francisco early in 1863 had given approval of the location of Camp Douglas, saying, "Brigham Young was exceedingly anxious that the troops should occupy Camp Crittenden, or some point remote from the city, but after mature consideration I came to the conclusion that the site of the present camp was the most eligible for the accomplishment of the objects in view. It is a commanding position, looking down on the city, and hence has been dreaded by the Mormon chief."[22]

The *Deseret News* reported in late June, 1862, that high water and floods had wreaked heavy destruction on bridges on the Jordan, the Big Cottonwood, and the Provo. However, the paper editorialized,

The California volunteers constituting Col. Connor's command, continue to elicit many remarks. . . . The pompous procession is expected to consist of the one thousand infantry, five hundred cavalry, a field battery, one hundred and fifty contractor's wagons and seventy others, besides them. To complete the arrangement, and render the scene superbly grand, several hundred head of cattle are to be driven in the rear of the procession. The Indians will of course be tremendously scared, and horse-thieves, gamblers, and other pests of the community wondrously attracted by the gigantic demonstration.[23]

The sarcasm of the *Deseret News* may have been a bit mild, but it grossly exaggerated the numbers. Connor's column could hardly be described as a "pompous procession." In the same issue of the paper, the possible amelioration of another annoying problem was discussed: "Things are beginning to assume a more cheering appearance in relation to the Eastern mails and the prospects are that they will be carried regularly for a time to come."[24] Interest was expressed in a July 9 edition of the same publication in the change in route of the Overland Stage and Mail to the Overland Trail through Wyoming rather than along the Oregon Trail, though both trails came through Utah.

The *Deseret News* kept the public posted on Connor's progress and on the Lot Smith expedition, and was critical of the eastbound telegraph line from Salt Lake City: it "has been an ineffective, crippled, diseased, dilapidated, crazy concern for a long time, so much so that it has been a very uncertain medium for the transmission of intelligence." [25] The Indians were causing trouble again in the Cache Valley, north of Salt Lake City. [26] In another issue Indian depredations were reported on Sublette's Cut-off, along with accounts of cricket matches in Salt Lake City and the problems of Garibaldi in Italy. [27]

But the item that aroused most interest in the paper of September 10 was the news that "Colonel P. E. Connor arrived in this city yesterday afternoon. The Colonel took a stroll about town and looked around with an air of familiarity that indicated that after all Salt Lake City was something of a place, and might not be unpleasant notwithstanding its desert surroundings." [28] It was when Connor got back to Ruby Valley that he penned his hypercritical message of September 14.

Connor was delayed in marching his command toward Salt Lake City by lack of supplies at Ruby Valley. [29] At the same time, Connor's mind was not entirely focused on supplies and Indian activities on the Humboldt. From Ruby Valley on September 24 he wrote to General-in-Chief Halleck in Washington:

The Third Infantry California Volunteers has been in service one year and marched 600 miles; it is well officered and thoroughly drilled; it is of no service on the Overland Mail Route, as there is cavalry sufficient for its protection in the Overland District. The regiment will authorize the paymaster to withhold $30,000 of pay now due if the Government will order it east, and it pledges General Halleck never to disgrace the flag, himself, or California. The men enlisted to fight traitors, and can do so more effectually than raw recruits, and ask that they may at least be placed on the same footing in regard to transportation east. If the above sum is insufficient we will pay our own passage from San Francisco to Panama. [30]

The same day Connor wired Halleck, "My regiment if ordered east would pay their own passage from San Francisco to Panama. Our services are not required here. We desire to strike a blow in this contest." [31] There seems no doubt that this was an honest aspiration of Connor and his men. After all, it was not unusual in the eastern states for regiments to want to be sent to the front and to request such service, especially this early in the war. Many men simply didn't want to miss being where the action was.

By October 1, fairly late in the season, Connor's force was still at Fort Ruby in eastern Nevada Territory. Although located well over halfway to Salt Lake City, and on the eastern edge of the Humboldt Mountains, Connor had to wait for supplies from the West. He also needed money to buy supplies, including those from the Mormons, for otherwise "Brigham may seize the want of it as a pretext to prevent his people from supplying me. The people of Utah are under the impression that I am to winter at Fort Crittenden, and I am credibly informed by letter this morning that the flag-staff at Fort Crittenden was cut down since my visit and hauled away by Brigham's order." [32]

In the meantime, on September 29, Connor ordered out Major Edward McGarry of the Second Cavalry California Volunteers to operate against Indians

who were concerned in the late murder of emigrants. . . . On the route from South Fork of Humboldt to Bear River you will spare no pains to discover the whereabouts of a band of traitors or guerrillas reported to be encamped in the vicinity of Humboldt, and who are believed to be the instigators, if not the participants, in the late Indian murders. If you should discover such a band you take them prisoners and convey them to headquarters near Salt Lake, but if they should resist you will destroy them without mercy. You will also destroy every male Indian who you may encounter in the vicinity of the late massacres. This course may seem harsh and severe, but I desire that the order may be rigidly enforced, as I am satisfied that in the end it will prove the most merciful. [33]

General Wright in San Francisco reported to Washington on November 18, "The swift retributive punishment which has been meted out to those Indians will doubtless have the effect of preventing a repetition of their barbarities. It is the only way to deal with those savages." [34] Connor agreed when he wrote to Wright on November 6 from Salt Lake City: "I am satisfied from verbal information received from officers of the expedition that the Indians who have been punished were a part of those who had committed the late murders, and that the punishment was well merited. I hope and believe that the lesson taught them will have a salutary effect in checking future massacres on that route." [35]

Major McGarry with Company H of the Second Cavalry of California Volunteers had left Fort Ruby September 29 and was at Camp Douglas near Salt Lake City October 29. He had joined

Captain S. P. Smith's company and moved north from Fort Ruby. For several days they found no Indians. They did entice into
camp on the Humboldt three armed Indians who attempted to recover their rifles. The Indians got the arms and attempted to escape, were wounded and then killed, as Major McGarry did not
wish to hazard the lives of his men "in recapturing them alive."
Captain S. P. Smith captured about fifteen Indians. These, too, attempted to escape and nine were killed. Several other Indians were
captured, and a few were released on condition they would bring
in the Indians "engaged in the massacre of emigrants." McGarry
threatened to kill the Indians kept in camp if the released ones did
not return. They did not, so "I put to death four of those remaining and released the squaws and children, telling them that we
were sent there to punish Indians who were engaged in the massacre of emigrants, and instructed them to tell all the Indians that
if they did not desist from killing emigrants that I would return
there next summer and destroy them." Eight more Indians were
killed on the expedition. McGarry believed the expedition a success, though to us today his actions seem excessive. However, it
should be noted that no "guerrillas," as Connor had suspected,
were found in the area.[36]

While this tragic and brutal sideshow was going on, Connor
moved eastward to Fort Crittenden, almost south of Salt Lake
City, arriving by October 17. He wired San Francisco: "Will cross
the Jordan to-morrow."[37] For some time and while he was on the
march, various individuals, many of them Mormon, who owned
property or commercial ventures at or near Camp Crittenden had
been importuning Connor to halt his command there and set up
headquarters, and, of course, to buy the property he needed as
well as supplies. Obviously Connor had no intention of halting.[38]

The *Deseret News* was keeping up a surprisingly accurate report of Connor's movements from other papers and from Mormon civilians along the route. Commenting on the volunteers'
efforts to join the war in the East, the paper reported from Ruby
Valley in the issue of October 15, "It seems that the 'Third,' officers and men, are becoming 'disgusted' with the duties they have
to perform on the plains and would like to go farther east, where
an opportunity might present itself for a display of their valor."
The same publication quoted from the San Francisco *Bulletin* of

September 24 from Ruby Valley: "The 3d Infantry California Volunteers wants to go home. . . . The glory which awaits the California Regiment that first lands on the Atlantic coast combines to make the 700 hearts camped in Ruby Valley pulse vigorously with the patriotic desire to serve their country in shooting traitors instead of eating rations and freezing to death around sage brush fires, which two are the only military duties to be performed hereabouts." It was reported that several companies subscribed considerable sums of money for their passage. The *News* goes on to quote the *Bulletin*: "As far as anybody can see, there is not a bit more use for infantry out here than there is for Topographical Engineers. Cavalry is the only efficient army against Indians; and the companies of the 2d Regiment, in the district, are fully competent to chastise all offenders. Brigham Young offers to protect the entire line with 100 men. Why we were sent here is a mystery. It could not be to keep Mormondom in order, for Brigham can thoroughly annihilate us with the 5,000 to 25,000 frontiersmen always at his command."[39]

The *Bulletin*'s correspondent was apparently John A. Anderson, who was chaplain of the Third California. He was later a superintendent of transportation under Grant in the 1864 Wilderness Campaign in Virginia and in the 1870s was president of Kansas State Agricultural College.[40]

The voice of the Mormons commented on Lincoln's Preliminary Emancipation Proclamation on October 22: "We demand to be informed whence the President derives his power to issue any such proclamation as he has now published. Not from the Constitution surely, for it is in plain violation of some of its leading provisions. . . . He is fully adrift on the current of radical fanaticism. We regret for his sake, we lament for the sake of the country, that he has been coerced by the insanity of radicals, by the denunciation of their presses, by the threats of their governors and senators."[41] Lincoln himself had characterized the proclamation as a war move, for he, too, worried about his constitutional power to issue it.

The arrival of Connor's command at Fort Crittenden elicited more of the *Deseret News*'s somewhat snide comment: ". . . contrary to the expectations of some, he manifested no disposition to make that desolate place his headquarters; and after camping near there . . . over night, moved on the next morning without consulting any of the patriots there assembled to serve their country in lucrative capacity, should opportunity present, as to what he had better do or even inquiring if their private interests would be effected there by, which, as represented, some of them took in high dudgeon."[42]

Connor did move rapidly across the Jordan, with its symbolic significance, right on into and through Salt Lake City and up to the bench above the city, where he at once established Camp Douglas, which would become a permanent U.S. Army post. On October 20 Connor wired San Francisco: "Just arrived. Encamped on site of new post. Command in good health and discipline."[43] He officially proclaimed the Department of Utah Headquarters at Camp Douglas on October 26.[44] By November 9 he told Washington of the camp, its location and facilities. "If it is contemplated to establish a permanent post in this Territory I know of no spot so desirable as this."[45]

The *Deseret News* told the story with its own details: "On Saturday night the command encamped near the point of the mountain on the west side of Jordan, and on Sunday night, near the bridge below the mouth of the Little Cottonwood. From thence, on Monday forenoon, the troops marched into the City; coming up the State Road to first South street, and then turned east passing the residence of Governor Harding, where a halt was made, and the troops were drawn up in two lines—the infantry in front, making quite a military display. . . ."

Governor Harding, who had met the troops outside the city, spoke to the command from his carriage in front of his home:

I am conscious, Soldiers, that your mission here is one of peace and security, not only to the government that gives you employment, but to every individual who is an inhabitant of this Territory. The individual, if any such there be, who supposed that the government has sent you here, that mischief might come out of it, knows not the spirit of our Government, and knows not the spirit of the officers who represent it in this Territory. . . . I confess that I have been disappointed somewhat, in your coming to this city. I have known nothing of the disposition that has been made of you. . . . But you are here, and I can say to you, God bless you, and God bless the flag you carry; God bless the Government you represent. . . . I do not know now what disposition is to be made of you, but I suppose you will be encamped somewhere, I know not where, but within a short distance of this city. I believe the people you have now come amongst will not disturb you if you do not disturb them.[46]

Harding urged them not to "break over the bounds of propriety." The command gave three cheers for the country, the brave old flag, and the governor. They then marched to the base of the mountain east of the city and encamped on the shelf near the springs between Red Butte and Emigration Canyon. The *Deseret News* commented: "How long the troops will remain where they now are, the speculators who seem to be most interested in the matter have not been able as yet to ascertain; neither where Col. Connor's headquarters will for the winter be established. The troops looked as they passed through the city like a hardy set of fellows; capable of performing any service that might be required. They were somewhat covered with dust, which was very abundant on that day. Some of their horses seemed a little jaded, and not in as good condition as might be desired for an Indian campaign."[47] Isaac L. Gibbs, the U.S. marshal for Utah Territory, arrived at about the same time.[48]

Further details of the march of Connor's command came from the San Francisco *Bulletin* of October 18, 1862. The correspondent reported that the expedition numbered 850 men and six guns. As they approached the city of the Saints, about twenty miles north of Fort Crittenden, they could discern white specks "which constitute the residences of the modern apostles; but at present we are more interested in the designs and doings of said apostles than in the general appearance of their habitations." There had been rumors in camp that the Mormons would not permit the troops closer than Fort Crittenden and that the banks of the narrow stream called Jordan, which empties the waters of Lake Utah into Great Salt Lake, would form the field of battle. At the time it caused "no further thought than as the starting-point of rambling conversation respecting Mormondom and the mission which the command has been detailed to execute—both subjects upon which we have had little information."[49] The reporter said there was "intense excitement" in Salt Lake City when the populace learned that Connor was not buying the buildings from the citizens at Fort Crittenden and staying there, but was coming on into the city.

The *Bulletin* story included reports on the Danites:

The Chief of the Danites—better known perhaps as the Destroying Angels, whose duty it is, if report be true, to place parties odious to the leaders where they can never tell tales—is represented as riding the streets offering to bet $500 that we would not and should not cross the river Jordan, the bet being untaken. Furthermore, not simple camp rumor, but reliable parties assert that Brigham Young would, when we near Jordan, have us met by Commissioners empowered to inform us that the Mormons objected to our close proximity to their city and would forcibly resist an attempt on our part to cross that stream. How much truth there may be in these advices, or how much the real state of affairs in Salt Lake is exaggerated I know not." [50]

The question of the Danites has become perhaps the second most controversial aspect of Mormonism, second only to polygamy. Allegedly the Danites were a form of secret police that did the bidding of Brigham Young and the Church leaders, even to the extent of murdering undesirables. On the other hand, there are those who deny that there ever were any Danites, or, if there were, they were assuredly not guilty of the dark deeds ascribed to them. But in the world beyond Utah there were many who avidly read anything available on the Mormons, polygamy, and the Danites.

According to the reporter of the *Bulletin*, Connor, in preparing to move to Salt Lake City, exercised "utmost prudence" and issued thirty rounds of ammunition to each man, and two six-pounders and a twelve-pound mountain howitzer were "amply supplied with shells." Fort Crittenden was on an open plain so no enemy could get to it "without a fair fight." Connor reportedly sent word to the head of the Danites that he would "cross the river Jordan if hell yawned below him." This statement cannot be authenticated, but it was not uncharacteristic of the flamboyant and determined Connor.[51]

The *Bulletin* reporter waxed editorial, and one might be surprised that the *Deseret News* printed the story:

Thus you see that whether we are to have a fight or not rests entirely with the Mormon rulers. And if it be true that United States troops, when ordered by Government to occupy United States territory are to be forcibly prevented, by those who live upon United States lands, from executing that order—if this principle is to constitute the national policy, then the nation has ceased to be a live nation, and the sooner it recognizes the

Southern Confederacy the better. But if our troops are to march on the United States territory wherever Government sends them, then those who resist their march, because of polygamy, are as really traitors as those who resist because of slavery and are to be dealt with as such.[52]

The correspondent stated,

This command, from the highest to the lowest, is disposed to treat the Mormons with true courtesy and the strictest justice, so long as they remain friendly to the Government; but the moment they become traitors the river Jordan will be as acceptable to us as the river Potomac, for we shall be fighting for the same precise principle—the flag and national existence—as are our Eastern brethren; and even should annihilation be our fate, of which we have no fears, the belief that our country men would think of our graves as they do those of Virginia, and that the Union men of California, our old friends, would swarm forth by the thousands to avenge us—such a hope and belief would nerve us for death.[53]

But, the writer added, "Unless he fails to exercise the statesmanship universally accorded to him, Brigham Young cannot but foresee the results which would flow from a war of his beginning."[54] Young had at least 8,000 well drilled and effective men and could perhaps call on 50,000, according to the reporter. Estimates of a possible Mormon army ranged widely. But Young could expect within two or three years that the federal government "could flood his valley with regiments, and sweep it with a gulf stream of bayonets." Despite the presence of some hotheads in Utah, this writer and others did not expect real war.[55]

The same San Francisco *Bulletin* correspondent, in another dispatch of October 20, graphically described the march from Fort Crittenden to Salt Lake City.

When Sunday's reveille awoke the command, it awoke expectant of battle ere another one should roll out upon the grey day-break. Blankets never were got from under and compactly strapped in knapsacks more promptly; cooks never prepared steaming breakfast with greater alacrity, and upon the principle that the aggregate strength of a regiment has a great deal to do with the aggregate prowess of a regiment, they never prepared a more bountiful repast. Upon the same principle, no breakfast during the whole march was ever stowed away in a more cool, nonchalant, jovial manner. The routine of months was dissipated, and, doubtless, each man's curiosity to know how he would personally stand fire, and the more general question—which side would whip—made everybody happy.[56]

There is a comparison here to similar scenes in Virginia and the Mississippi Valley. It was a rare opportunity to experience pre-battle emotions in the West, where war was considerably different. But in this instance, the Californians' reactions approximated those of their brothers on fields of battle to the east. Connor himself sat on a log and calmly loaded his revolvers while playing with his toddling child. Some men popped caps or even fired to make sure their arms were in shape. Others spent time in polishing their weapons.[57]

Cavalry preceded the staff and infantry. They moved forward steadily and compactly with the carriages behind the staff. With the carriages so close up to the van, it was clear to the men that the officers felt a fight was improbable. After marching fifteen miles the command crossed the Jordan. Here, too, was what was described as "a magnificent place for a fight." But there was no fight. In camp it was discussed that probably many of the Mormons were glad of the troops' presence "as it would bring many a dollar into the city circulation."[58]

The day after crossing the Jordan, the troops were not sure where they were going, but it was clearly toward Salt Lake City. There was still some fear of Mormon armed opposition. The San Francisco *Bulletin* reporter wrote: "A large and influential party was avowedly opposed to any near approach, and, in view of the advices received by our commander . . . the precise *animus* of the people and the treatment that would meet us, we did not know." There was still concern that the Utahans far outnumbered the troops and could annihilate the volunteers, who were 600 miles from reinforcements. All this uncertainty obviously created uneasiness and tension. The troops thought they would pass around the city, but the men did not yet understand the aggressive determination of their commander. To Connor a show of strength in Salt Lake City was imperative. So they marched right through the heart of the city, with a pause at Governor Harding's house.[59] "Every crossing was occupied by spectators, and windows, doors and roofs had their gazers. Not a cheer or a jeer greeted us. . . . A carriage, containing three ladies, who sang John Brown as they drove by, were heartily saluted. . . . There were none of those manifestations of loyalty that any other city in a loyal Territory would have made. The sidewalk by the mansion was thoroughly packed with Mormons, curious to know what would be the next feature. The bands continued their flood of music" on the march out to the future Camp Douglas. This was not far from where Brigham Young was supposed to have declared, "This is the place," when he first saw the Salt Lake Valley.[60]

Connor and his men immediately began to establish their camp as rapidly and as permanently as they could in the face of the coming Wasatch Mountain winter. Dugouts with tents for roofs, small log and adobe buildings had to suffice.[61] In his official orders of October 26 setting up the military post, Connor described the limits of the camp and announced that it contained some 2,560 acres.[62]

Brigham Young was, as always, active during the autumn. He continued to seek payment for the Mormon volunteers and their expenses for service guarding the Overland Trail. He wrote to Bernhisel in Washington on October 3: "If the Department are going to haggle, postpone and vexatiously delay the payment of expenses, we are able to make a present thereof to the government, if we should see proper to do so."[63] To the congregation in the Bowery on October 6, Young continued his criticism on a broader theme: "A Republican Government in the hands of a wicked people must terminate in woe to that people, but in the hands of the righteous, it is everlasting, while its power reaches to the heavens."[64] He was disturbed by the coming of Connor's men and issued what amounted to his instructions to his people in a meeting at President Young's School House October 26. He

considered it important that some regulations should be made in each ward of this city by which the people might be kept from association with the troops that have come into our city. To this end he recommended that the Teachers of the several Wards should be constituted policemen to look after the interests of the people . . . that if these Teachers become suspicious of any person in their Wards they should watch them day and night until they learned what they were doing and who frequented their houses. If they found any of the sisters going to Camp, no matter under what pretence, they should cast them forth from the Church forthwith.

He also appointed a central committee to establish standard prices for articles that might be sold to the army.[65]

But by October 30 Young was a bit less apprehensive. He is quoted as saying at a council meeting of the First Presidency:

Now, right in the time of war there could not be a greater insult offered, nor one of a higher character than the Government have already offered to this corporation by locating that army within the limits of the corporation without asking leave. And then after doing this, tell this community that they must take an oath of allegiance before they can be allowed to sell anything to the army; for say they, "We rather mistrust that you are not loyal and we shall not allow you to bid at all." In regard to their location I wish to say, that after all the insult that has been offered, they are in the best place they can be in for doing the least injury. If they were at Camp Floyd or Camp Bridger they would go unrestrained, but here they cannot do much hurt. I feel that they will dwindle away. Col. Connor started, I am told, with 1,600 men and got here with a little over 600. . . . I cannot say what we shall do next time we hear of an army coming here, but hope we shall do right. . . . I hope the brethren will keep their families from that Camp; and let them alone and politely ask for what they want. To take the oath to furnish a dozen of eggs! I wonder who would do it for the privilege of selling a dozen of eggs! They make manifest their folly in all they do. . . . Let them come and say "Will you sell me a bushel of potatoes?" Then comes the answer "Do you want me to take the oath of allegiance? If you do, go to hell for your potatoes."[66]

To George Cannon, back in Liverpool, Young wrote on November 13 about the new army and its camp, "Whatever may be the designs in making an encampment of troops where their trains and post will be expanded in a manner devoid of accomplishing what they were ostensibly ordered out for, it is certain that those designs and plans will result in benefit to the wise and in the advance of true principles. Thus far the troops have stayed quietly in their camp, attending to their own affairs, the citizens also attending to theirs; in so much that one does not notice and scarcely even thinks of their proximity."[67] However, this happy situation of separation was soon to change.

On November 29 Young went into more details in a letter to Bernhisel:

Col. Connor and his command, ostensibly ordered to Utah for the protection of the overland mail and telegraph lines, have, except a company or two left at Ruby Valley, safely encamped on the bench land near the mouth of Red Butte Canyon, and within the corporate limits of this City. What such an uncalled for, utterly useless, extravagant, and non-sensical operation means is probably more than Col. Connor and all his command can explain, though may be in keeping with the Cabinet views of economical expenditures for ordered services, since the command is within sight of a short portion of the line professed to be in want of the protection they are professedly ordered to tender, and they are safely ensconced within the limits of a large city, secure from depredation and attack by Indians . . . it is written that "the well laid plans of mice and men gang aft agee" and so will theirs in all their plottings and acts to thwart the purposes of Jehovah. Does Government expect revenue from taxes, imposts, and all sources sufficient to enable them to keep so many troops rusting in camps, within a City, when they are so much needed in active service? And if they are so foolishly improvident, do they expect to long keep such conduct from the knowledge and just comments of an abused and insulted public? Thus far Colonel Connor has maintained strict discipline in camp, as far as I am informed, but why are they where they are? This is a question that we are much satisfied *we* can correctly answer, but at the same time would be much pleased if you could induce the Secretary of War to give an answer equally correct, or even any answer.[68]

To his son, Brigham Young, Jr., in Liverpool, on January 3, 1863, the Church president went over the same ground, but added: ". . . as heretofore, the plans of those who ordered them where they are will be frustrated, and they, also as heretofore, will be filled with wrath and wonder" that their efforts "against the truth" have failed.[69]

Brigham Young was reported as commenting on the order for California troops: "Lincoln has ordered an army from California, for the Order has passed over these wires," thus indicating that government orders and other telegraphic communications were reported to the Mormon leaders.[70]

Meanwhile, there were forces at work apparently to try to bring about the removal of Connor and his command from Salt Lake City to Fort Bridger to the east. General-in-Chief Halleck in Washington told General Wright in San Francisco on December 9, by telegraph, that "All communications received at the War Department from Overland Mail Company, Post Office Department, and Department of the Interior urge the removal of Colonel Connor's command to Fort Bridger and Ham's Fork, as a check upon the Indians."[71] Wright replied the same December 9 that the neighborhood of Fort Bridger was quiet, but he had directed Connor to detach one or two companies to occupy the fort. Wright added, "I am fully satisfied that we should have a force in the Salt Lake Valley of at least 2,000 men, commanded by a firm and discreet officer. Without entering into details I am well convinced that prudential considerations demand the presence of a force in that country strong enough to look down any opposition."[72] It is not reading too much into this to say that Wright, egged on by Connor, felt that the Mormons had to be watched, though he did not come out and say so.

By December 12 Wright informed Washington that he "would not recommend the entire abandonment of the position now occupied by Colonel Connor, in close proximity to Salt Lake City, where he is erecting temporary shelter for his men."[73] Wright continued his strong support of Connor, observing that "he is taking every precaution to guard effectively the Overland mail Route, and also the telegraph stations; and to his energy and sound judgment may safely be confided that important duty."[74]

Late in the year there were reports of Indian outbreaks around the Cache Valley to the north of Salt Lake City, around Pacific Springs, and along the Humboldt, far to the west of Salt Lake City. In November an expedition went from Camp Douglas to the Cache Valley with a skirmish against Indians on November 23.

The expedition was undertaken by Major Edward McGarry and the Second Cavalry California Volunteers. As Connor explained to headquarters, the uncle of Reuben Van Orman, a young boy who had been captured by Indians, reported he had been looking for the youth for two years. Three sisters taken at the same time in 1860 were dead. Two expeditions from Oregon had been unsuccessful in finding the boy.[75] Connor further reported that "The Indians are threatening the Overland Mail Route east and west of here. I have no fears of the western end, as the lessons I have been teaching them and the message I sent them make them fear me." However, he had sent ten men east to protect the telegraph station at Big Sandy. About 100 horses belonging to some mountaineers had been stolen from the Fort Bridger Reserve. So he sent Company I of the infantry to garrison Bridger during the winter. Pacific Springs had been garrisoned by troops from the Department of the West, and the telegraph station at Big Sandy was actually in the District of Oregon.[76]

Major Edward McGarry reported that he left Camp Douglas

with about sixty men November 20 and went north to Cache Valley, near Providence. After skirmishing, with three Indians killed, McGarry met with the Indians who came in, including Chief Bear Hunter. The Indians brought in the captured boy and McGarry released Bear Hunter and four warriors. He returned to Camp Douglas on November 27.[77] This was typical of small actions Connor's men engaged in to protect the trails against Indians.

A few days later, on December 4, Major McGarry led another expedition to the north to attempt to recover stock stolen by Indians. An Indian camp was found on Bear River. Four captives were reportedly taken by the soldiers, and the return of the stock was demanded. According to the *Deseret News*, the stock was not returned and the captives were put to death.[78]

Wright commended Connor on the Cache Valley expedition: "All that you have done and propose to do is approved by the general, who feels that he can safely rely upon your sound judgment for conducting to a favorable issue the delicate duty assigned you."[79]

Near the end of 1862, on December 20, Connor wrote at length to San Francisco headquarters:

I have been aware that efforts were being made to dissever my command. The real governor of this Territory, Brigham Young, and his satellites on the one hand, and agents and contractors on the other, have since my arrival here constantly worked to separate this command, the former with his usual sagacity, for the attainment of his own purposes, and without the least doubt of his success (high authority states that he has openly boasted, and in fact, that he would drive me away from here before spring), and the latter from a desire to make money out of the Government.

Connor complained that Judge William Alexander Carter, Overland agent at Fort Bridger, and others "have not so much the interests of the Government or the Overland Mail company at heart as a desire to speculate upon the necessities of this command by selling to it supplies, of which Judge Carter has large quantities on hand." Connor continued,

I am reliably informed that the so-called President Young is making active preparations indicating a determination on his part to oppose the Government of the United States in the spring, provided Utah is not admitted into the Union as a State, or in case of a foreign war or serious reverse to our arms. It is constantly asserted by him and his agents that this command should be moved and scattered along the line of the Over-land Mail Company as a "check against Indians," who they say are ready to attack the property at any moment; and many willing converts to this fear are found among Brigham's hosts. But no one having the interest of the Government or the company in view can be found here credulous enough to be blind to the real motives which actuate their desires. Brigham Young is now engaged in mounting cannon for the purpose of resisting the Government, and has reports circulated, which have reached the ears of those highest in authority, in order to mature his plans, gain time, and prepare his cannon. Desirable as this would be to him I hope to defeat his intentions.[80]

Connor was satisfied that he occupied every necessary position on the Overland. He controlled the entire line from Ruby Valley to Ham's Fork. He did not feel troops were needed at Fort Bridger, but, obeying orders, he would garrison it. His position at Camp Douglas commanded all avenues to and from Salt Lake City itself. "The presence of this command here, which the informants of the General-in-Chief desire so much to have removed, indicates that my information regarding the real intentions of these people is correct." Connor was perhaps being a bit sarcastic here, insinuating that the Mormon and other efforts to remove his troops proved the necessity of their presence in Utah and Salt Lake City. He went on:

I am truly glad that the department commander has given me discretionary powers in the premises. I am creditably informed and believe that the Mormons have instigated the late attack by Indians on the telegraph station at Pacific Springs in order to draw my forces to that point. Mormons also, in the northern part of this valley, encourage depredations by the Humboldt Indians by purchasing of them property of which massacred immigrants have been despoiled by giving them in exchange therefor powder, lead and produce.[81]

General Wright sent Connor's communication to Washington, with the comment that "Colonel Connor is a man of observation, undaunted firmness, and self-possession under all circumstances, and his views of the state of affairs in Utah can be relied on. . . . With the small force now in the Territory the greatest prudence is required, and in the early spring I propose to throw forward to Salt Lake such a re-enforcement as will insure respect to our flag and a due observance of the laws of the United States."[82]

On the last day of the year the *Deseret News* called the Emancipation Proclamation "this ultra measure," and the paper felt it would benefit the Confederacy. As to the Indians, the "aborigines in the vicinity of the northern settlements have, as reported, been very hostile in their demeanor." This attitude they blamed on Major McGarry's expedition.[83]

The year 1862 ended with what amounted to a standoff between Connor and his men and Brigham Young and the Mormons. There had been a sort of feeling-out process. All was not animosity by any means, but there was mutual distrust and maneuvering for advantage. It was clear that the federal government had decided to put the protection of the mail and telegraph lines in the hands of California Volunteers rather than in those of the Utah or Mormon militia. As one observer put it, "Utah was placed under a military surveillance during the war, and California was made her sister's keeper. At least, such was the interpretation placed upon the military mission of General Connor and his command."[84]

Admission of Utah was still not entirely a dead letter as far as the Mormons were concerned. In Washington Delegate Bernhisel was still doing what he could to obtain admission, but his efforts were fruitless. On December 12 he told Brigham Young that there was a proposed enabling act to admit Nebraska, Colorado, Utah, and Nevada at one time. Bernhisel wrote: "Though candor compels me to state I do not regard the prospect of passing a bill of this character as very brilliant, yet Utah being in the same bill with the other Territories will give us strength. The principal obstacle to the admission of Utah is, as you are doubtless aware, 'the peculiar institution.'"[85] Of course, Bernhisel was reiterating that polygamy was the main obstacle, and he was undoubtedly correct.

Again on December 26 Bernhisel reported on the omnibus bill:

That portion of the bill relating to Utah created a good deal of excitement and the Committee [House Committee on Territories] broke up almost in a row. The committee requested the chairman to propose a separate bill for each Territory which he has accordingly done. . . . The indications are that Utah could be admitted into the Union of the States, on condition that the people of the Territory would covenant to abolish the "peculiar institution." On Monday morning I called on the President and informed him that a regiment of volunteers, under the command of Colonel Connor had been ordered from California for the protection of the telegraph line, and the overland emigration and that they were encamped within the limits of the city, and stated to his Excellency in pretty strong terms that they were not needed there and might be elsewhere. The President gave me a line to the Hon. Edwin M. Stanton, Secretary of War, requesting him to see me. I went immediately to the War Office.[86]

Bernhisel could not see Stanton that day and had not done so by the date of the letter. However, by January 2, 1863, he had had an interview with Stanton. The Secretary promised to talk to Halleck, which it seems he did, "for General Halleck informed me last Saturday that he had telegraphed to General Wright to order their removal, but he did not know to what point they should be removed. This military force has perhaps already taken their departure, but if not, it probably will long ere this reaches you."[87] Bernhisel, of course, was far off base in his information. Halleck had ordered removal, but General Wright interceded and Connor and his men spent their first winter at Camp Douglas.

Young and the Mormons had still other problems by fall and early winter of 1862, aside from admission and the presence of Connor and his men. Citizens and Mormon leaders had seemed pleased with Governor Harding's statements upon his arrival in Utah in July, but this euphoria was not to continue. Harding himself showed, at least privately, that he was becoming suspicious of the Mormons. He wrote to Secretary of State Seward in late August of 1862, "It is my deliberate opinion that no communications from this Department of the General Government can be sent from this point, through the P.O. without danger that its contents will be known here at *Head Quarters*, by which I mean the *power* that rules the people here, with an absolutism scarcely to be conceived, by those not in a situation to see and hear for themselves." The governor felt the Mormons were disloyal to the government of the United States: "Brigham Young and other leaders are constantly inculcating in the minds of [the] . . . audience who sit beneath their teachings every sabbath that the Government of the United States is of no consequence, that it lies in ruins, that the prophecy of Joseph Smith is being fulfilled to the letter." After both sides in the Civil War are exhausted "then the Saints are to step in and quietly enjoy the possession of the lands and all that is left of the ruined cities and desolated fields and that 'Zion is to be built up' not only in the valley or the mountains but the great centers of their power and glory, is to be in Missouri, where the Saints under the lead of their prophet, were expelled many years hence [*sic*]." He wrote that he had not heard one prayer or word offered up for the success of the Union cause or the restoration of peace. He emphasized the insistence upon absolute obedience to Brigham Young, "These people are taught to believe that the President (That is Brigham Young and his counselors) hold the key of all rightful power extending over all things both in earth and in heaven, and that life and death are subject to the will of the 'Lord's annointed' (that is Brigham Young)."

He complained that Mormons were not attacked by Indians, but Gentiles on the same road were. Governor Harding went on to urge that a military force be posted in the area that would "make treason dumb."[88] The governor again wrote to the Secretary of State on September 3 that he had attended the service at the Bowery and he quoted Brigham Young as saying: "Nothing I can say can save the Government of the United States. It could have been saved if the people had accepted Joseph Smith for their President." Harding accused Young of implying that the main reason the army was coming was not to protect the Overland Mail but to act against the Mormons.[89]

Secretary of State Seward had forwarded two of Harding's letters to the President on September 20. Seward suggested sending some paroled troops to Utah. Lincoln sent the letters on to the Secretary of War, whose office referred them to General Halleck. There was no action on this idea, but of course Connor's men were moving toward Salt Lake City.[90]

Brigadier General James Craig telegraphed General Halleck from Fort Laramie on August 25 that "Governor Harding, of Utah, in dispatch today in relation to re-enlistment of Mormon troops, after saying he had interview with Brigham Young, closed dispatch as follows: 'You need not expect anything for the present. Things are not right.'"[91] As we have seen, nothing came of any proposed reenlistment of Mormon soldiers.

Brigham Young had had his fill of Harding by fall. At a council meeting of the First Presidency on October 30 he is quoted as saying, "And that thing that is here that calls himself Governor. . . . If you were to fill a sack with cow shit, it would be the best thing you could do for an imitation, and that would be just as good as he is."[92]

On November 22 Colonel Connor put up a flagpole at Camp Douglas with Governor Harding, the three justices, and the U.S. marshal present. The governor is quoted in a Mormon source as making a "speech in which he shed tears for his country; desired all the sins of the nation could be put on his head; he could put his hand on his mouth and his mouth in the dust and cry Unclean! Unclean! Judge Kinney was said to be near the Governor and the smoke from the judge's cigar nearly suffocated his Excellency, and it is said his Excellency and the judge were both gentlemanly drunk."[93]

Mormon historian Whitney wrote that something occurred soon after Harding's arrival "to turn him against the vast majority of the citizens and cause him to take a stand diametrically opposite to that which he at first assumed."[94] Some felt he changed with the advent of the army and Connor, but it is clear that Harding became disenchanted soon after his arrival.

The first main public explosion of criticism was what the Mormons termed an "attack" when Harding addressed the territorial legislature on December 10, 1862. In a long and involved address which covered many fields, Harding praised the material progress of the citizens of the Territory. Going into the causes of the civil conflict in the nation, he blamed African slavery: "That it is the duty of every lover of human liberty and friend of republican institutions on this continent to stand by the government in its present trials is, to my mind, a proposition too clear for argument." Harding went on to support emancipation, before getting into the admission of the state of Deseret. He felt Congress would take up the question of admitting Utah in the future, and then he rebuked his hearers:

I am sorry to say that since my sojourn amongst you I have heard no sentiments, either publicly or privately expressed, that would lead me to believe that much sympathy is felt by any considerable number of your people in favor of the government of the United States, now struggling for its very existence. . . . If I am mistaken in this opinion, no one will rejoice more than myself in acknowledging my error. . . . I regret, also, to say I have found, in conversing with many gentlemen of social and political influence, that because the question of the admission of this Territory into the Union was temporarily postponed, distrust is entertained in regard to the friendly disposition of the federal government, and expressions have been used, amounting to innuendoes at least, as to what the result might be in case the admission should be denied or postponed.[95]

And then Harding plunged into the Mormon institution of polygamy. He called it an "anomaly throughout Christendom. . . . I lay it down as a sound proposition, that no community can happily exist with an institution so important as that of marriage, wanting in all those qualities that make it homogenial with institutions and laws of neighboring civilized communities having the same object." He urged Mormons to guard against flagrant abuses of polygamy: "That plurality of wives is tolerated and believed to be right may not appear so strange; but that a mother and her daughters are allowed to fulfil the duties of *wives* to the same husband, or that a man could be found in all Christendom who could be induced to take upon himself such a relationship, is, perhaps, no less a marvel in morals than in matter of tastes. . . . No community can long exist without absolute social anarchy unless so important an institution as that of marriage is regulated by law."[96]

The territorial governor then spoke out on the anti-polygamy law passed by Congress: "I am aware that there is a prevailing opinion here that said act is unconstitutional, and therefore it is recommended by those in high authority that no regard whatever should be paid to the same; and, still more to be regretted, if I am rightly informed, in some instances it has been recommended that it be openly disregarded and *defied*."[97] He warned the people against "such dangerous and disloyal counsels. . . . The individual citizen, under no circumstances whatever, has the right to defy any law or statutes of the United States with impunity. . . . To forcibly resist the execution of that act would be, to say the least, a high misdemeanor, and if a whole community should become involved in such resistance would call down upon it the consequences of insurrection and rebellion."[98]

The governor admitted the liberty of conscience and the right to worship God as one chooses. But the rights of freedom of religion must not be abused: "when religious opinions assume new manifestations, and pass from the condition of *mere sentiment* into *overt acts*, no matter whether they *be acts of faith* or not, they must not outrage the opinions of the civilized world, but, on the other hand, must conform to those usages established by law, and which are believed to underlie our very civilization."[99] Harding went on to call for a revision and codification of the Utah statutes and voting by secret ballot instead of having voters sign ballots. As to Indian troubles, the governor believed that "the presence of a military command would prevent Indian horrors."[100]

To say that this speech caused a great stir among the Mormons is understating the event. Editor Stenhouse wrote that the governor's message "was the tocsin of war, and was considered a very offensive document. . . . The *manner* of delivery of the message was worse than the matter, and probably no Legislature ever felt more humiliated and insulted. It was painful to observe the legislators, as they sat quiet and immovable, hearing their faith contemned. It was interpreted as an open and gratuitous insult on the part of the Executive."[101] One member of the audience said Harding's message reminded him of the man feeding his cow. The man started with sweet apples and then threw in the onions.[102]

The legislature did not order the printing of the governor's message as was (and is) customary. It passed some twenty measures of which Harding vetoed fourteen. The reports were rife early in 1863 that Harding and Judges Waite and Drake were writing to members of the government in Washington and were said to be working against the people of Utah. As spring came on, public meetings were held protesting Harding and the two magistrates.

If the legislature would not print Harding's message, the U.S. Senate would and did. Senator Benjamin Wade of Ohio submitted to that body a report from the Committee on Territories dated February 13, 1863, with a resolution that a thousand copies of the message of the governor be printed and sent to Harding for distribution. This was done. But the committee report went further; it stated that sources of information

disclose the fact that the customs which have prevailed in all our other Territories in the government of public affairs have had but little toleration in the Territory of Utah; but in their stead there appears to be, overriding all other influences, a sort of Jewish theocracy, graduated to the condition of that Territory. This theocracy, having a supreme head who governs and guides every affair of importance in the church, and practically in the Territory, is the only real power acknowledged here, and to the extension of whose interests every person in the Territory must directly or indirectly conduce.[103]

The report also said:

Contrary to the usages of the whole country, the affairs of this Territory are managed through church instrumentalities, and no measure is permitted to succeed in the Territory which will, for one moment, conflict with the interests of the church; in other words, we have here the first exhibition within the limits of the United States of a church ruling the State. . . . Another opinion—the subject of both public and private teaching—is that the government of the United States will not and ought not to stand. They make a difference between the Constitution and the government of the United States; to the Constitution they claim to be very loyal, but to the government they owe no particular allegiance.[104]

The report pointed out that in Utah Territory there was only one newspaper, the *Deseret News*, which was an organ of the Church, and that Harding's message was suppressed. The report charged that "Polygamy of the most unlimited character, sanctioning the cohabitation of a man with the mother and her daughters indiscriminately, is not the only un-American thing among them."[105] The voting system was also soundly criticized.

Rumors and false reports were still common regarding the Mormons. Acting Governor of New Mexico Territory W. F. M. Arny wired Secretary of State Seward on December 13 that he was informed some 5,000 Rebel troops were preparing to invade New Mexico from Texas "with the intention of obtaining possession of this territory and Colorado, and then, with Utah under Brigham Young, to establish a number of slave states." Of course there was nothing to the report, at least so far as Utah was concerned.[106]

Yet all these rumors of marching men, the parochial events, and local political maneuverings could be of little moment to most of the nation's populace. The conflicts of opinion in Utah were puny in comparison with the titanic and tragic struggles of 1862 at Second Manassas, Antietam, Fredericksburg, and the start of the Vicksburg campaign in the fighting war, not to mention the controversy raging over emancipation.

NOTES

1. O.R., vol. L, pt. 1, pp. 548–50.
2. Ibid., p. 543.
3. H. H. Bancroft, Biographical Sketch of General P. E. Connor (San Francisco: n.p., 1887), microfilm of typescript of pamphlet, in Bancroft Library, Berkeley, Cal., p. 1.
4. The primary sources for background on Connor are Rogers, Soldiers, pp. 1–5; Dictionary of American Biography, vol. IV, pp. 352–53; Heitman, Historical Register and Dictionary of the United States Army, vol. I, pp. 321–22; Leo P. Kibby, "Patrick Edward Connor, First Gentile of Utah," Journal of the West, 2 (Oct., 1863), 425–26; and Bancroft, Connor. There is no major known collection of Connor papers, so far as research shows.
5. Connor's own account of the incident is in the Sacramento Transcript, Apr. 20, 1850, with more details in the Daily Alta Californian, Apr. 17, 1850, from Rogers, Soldiers, pp. 5–8; see also Bancroft, Connor, pp. 1–4.
6. Rogers, Soldiers, pp. 8–11; Dictionary of American Biography, vol. IV, pp. 352–53; Bancroft, Connor, p. 4.
7. Rogers, Soldiers, pp. 12–13; Bancroft, Connor, p. 4.
8. Rogers, Soldiers, p. 13.
9. Orton, Records of California Men, p. 12.
10. Bancroft, Connor, pp. 4–5.
11. O.R., vol. L, pt. 1, p. 960.
12. Orton, Records of California Men, p. 506.
13. O.R., vol. L, pt. 1, pp. 1164–65.
14. O.R., vol. L, pt. 2, pp. 19, 31.
15. Ibid., pp. 48–49.
16. Ibid., p. 55.
17. Ibid., pp. 60–61.
18. Ibid., pp. 67, 97.
19. Ibid., pp. 119–20.
20. Ibid.
21. Utah Territorial Papers, U.S. Department of State, Record Group 59, Wootton to Seward, Sept. 5, 1861.
22. Orton, Records of California Men, p. 512, Mar. 30, 1863.
23. Deseret News, June 25, 1862.
24. Ibid.
25. Ibid., July 23, Aug. 13, 1862.
26. Ibid., Sept. 10, 1862.
27. Ibid., Oct. 1, 1862.
28. Ibid., Sept. 10, 1862.
29. O.R., vol. L, pt. 2, p. 128.
30. Ibid., p. 133.
31. Ibid., p. 33.
32. Ibid., pp. 143–44.

33. *Ibid.*, p. 144.
34. *Ibid.*, vol. L, pt. 1, p. 177.
35. *Ibid.*, p. 178.
36. *Ibid.*, pp. 178–79.
37. *Ibid.*, vol. L, pt. 2, p. 180.
38. Bancroft, *Connor*, p. 6.
39. *Deseret News*, Oct. 15, 1861.
40. Rogers, *Soldiers*, p. 261n.
41. *Deseret News*, Oct. 22, 1862.
42. *Ibid.*
43. O.R., vol. L, pt. 2, p. 187.
44. *Ibid.*, p. 195.
45. *Ibid.*, p. 218.
46. *Deseret News*, Oct. 22, 1862.
47. *Ibid.*
48. *Deseret News*, Oct. 29, 1862.
49. *Deseret News*, Nov. 12, 1862, from San Francisco *Bulletin*; Bancroft, *Connor*, pp. 7–9.
50. *Deseret News*, Nov. 12, 1862, from San Francisco *Bulletin*; one source identifies the alleged Danite chief as Bill Hickman: Linn, *The Story of the Mormons*, p. 545.
51. *Deseret News*, Nov. 12, 1862, from San Francisco *Bulletin*.
52. *Ibid.*; Bancroft, *Connor*, pp. 8–9.
53. *Deseret News*, Nov. 12, 1862, from San Francisco *Bulletin*.
54. *Ibid.*
55. *Ibid.*
56. *Ibid.*; Bancroft, *Connor*, pp. 10–11.
57. *Ibid.*
58. *Ibid.*
59. *Deseret News*, Nov. 12, 1862; Bancroft, *Connor*, pp. 12–13.
60. *Ibid.*; Bancroft, *Connor*, p. 13.
61. Leonard J. Arrington and Thomas G. Alexander, "The U.S. Army Overlooks Salt Lake Valley, Fort Douglas, 1862–1865," *Utah Historical Quarterly*, 33 (Fall, 1965), 329.
62. O.R., vol. L, pt. 2, p. 195.
63. Brigham Young Letter Books, Church Archives.
64. *Journal of Discourses*, vol. X, p. 15.
65. Journal History, Oct. 26, 1862.
66. *Ibid.*, Oct. 30, 1862.
67. Brigham Young Letter Books, Church Archives.
68. *Ibid.*
69. *Ibid.*
70. Roberts, *Comprehensive History*, vol. V, p. 17; date of Young's comment is uncertain.
71. O.R., vol. L, pt. 2, p. 244, Dec. 9, 1862.

72. *Ibid.*, p. 245.

73. *Ibid.*, p. 249.

74. O.R., vol. L, pt. 1, p. 181, Dec. 15, 1862.

75. *Ibid.*, pp. 181–82; Newell Hart, "Rescue of a Frontier Boy," *Utah Historical Quarterly*, 33 (Winter, 1965), 51–52.

76. *Ibid.*

77. O.R., vol. L, pt. 1, pp. 182–83; Hart, "Rescue of a Frontier Boy," pp. 51–52.

78. *Deseret News*, Dec. 10, 17, 1862. There is no report of this action in O.R.

79. O.R., vol. L, pt. 2, pp. 253–54, Dec. 20, 1862.

80. *Ibid.*, pp. 256–57.

81. *Ibid.*

82. *Ibid.*, p. 275, Jan. 3, 1863.

83. *Deseret News*, Dec. 31, 1862.

84. Tullidge, *History of Salt Lake City*, p. 273.

85. Bernhisel Papers.

86. *Ibid.*

87. *Ibid.*, Bernhisel to Young, Jan. 2, 1863.

88. Utah Territorial Papers, U.S. Department of State, Record Group 59, National Archives, Harding to Seward, Aug. 30, 1862.

89. *Ibid.*

90. O.R., vol. XIII, p. 596.

91. Lincoln, *Collected Works*, vol. V, p. 432.

92. Journal History, Oct. 30, 1862.

93. Journal History, "History of Brigham Young," Nov. 22, 1862.

94. Whitney, *History of Utah*, p. 82.

95. Stephen S. Harding, "Message to the Territorial Legislature of Utah," *Senate Miscellaneous Document*, No. 37 (Washington, D.C., 1863), pp. 1–5.

96. *Ibid.*, pp. 5–6.

97. *Ibid.*

98. *Ibid.*, p. 7.

99. *Ibid.*, p. 8.

100. *Ibid.*, pp. 14–15.

101. Stenhouse, *Rocky Mountain Saints*, p. 603.

102. Tullidge, *History of Salt Lake City*, p. 305.

103. "Report of the Committee on Territories," *Senate Committee Report*, No. 87 (Washington, D.C., 1863), p. 1.

104. *Ibid.*, p. 2.

105. *Ibid.*

106. O.R., vol. XV, p. 641.

CHAPTER

VII

Tragedy on Bear River

By the winter of 1862–63, a more severe one than usual, the intricacies of the Civil War period were extremely complicated even in such apparently isolated places as Utah Territory. The din, blood, and death in the great battles did, however, provide a primary focus of interest in the East, where the war itself held center stage and eclipsed all lesser events. Not so in the far West: there were real enemies, suspected enemies, cantankerous friends, and a shadowy third or even a fourth world. People's attention had to be divided in many directions.[1]

All during autumn, reports came in of Indian troubles in Utah, laid mainly to the Bannock and Shoshone tribes. The columns of the *Deseret News* were full of such incidents. Some of the reports were patently false; others were exaggerated; a few were true. Utah Indian Superintendent James Duane Doty reported to U.S. Commissioner of Indian Affairs William P. Dole on October 6, 1862, of continued Indian depredations extending from the northwestern part of Utah Territory far into Nevada Territory. He felt it necessary to visit the governor of Nevada to try to devise some means of protection.[2] Army patrols went out constantly from Camp Douglas. They moved out temporarily to Fort Bridger and farther east along the Oregon Trail. Westward they protected the route across the Great Basin to Fort Churchill in Nevada Territory. Vigilance had to be maintained to the south as well.

Generally speaking, white civilization in Utah was limited to a lengthy strip of Mormon settlement in the Great Salt Lake Valley along the western edge of the Wasatch Range and in southern Utah. To the north of Salt Lake City there were other Mormon communities which thinned out near the border between Utah Territory and what was in 1862 part of Washington Territory, soon to become Idaho Territory.

Commissioner of Indian Affairs Dole, in his 1862 report to Congress, wrote of the Utah Superintendency:

Our relations with the Indians of this superintendency are still in an unsatisfactory condition. But little progress has been made in subjecting the Indians to the policy we have adopted for their government. The efforts of the superintendent and agents to ameliorate the condition of the Indians are very much restricted for want of adequate means, and I have no little doubt that many of the depredations committed by Indians are induced by want and privation. Another cause for the restless and rebellious spirit manifested by the Indians is attributed to an unwarrantable interference, on the part of the Mormons, with the legitimate discharge of the duties of superintendent and agents.[3]

Dole felt that the most numerous, powerful, and troublesome Indians were the Shoshone or Snakes, who had created serious disturbances on the overland emigrant and mail routes. Lives had been lost, vast numbers of horses, cattle, and mules had been stolen, and much property had been destroyed. While appropriations had been made to negotiate treaties with the Indians, it was too late in the season to negotiate very rapidly. Prospects for peace were not good, and more appropriations were needed.[4]

Superintendent Doty agreed with this and went into considerable detail, as did the clerk of the superintendency Amos Reed.[5] In his 1863 report, Doty wrote: "During the year 1862 and the winter months of this year many of the Indians in this superintendency manifested decided evidences of hostility toward the whites. The numerous murders and depredations upon property which they committed, as also their language, indicated a determination to stop all travel upon the overland routes and upon the roads leading to the gold mines in Idaho Territory. It became unsafe even for the Mormon settlers to go into the canyons for wood; and the Bannock prophet said the Indians would combine and drive the white man from the country."[6] Chief Washakie, astute leader of the Shoshones, was apprehensive of a general Indian outbreak. He recommended that Fort Bridger be garrisoned and that his band be put on a reservation. It appears that Washakie's authority had apparently declined at this time and that a number of the Shoshone warriors were renegades.[7]

It must be said that the attacks, killing, and stealing occurred on both sides. Peaceful Indians had sometimes been attacked by the fearful emigrants, and Connor's troops had been far from gentle in their chastisement of the Indians. The year 1862 had seen some increase in white emigration, which aroused the Indians' ire, and they were also unhappy with the inefficiency of the various Indian agents. On December 10, 1862, the *Deseret News* reported, "The Shoshone had already announced their intention of killing 'every white man they should meet with on the north side of Bear River, till they should be fully avenged for the Indian blood which had been shed.'" The settlers, especially to the north of Salt Lake City, had gathered in their stock and prepared for defense.

There is disagreement among historians as to how many of the band on Bear River in northern Utah were Bannock and how many were Shoshone. From the inconclusive information available, it would seem that the majority were Shoshone.[8]

The always wary, aggressive, and perceptive Connor was acutely conscious of the situation as winter crowded in on the Wasatches. He was aware that major action must be taken against the Indians to assure travelers and settlers some degree of safety. In his official report he said he had information, from various sources, of the encampment of a large body of Indians on the Bear River, about 140 miles north of Salt Lake City. "These Indians," he wrote, "had murdered several miners during the winter; passing to and from the settlements in this valley to the Beaver Head mines, east of the Rocky Mountains." He was satisfied "they were a part of the same band who had been murdering emigrants on the Overland Mail Route for the last fifteen years, and the principle [*sic*] actors and leaders in the horrid massacres of the past summer."[9] Connor then told of his decision: "I determined, although the season was unfavorable to an expedition in consequence of the cold weather and deep snow, to chastise them, if possible."[10] Connor had apparently planned his expedition at the same time or before Utah Territorial Chief Justice Kinney on January 19 issued a warrant for the arrest of Chiefs Bear Hunter, San Pitch, and Sagwitch and had given it to Marshal Isaac L. Gibbs to serve. Miner William Bevins had told the judge that his party coming from the Grasshopper Gold Mines had been attacked by Indian bands and one John Henry Smith had been killed. Connor told Marshal Gibbs that he could come along on the expedition but that the army was not going just to help serve the warrant.[11] Connor made it clear that it was not his "intention to take any prisoners."[12] Actually, jurisdiction lay with the authorities of Washington Territory in this case, but in the West such geographic legalities were shadowy. Connor did not want the band of Indians reported to be on the Utah border north of the Cache Valley to scatter. "Feeling assured that secrecy was the surest way to success," he reported, "I determined to deceive the Indians by sending a small force in advance, judging, and rightly, they would not fear a small number."[13]

Upon the departure of the army, the *Deseret News* said of the Indians: "We wish this community rid of all such parties, and if Col. Connor be successful in reaching that bastard class of humans who play with the lives of the peaceable and law abiding citizens in this way, we shall be pleased to acknowledge our obligations." This and other statements indicated that at least some of the Mormons were getting tired of their traditional policy as pronounced by Brigham Young that it was "manifestly more economical and less expensive to feed and clothe than to fight the Indians."[14]

A correspondent using the pseudonym "Verite" wrote in the *Daily Alta Californian* that since the fall of 1862 the "Indian attacks upon the whites, traveling to and from the Dakota Mines, have only added determination to determination to rid the country of this terrible scourge—this perpetual reign of terror."[15]

On January 22, 1863, Connor sent Company K of the Third California Volunteer Infantry northward from Camp Douglas with two howitzers, and twelve cavalrymen with fifteen supply wagons, all under Captain Samuel N. Hoyt. Two days later Connor himself followed with the main force of some 225 cavalry.[16] The night marching was an attempt at deception. On the second night Connor overtook the advance party at Mendon and ordered them to march again at night. Connor with his cavalry units again overtook the foot troops at Franklin, the northern Utah settlement now in Idaho, only twelve miles from the Indian camp on Bear River.[17]

While abominable winter weather was suffered by both sides, it perhaps affected the defending Indians a little less than it did the advancing soldiers. The hands of some of the federals were benumbed so that they could barely load their arms. Connor later reported that their "suffering during the march was awful beyond description, but they steadily continued on without regard to hunger, cold, or thirst, not a murmur escaping them to indicate their sensibilities to pain or fatigue. Their uncomplaining endurance during their four nights' march from Camp Douglas to the battlefield is worthy of the highest praise." No less than seventy-five men had frozen feet and there was fear some would be permanently disabled.[18]

Captain Charles H. Hempstead described the march:

Those who were there at that time or participated in the events recounted can well remember—how can they ever forget—that fearful night march. . . . The shrill north wind swept over the valleys and down the mountain sides freezing with its cold breath every rivulet and stream. The moistened breath freezing as it left the lips, hung in miniature icicles from the beards of brave men. The foam from their steeds stood stark and stiff upon each hair and motion only made it possible for them to endure the biting freezing blast. . . . The sufferings of that night march of 68 miles can never be told in words. Many were frozen and necessarily left behind, but the troops after a halt by day, again faced the severity of winter in the mountains and pressed on, the Infantry by day and the Cavalry by night, to deceive the wiley foe.[19]

Connor's elaborate secrecy probably did no good, although correspondent Verite felt it was successful.[20] Such a march could hardly be kept secret from the usually observant Indians, although they might have been uncertain as to the size of the federal force.

Chief Bear Hunter and some of his men were in Franklin on January 27 and did a war dance around the home of the Mormon bishop, demanding more wheat. On the 28th they came back to collect the grain and observed approaching soldiers. A citizen said, "Here come the soldiers. You may get killed." Bear Hunter is said to have replied, "May-be-so soldiers get killed too."[21] It seems clear the Indians did not feel it necessary to flee their Bear River camp. One authority feels that Colonel Connor "made full use of surprise in his march. . . . If Bear Hunter had seen the cavalry he would have scattered his band."[22]

After some delays during the night of January 28 at Franklin, Connor moved with the cavalry, passing the infantry, artillery, and wagons about four miles from the camp of the Bannock and Shoshone. The location of the camp was determined by the smoke rising from the lodges. An open, treeless plain extended from Connor's position toward the camp, while the hills around held stunted cedars.[23] Connor was fearful still that the Indians would find out his strength and flee. So, at daybreak on the 29th, he moved rapidly forward with the cavalry, reaching the bank of Bear River just after daylight. The troops were in full view of the Indian encampment about a mile away. The colonel surveyed the Indian position through his field glasses and then sent Major Edward McGarry to advance with cavalry and surround the camp, if possible. Connor remained temporarily in the rear to give orders to the infantry and artillery.[24]

Correspondent Verite wrote, "The passage of the river was extremely difficult, from the hard ice at its bottom, underlying the current that carried also broken sheets of ice with it, to the incessant noise and danger of upsetting the horses and their riders."[25]

By the time Connor got to the field, McGarry had dismounted his men and engaged the Indians. McGarry had been unable to carry out his orders to surround the Indians, so he had accepted their challenge and had charged. According to Connor, the enemy "had sallied out of their hiding places on foot and horseback, and with fiendish malignity waved the scalps of white women and challenged the troops to battle, at the same time attacking them."[26] According to the eyewitness account in the *Deseret News*, "the Indians seemed to look upon the coming struggle with particular good humor. While one of the chiefs rode up and down in front of the ravine, brandishing his spear in the face of the volunteers, the warriors in front sang out: 'Fours right, fours left; come on you California sons of b____hs!"[27]

The Indian position was a strong one and naturally so, according to all eyewitnesses. Connor described it as "almost inaccessible to the troops, being in a deep, dry ravine from six to twelve feet deep and from thirty to forty feet wide, with very abrupt banks and running across level table-land, along which they had constructed steps from which they could deliver their fire without being themselves exposed. Under the embankments they had constructed artificial covers of willows thickly woven together, from behind which they could fire without being observed." [28] Witnesses put the ravine as being deeper than did Connor. The Indians had prepared embankments constructed of rock and earth, and had rammed forked sticks into the ground to serve as rifle rests, defensive preparations unusual for Indians. The location had probably been chosen originally for protection from the sharp winter winds, but its advantage as a defensive position was obvious. It was compared, with some exaggeration, to a "miniature Sebastopol." [29]

The ravine where the Indians were encamped was open only to the south and branched off another and longer ravine through which flowed a stream, later known as Battle Creek. Bear River at this point runs almost due east and west and the Indian ravine was to the north of it. The troops had to cross two benches, or ascending terraces, to get to the ravine. According to Verite, the volunteers told him that "with the same number of troops as Indians in such a position, they could have held at bay two thousand soldiers." [30] The *Deseret News* reported that the Indians retired into the entrance of the ravine and, as the troops charged, awaited "calmly their approach and sent at them a murderous fire that was sensibly felt everywhere. A large number of men fell dead, several fell mortally wounded and others threw themselves to the ground to bide their time and to adopt another style of fighting. The word was passed along the line for the men not to waste their ammunition and to protect themselves as much as possible." As Company K advanced, Lieutenant Chase, a former Mormon elder, was wounded in the wrist and then in the chest. He kept on fighting for twenty minutes more, mortally wounded, yet urging his men forward. The Indians fired with deadly effectiveness. [31]

After more than twenty minutes of ferocious fighting, Connor, now on the field, ordered McGarry with twenty men to turn the left flank of the Indian position in the ravine. About this time Captain Hoyt arrived at the riverbank, but his infantry found the stream impossible to cross. Connor sent the infantry some of the cavalry horses to carry the foot soldiers over. Part of the newly ar-

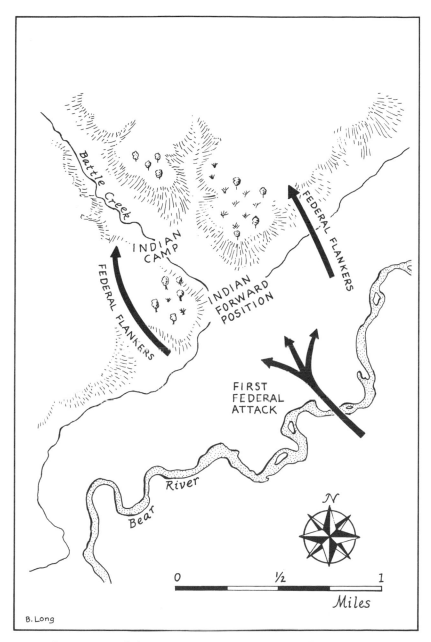

General concept of the area of the engagement of Bear River, based on the present-day Geological Survey map of the area and on visual on-the-scene information supplied by Thomas Lindmier.

rived infantry were sent in support of McGarry's flankers, who were soon successful in their surrounding operation. According to eyewitness accounts recorded in the *Deseret News*, the infantry "succeeded in scrambling up the hill—skirmishing as they went till they finally reached the west side, where, with the troops north and east they kept up an enfilading fire on the Indians that ultimately drove them down into the central and lower portions of the ravine."[32]

Connor put it succinctly when he reported, "Up to this time, in consequence of being exposed on a level and open plain while the Indians were under cover, they had every advantage of us, fighting with the ferocity of demons."[33] Federal soldiers, either regular or volunteers, were not accustomed to charging entrenched Indians. "My men fell fast and thick around me, but after flanking them we had the advantage and made good use of it," Connor reported. The flanking party was ordered to advance down the ravine on either side, giving the volunteers the advantage of enfilading fire. Some of the Indians now gave way and fled toward the north end of the ravine. A company of troops shot them as they ran out. Cavalry was ordered to cut off the retreat of any others who might try to escape.[34] According to Connor, relatively few Indians attempted to get away, but "they continued fighting with unyielding obstinacy, frequently engaging hand to hand with the troops until killed in their hiding places." Some who did attempt escape were shot while trying to swim the frigid river, or were killed while fighting from the cover of the dense willow thicket along the banks. Among those who did flee was Chief Sagwitch. Bear Hunter, however, was killed while crouching by a fire to prepare his ammunition.[35]

As the *Deseret News* put it, "The Indians bravely as they fought, could not withstand the indomitable will and bravery of the troops."[36] Corporal Tuttle of the volunteers later recorded that as soon as "the squaws and children saw that the soldiers did not desire to kill them, they came out of the ravine and walked to the rear." There they sat down in the snow, "like a lot of sage hens."[37]

The battle, or engagement, of Bear River lasted from approximately 6 A.M. to 10 A.M. "The position of the Indians," Connor reported, "was one of great natural strength, and had I not succeeded in flanking them the mortality in my command would have been terrible."[38]

Soon, according to Verite, "The silence of grim death began to reign, where before the hills had reverberated with the incessant crack of the rifle."[39] Corporal Tuttle, with his own spelling, described the post-battle scene:

I never shal far get (how can I). There we camped on the bank of Bear River with our dead dieing wounded and frozen 2 feet of snow on the ground nothing for fire but green willows which would burn about as well as the snow oh! the groands of the frozen it seems to ring in my ears yet the poor feelows some lost their toes some a portion of their feet I worked near all night bringing water from the river to wett cloths to draw frost from their frozen limbs. I had not sleep any for two nights befor it was a dreadful night to me but managed to get through the night some never saw the morning.[40]

Mormon guide Porter Rockwell went to Franklin to get teams to haul the wounded. The return journey to Salt Lake City was a slow one for the troops because of storms, mud, ice, and snow. The wounded had to be transferred from sleighs to wagons and were hurried to the Camp Douglas hospital. By the evening of February 4 the walking wounded and uninjured men arrived. Connor came back in a buggy with the guide Rockwell, bringing in over a hundred head of Indian horses.

After the return of the troops, a solemn funeral was held for the sixteen slain men. Sixteen riderless horses draped with black blankets led the procession. (Today there is a monument to the federal soldiers of Bear River in the Camp Douglas cemetery.) One eyewitness described the burial as "a solemn occasion to the city as well as to the camp. The day was cold and raw, yet a large number of our citizens were present. . . . Up to that time scarcely any of the citizens had set foot within the encampment, but now there was quite a score of carriages from the city, many equestrians and a large concourse of people on foot." Three volleys were fired. Connor sat motionless on his horse.[41]

Connor, who was forever suspicious of the Mormons, reported that in his march from Salt Lake City, "no assistance was rendered by the Mormons, who seemed indisposed to divulge any information regarding the Indians and charged enormous prices for every article furnished my command."[42] Mormon writers disagreed with this statement, the Logan Branch records of the Mormon Church showing a different story. "We the people of Cache Valley, looked upon the movement of Colonel Connor as an intervention of the Almighty, as the Indians have been a source of great annoyance to us for a long time, causing us to stand guard over our stock and other property the most of the time since our first settlement." Other records show sympathy on the part of the people of the Cache Valley for the volunteers, and eyewitnesses describe the aid given by the Mormons to the wounded and frozen soldiers after the battle. One resident told of soldiers being taken into homes in Logan during the return, where they were fed and could get warm. Peter Maugham, presiding Mormon bishop of the country, pronounced victory the "interdisposition of Providence in behalf of the settlers."[43]

As commander of the expedition, Connor praised the work of many officers. It does seem that the California Volunteers did an admirable job with their assignment. In his order of congratulation, Connor wrote,

After a rapid march of four nights in intensely cold weather, through deep snow and drifts which you endured without murmer or complaint, even when some of your number were frozen with cold and faint with hunger and fatigue, you met our enemy, who have heretofore on two occasions, defied and defeated Regular Troops, and who have, for the last fifteen years, been the terror of the emigrants, men, women, children and citizens, of these vallyes—murdering and robbing them without fear of punishment. At daylight on the 29th of January, 1863, you encountered the enemy greatly your superior in numbers, and in a desperate battle, continued with unflinching courage for over four hours, you completely cut him to pieces, captured his property and arms, destroyed his stronghold, and burned his lodges.[44]

As usual, casualty figures are in part a matter of conjecture. Connor reported they found 224 Indian bodies on the field, including that of Bear Hunter. Others put Indian deaths up to 300 or more, counting women and children. But accurate figures are impossible.

After the battle, Mormons went out to search for survivors. One William Hull related in the *Deseret News*, "Never will I forget the scene, dead bodies everywhere. I counted eight deep in one place, in several places they were three to five deep; all in all we counted nearly four hundred; two thirds of this number being women and children," probably an exaggeration.[45] The *Deseret News* reported,

A thousand bushels of wheat and a large amount of beef and provisions, together with an abundant supply of powder, lead, bullets, and caps were found in the encampment. There were numerous evidences of emigrant plunder, such as modern cooking utensils, looking glasses, combs, brushes, fine rifles and pistols, and such things as the Indians were likely to consider worthy of preservation, when they had attacked and robbed the emigrants. Wagon covers, with the names of their unfortunate owners, were lying around and patching up the wick-i-ups.[46]

Connor reported capturing 175 horses and some arms, and destroying over 70 Indian lodges, along with a considerable amount of wheat and other provisions. He did leave "a small quantity of wheat for the sustenance of 160 captured squaws and children, whom I left on the field."[47] Connor regretted that Chiefs Pocatello and Sagwitch "with their bands of murderers, are still at large." He hoped to be able to kill or capture them by spring.[48] He felt if he succeeded in rounding up the chiefs, "the Overland Route west of the Rocky Mountains will be rid of the bedouins who have harassed and murdered emigrants on that route for a series of years."[49]

The commanding colonel said that because of men left on the route of march with frozen feet and as guards for the train, howitzers, and cavalry horses, he had had about 200 engaged. He put the Indian total at about 300 warriors, mostly well armed with rifles and ammunition.[50]

In forwarding Connor's report to Washington from San Francisco, Brigadier General Wright put the federal loss, out of 200 engaged, as fourteen killed on the field and four officers and forty-nine men wounded. Of the wounded, one officer and five men died later. Wright called Bear River "that terrible combat" and commended the conduct of the column from California and its commander.[51] In Washington on March 29, 1863, General-in-Chief Henry Wager Halleck referred Wright's communication to Secretary of War Edwin M. Stanton with the recommendation that Colonel Connor be made a brigadier general of volunteers "for the heroic conduct of himself and his men in the battle of Bear River."[52] Connor was so promoted.

Superintendent of Indian Affairs Doty reported, "The battle with the Shoshones on the bank of Bear River in January, and the subsequent engagements with the Utahs on Spanish Fork, and with the Goaships in their country, effectually checked them, and severely and justly punished them for the wanton acts of cruelty which they had committed. . . . The fight on Bear River was the severest and most bloody of any which has ever occurred with the Indians west of the Mississippi. . . . It struck terror into the hearts of the savages hundreds of miles away from the battle-field." Doty then detailed meetings between him and the Indians and Connor after Bear River and the treaties of peace that were entered into. Doty felt these treaties "could not have been made without the aid of the appropriations made by Congress for this superintendency, which have been wholly applied to the great object of restoring peace; and also to the presence of the military, who have rendered distinguished and lasting service to the government in subduing the Indians throughout this Territory."[53]

Doty wrote to Commissioner of Indian Affairs Dole on February 16, 1863, that the Indians reported there were 255 men, women, and children killed in the Bear River engagement. "Their camp was well filled with provisions, bacon, sugar, coffee, &c, and with various other articles, all of which had obviously been taken from the trains which they had robbed during the past season." He also said he had reports that some of the Shoshones were disposed to be friendly and that they should be separated "from those who are hostile who I suspect will soon be attacked or pursued by the soldiers."[54]

Doty in mid-summer of 1863 reported that he had met the Bannock and Shoshone and "I am satisifed they are disposed to be peaceable and friendly. The exhibition of a cavalry force among them apparently satisfied them that they could be reached by the power of the government and that they would certainly be punished if they committed depredations upon the white men. There are undoubtedly, as they say, some bad men among them, who will not be controlled by the chiefs, but efforts are made by the peaceable Indians to restrain them."[55] During the summer and fall of 1863, five treaties were made in the area with the Shoshone and Bannock.[56]

Historians vary in assessing Bear River. Authority Robert M. Utley termed it a "signal victory" for the volunteers, with various chiefs begging for peace afterwards.[57] Brigham D. Madsen, another Indian expert, wrote, "The battle was a natural and perhaps inevitable consequence of 15 years interaction between oppor-

tunistic and aggressive white pioneers and warlike and equally aggressive tribesmen of the plains and mountains."[58] Salt Lake City
historian Edward W. Tullidge wrote, probably exaggerating, "that
famous victory forever put a quietus to Indian hostilities in northern Utah and Southern Idaho."[59] Fred B. Rogers characterized it as
"one of the most successful expeditions of the West against hostile
Indians. The emigrant route in the general vicinity was made comparatively safe, and Cache Valley was practically freed from serious Indian depredations. The assistance rendered after the battle
by the people of the valley was the means of saving the lives of
many soldiers."[60]

The engagement of Bear River did not solve the Indian problem
in the area on any permanent basis; no one action was going to do
that. But it did result in several treaties, and certainly was a blazing
sign to the Indians that Connor and his men meant business and
were opponents to be feared. Eventually the Indians of the area
and the emigrants renewed their violent animosity. It does seem,
however, that Connor's action relieved depredations on the trails,
at least temporarily. The federal army had unmistakably established its authority in the northern Rockies. It had indicated to
high army officials that it was willing and able to carry out its assignment. Furthermore, the volunteers had shown the Mormons
that they were an effective body and would protect Mormon and
Gentile settlers alike from Indian forays. The Mormon Church
and the civilian population generally seemed pleased with Connor's action. While the engagement did not create complete mutual trust, it did elicit from the Mormons some reluctant admira-
tion for the occupying troops.

While there may well have been excessive killing during the latter part of the engagement, Bear River cannot be termed a massacre. Tactically it was more a traditional fight of advancing
troops against an emplaced enemy. Thus it was out of the pattern
usual in western Indian fights. As to the generalship on both sides,
Connor probably should not have attempted the frontal attack on
the mouth of the ravine. If he had engaged the Indians from a distance and then carried out his encirclement, he might well have
suffered fewer casualties. Nonetheless, he defeated a well-armed
force superior in numbers and entrenched in a strong position.
The Indians, in their unusual defensive position, apparently did

not foresee the volunteers' fairly obvious tactics in time to make a mass escape. They failed fatally to protect their flanks.

Bear River did not win or lose the Civil War, even in the West, and perhaps some of the reports have exaggerated its size. Yet it has not received the attention it deserves and has suffered from comparison with Sand Creek in Colorado Territory or with Civil War fighting farther east. But there is no doubt that it was a violent clash in abysmal weather, with heavy casualties and a display of bravery and fortitude on both sides. It did serve as an example to the Indians and helped to confirm the authority of the United States. It was a part of the taming, or conquest, of the West. It is conceivable that if there had not been something like Bear River in the winter of 1862–63, the summer of 1863 would have seen vastly increased depredations by the Indians, even a prolonged blockade of the trails and disruption of the telegraph. The opening of the mines of Idaho and Montana Territories, so valuable to the Union, might have been slowed. More federal troops might have been required, with even more fighting and casualties. And the Mormons, ever watchful, might have grown more suspicious and perhaps even more resentful of the federal presence. But, with Bear River and other operations, the trails and the telegraph were never permanently broken. Overland communications with the isolated states of California and Oregon were largely maintained; mines in the northwest brought gold to the federal Union; and a religious and resourceful people stayed with the Union physically and even, it may be said, spiritually. Bear River may well be one incident in what has been called the Americanization of Utah, but it is one which might better be termed an event in the closer unionization of Utah and the upper Rocky Mountains.

NOTES

1. The present chapter is an extended, considerably revised version of my earlier essay, "The 'Terrible Combat' at Bear River," *Civil War Times Illustrated*, 15 (Apr., 1976), 4–11, 40–43.

2. Letters Received, U.S. Department of the Interior, Office of Indian Affairs, Record Group 75, National Archives and Records Center, Denver, Colo.

3. William P. Dole, Commissioner of Indian Affairs, "Report of the Commissioner of Indian Affairs," Nov. 26, 1862, *Executive Documents* (Washington, D.C., 1862), pp. 185–86.

4. *Ibid.*

5. *Ibid.*, pp. 342–46.

6. James Duane Doty, Acting Superintendent of Indian Affairs, Utah Territory, "Report," Oct. 24, 1863, in "Report of the Commissioner of Indian Affairs," *Executive Documents* (Washington, D.C., 1864), pp. 539–40.

7. Grace Raymond Hebard, *Washakie* (Cleveland: Arthur H. Clark Co., 1930), p. 107.

8. Rogers, *Soldiers*, p. 67.

9. O.R., vol. L, pt. 1, p. 185.

10. *Ibid.*

11. *Deseret News*, Jan. 28, Feb. 11, 1863.

12. O.R., vol. L, pt. 1, p. 187.

13. *Ibid.*, p. 185.

14. *Deseret News*, Dec. 14, 1864, Jan. 28, 1863; Brigham D. Madsen, "Shoshone-Bannock Marauders on the Oregon Trail, 1859–1863," *Utah Historical Quarterly*, 35 (Winter, 1967), 4.

15. Orton, *Records of California Men*, p. 75.

16. O.R., vol. L, pt. 1, p. 185.

17. *Ibid.*

18. *Ibid.*, p. 186.

19. Rogers, *Soldiers*, pp. 69–70.

20. Orton, *Records of California Men*, p. 175.

21. Madsen, "Shoshone-Bannock Marauders," p. 25, quoted in Franklin County (Idaho) Historical Society, *The Passing of the Redman* (Preston, Idaho, 1970), p. 70.

22. Rogers, *Soldiers*, pp. 69, 76–77.

23. Rogers, *Soldiers*, p. 71, and report of researcher Thomas Lindmier to author, Mar., 1975, on condition of battlefield today.

24. *Deseret News*, Feb. 11, 1863.

25. Orton, *Records of California Men*, pp. 175–76.

26. O.R., vol. L, pt. 1, p. 186.

27. *Deseret News*, Feb. 11, 1863.

28. O.R., vol. L, pt. 1, p. 186.

29. *Deseret News*, Feb. 11, 1863.

30. Orton, *Records of California Men*, p. 176.

31. *Deseret News*, Feb. 11, 1863.

32. *Ibid.*

33. O.R., vol. L, pt. 1, p. 186.

34. *Ibid.*

35. *Ibid.*

36. *Deseret News*, Feb. 11, 1863.

37. Rogers, *Soldiers*, p. 73.

38. O.R., vol. L, pt. 1, p. 187.

39. Orton, *Records of California Men*, p. 177.

40. Rogers, *Soldiers*, p. 75.

41. Tullidge, *History of Salt Lake City*, pp. 287–88.

42. *O.R.*, vol. L, pt. 1, pp. 186–87.

43. Tullidge, *History of Salt Lake City*, pp. 289–90.

44. *Deseret News*, Feb. 11, 1863.

45. Brigham D. Madsen, *The Bannock of Idaho* (Caldwell, Idaho: Caxton, 1958), p. 137, quoted in Daughters of Idaho Pioneers, *History of the Development of Southeastern Idaho* (n.p., 1930), p. 13; *O.R.*, vol. L, pt. 1, p. 187.

46. *Deseret News*, Feb. 11, 1863.

47. *O.R.*, vol. L, pt. 1, p. 187.

48. *Ibid.*

49. *Ibid.*

50. *Ibid.*

51. *Ibid.*, p. 184.

52. *Ibid.*, pp. 185, 187.

53. Doty, "Report," Oct. 24, 1863.

54. Letters Received, U.S. Department of the Interior, Office of Indian Affairs, Record Group 75, National Archives, Washington, D.C., from microfilm in National Archives and Records Center, Denver, Colo.

55. *Ibid.*, Doty to Dole, June 25, 1863.

56. Hebard, *Washakie*, p. 109.

57. Robert M. Utley, *Frontiersmen in Blue* (New York: Macmillan, 1967), p. 224.

58. Madsen, "Shoshone-Bannock Marauders," p. 4.

59. Tullidge, *History of Salt Lake City*, p. 283.

60. Rogers, *Soldiers*, p. 76.

Brigham Young at age sixty-five (Carter Collection Church Archives, Church of Jesus Christ of Latter-day Saints).

General Patrick Edward Connor at the height of his career (Carter Collection Church Archives, Church of Jesus Christ of Latter-day Saints).

Judge John F. Kinney, chief justice of Utah Territory and Utah territorial delegate to the House of Representatives (National Archives).

Dr. John M. Berhnisel, territorial delegate for Utah to the House of Representatives (Utah State Historical Society).

W. H. Hooper, Utah's second delegate to Congress (Utah State Historical Society).

John W. Dawson, the controversial governor of Utah Territory in 1861 whose sudden departure raised many questions (Church Archives, Church of Jesus Christ of Latter-day Saints).

Editor T. B. H. Stenhouse of the *Deseret News* (Utah State Historical Society).

Alfred Cumming, governor of Utah Territory in 1861 (Utah State Historical Society).

Stephen S. Harding, governor of Utah Territory in 1862–63 (Utah State Historical Society).

James Duane Doty, Indian agent and governor of Utah Territory, 1863–65 (Church Archives, Church of Jesus Christ of Latter-day Saints).

Typical Indian warriors of the approximate period (Special Collections, Marriott Library, University of Utah).

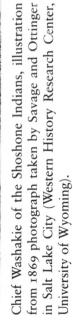

Chief Washakie of the Shoshone Indians, illustration from 1869 photograph taken by Savage and Ottinger in Salt Lake City (Western History Research Center, University of Wyoming).

View of commanding officer's headquarters at Camp Floyd (Crittenden) in 1859 (Utah State Historical Society).

Quarters of General Connor at Camp Douglas in 1864 (Utah State Historical Society).

Site of the engagement at Bear River long after the event, looking east from the Indian camp. General Connor came down the slope. The old road is in the center of the picture (Utah State Historical Society).

Mormons and Indians going through Echo Canyon near Salt Lake City (Western History Research Center, University of Wyoming).

Panoramic view of Salt Lake City looking northwest (Utah State Historical Society).

The Mormon Bowery (right) and old Tabernacle in Salt Lake City, 1855 (Utah State Historical Society).

View of East Temple Street (now Main Street) looking north toward Wasatch
Mountains (Savage and Ottinger Collection, Church Archives, Church of
Jesus Christ of Latter-day Saints).

Typical busy Salt Lake City street scene (Western History Research Center,
University of Wyoming).

Foundation of the Mormon Temple with Tabernacle in background, mid-1860s (Savage and Ottinger Collection, Church Archives, Church of Jesus Christ of Latter-day Saints).

The famed Eagle Gate and Brigham Young schoolhouse in Salt Lake City in the early 1860s (Savage and Ottinger Collection, Church Archives, Church of Jesus Christ of Latter-day Saints).

CHAPTER

VIII

To Arms—With Words

☆

B EAR RIVER WAS SPECTACULAR, the most spectacular single event
of the Civil War years in Utah. And it did divert attention for a
short time from other issues such as the federal officials and army
in the midst of a still somewhat hostile Utah Territory, and the
continuing but losing battle over statehood.

For a while early in 1863 Brigham Young felt no direct threat
from the soldiers, despite his opposition to their presence. Even
before the engagement at Bear River he wrote to Bishop Cannon,
now back in Liverpool, "As yet Colonel Connor and his companies have conducted themselves very properly, so far as their intercourse with the citizens is concerned, though they have had
some little trouble with the Indians north of us."[1] Young went on
to say, hopefully, if inaccurately, that Bernhisel had written that
Secretary of War Stanton had telegraphed to order the removal of
troops, but, as Young put it, "even if that is so, they cannot well
move at present."[2]

Governor Harding's December message to the legislature was
exciting more and more censure and denunciation from the Mormon community. As usual Brigham Young had some sharp comments when he wrote Deseret Senator-elect Hooper in New York
on February 21: "In regard to Governor Harding's message, the
assembly were not only offended with his style of reading certain
very objectionable passages, but they also deemed the document
malicious, meddlesome, and mischievous, for which reasons, as
the shortest and easiest method, they simply declined ordering it

printed in pamphlet form, though agreed to its being printed in the journals." Young called the message "unjustifiable attack, slander, and other grievous aggravation." As to admission,

Better not to be admitted than be admitted but at the sacrifice of even social or political rights, much less of a right pertaining to freedom of conscience in the worship of our God, in accordance with his revelations and commandments. Where do Congress get the right to place such restrictions or conditions upon the admission of a Territory? The answer is obvious, nowhere. Why is it sought to be imposed in the case of Utah? Because the majority of her population are or are trying to be faithful servants of the true and ever living God. Well, let them plan, devise and debate, they cannot hinder the purposes of Jehovah, nor prevent his overruling the results of their acts to his glory. Of course Harding, Waite and others have been and are doing all they can to create strife between us and the Government. This is so generally the case with government officials sent here, that it gives a person reason for supposing that there is a design in sending such characters as are the majority of those they have sent. But rest content, they will not be able to accomplish their designs one hair's breadth farther than the Lord in his wisdom may see fit to permit. . . . In the mean time and all the time it behooves us to be ever on the alert to prevent and avert, so far as in our power, the evil designs of the enemies of truth.[3]

Reportedly the Mormon leader, after hearing the governor's speech, gave his opinion that it should not be printed nor should the minutes connected with it be printed.[4]

Elder George A. Smith also wrote to Delegate Bernhisel regarding Harding's speech:

He then solemnly declared what he said he regretted to state, that he had heard no sentiments of sympathy between the citizens of this Territory and the United States, and called upon the legislature to pass such resolutions as would compel him to retract—next a long dissertation upon the horrors of polygamy, coupled with threats and inuendoes and most apparently solemn and hypocritical shutting of the eyes to the consequences of our continuing in our anomalous course. He denounced our Territory laws almost en masse, and was especially dreadful on that law which allows a man to protect his family from the seducer, without being hung therefore; he made an attack upon the authorities as urging men into polygamy on purpose to trample the sacred laws of Congress under foot.[5]

The uproar over Governor Harding and two of the three judges continued. The governor was aware of the protest over his remarks to the legislature. He wrote Secretary of State Seward on February 3, "I do not desire to create any unnecessary alarm still I deem it my duty to say to the President that political affairs in Utah are far from being quiet." He felt there was a "peculiar element of disloyalty and religious fanaticism in Utah" that was difficult for anyone outside the Territory to realize. He felt the Mormon leaders worked cunningly in an almost "supernatural" way upon "the superstitions of an ignorant, credulous and dependent people. . . . Brigham Young has been able to work upon his followers and make them believe that the only rightful authority to govern rested in his hands by the special gift of the Holy Ghost— all other governments are mere usurpations." Harding also said of Young, "There can be no mistaking his ultimate purpose. He is aiming if not at universal empire on this continent at least in this Territory." Harding's denunciations became even more censorious, vindictive, almost hysterical.[6]

On February 16, 1863, Harding wrote to General Wright in San Francisco:

For a few days past there has been a rumor (perhaps it is nothing else) that Col. P. Edward Connor, whose command is stationed near this city, is to be called elsewhere with the troops. I cannot believe that such an order would be given if the true condition of things here was understood. Indeed, in my opinion, the withdrawal of his force at this time would make his advent into this Territory a great misfortune to those who have evinced a kindness to him and loyalty to the General Government, for I am not mistaken as to what will follow upon such an act. It would not be safe for these persons to remain in this city. They, at least, will have subjected themselves to insult and contumely, if nothing worse. The recent brilliant victory over the hostile Indians north of here, on Bear River, instead of becoming a cause for future safety to emigrants would only have a tendency to enrage those still banded together for the purpose of murder and plunder, inasmuch as the dread of punishment would be thereby removed from their minds, and the fact that so terrible a chastisement had been administered by U.S. troops, and not by Mormons, would become a subtle and plausible argument in the mouth of the powers here to induce them to form a still closer alliance with that power for common mischief in keeping out in future all troops whose presence was not desired.[7]

Harding said the Mormons were in the habit of visiting the band annihilated by Connor and were enabled to pass through Indian lands where Gentiles would have been robbed and murdered. "Secret agents of the church are employed to form a league for a common safety and a common purpose." If Connor were ordered away, it would be "the last time that U.S. soldiers will have the privilege of entering this Territory peaceably." While the Mormons might not openly meet U.S. troops, the Indians would be encouraged to do so. If the troops were ordered away, the federal officers should be also. Harding wanted additional troops and concluded, "I will only add that in withdrawal of the troops the General Government virtually abandons here sovereignty over this Territory." [8]

Connor added his even more strident voice on February 19:

I can only allude briefly to the frequent and flagrant violations of the law and the audacious interference with its operations. The law for the prohibition of polygamy is daily violated under the very eyes of the Federal courts by citizens and members of the Mormon Church, who are composed chiefly of the very lowest class of foreigners and aliens. Naturally opposed to our laws, they do not hesitate at violating them, and are willing tools in the hands of their leaders, hesitating at the commission of no crime. Political machinations, plundering expeditions, Indian barterings, and intrigues are things of daily occurrence and are constantly brought to my notice. Not the least respect is paid to the marriage relation; instances of incestuous connections and the crime of bigamy are not only tolerated but encouraged by the Mormon creed, which is inimical to the U.S. laws, winks at murder, pillage, and rapine, and is the very embodiment of hypocrisy; mocks at God and insults the nation. Civil law is a perfectly dead letter in the statute books; they have the right of trial by jury, and under their rule it becomes the instrument of oppression to those who are so independent as to be without the pale of the church and so unfortunate as to need its aid. [9]

Connor continued at length in this vein. He flatly declared, "The people, from Brigham down to the very lowest, are disloyal almost to a man, and treason, if not openly preached, is covertly encouraged and willful and infamous misrepresentations as to the intention of the Government toward this people constantly made under the guise of heavenly revelations." [10] Connor complained that Brigham Young was mounting cannon supposedly for protection against the Indians but "by this means has placed himself in a position of formidable importance as an enemy." There were fifteen guns including nine, twelve and twenty-four pounders. Mormon workmen were engaged in manufacturing fixed ammunition for various types of arms. Connor felt this and other developments indicated that Young "only awaits a serious reverse to our arms, or a foreign war, to break out into open rebellion, and if I understand the significance of his preparations they mean rebellion and nothing else."[11]

The charges by Connor were fierce: "From the time of my arrival in this district until the present Brigham has shown unmistakable evidences of hatred and disloyalty to the Government, and a disposition to embarrass my command by charging enormous prices for such articles as he knew I would require, and forbidding their sale at a less price than that fixed by himself or his bishops." Connor enclosed a list of the offending prices.[12] Never short of words, Connor continued his caustic diatribe:

. . . if the crimes and designs of this people were known and understood by the people of the United States as I understand and know them, it would cause such a burst of indignation as would result in the utter annihilation of this whole people, and if the present rebellion is a punishment for any national sin, I believe it is for permitting this unholy, blasphemous, and unnatural institution to exist almost in the heart of the nation, ignoring its horrid crimes and allowing it to extend its ramifications into every grade of society in defiance of laws human and divine. To relate the revolting crimes and the numerous outrages which are daily perpetrated by Brigham and his church were superfluous. Suffice it to say, then, if the social and political attitude of this people is such as I believe it is, the sooner we are rid of the evil, and the nation of the stigma, the better it will be for us.[13]

Connor suggested two ways to resolve the situation. First, he would divide the Territory into four parts and add the parts to the four adjoining territories. Second, he would declare martial law and his force should be increased to 3,000 with a light battery and three heavier guns. If he received such reinforcements, he wrote, he would "guarantee to take measures such as will give Brigham no alternative but to obey the law, and then put a brief end to the institution of polygamy." He had learned, he said, that Brigham's agents were strenuously trying to get the troops removed from Utah. Connor would agree with that unless he were reinforced. If the troops were removed "it will cost the Government a treasure of money and blood before it could regain the position and advantages we now possess. Individually I would prefer to serve in another field. At the same time there is much to do here, and it would give me great pleasure to contribute my humble services to blot out this stigma on our national honor."[14]

Thus Connor, in language strenuous even for him, laid down the gauntlet. He had said some of this before and was to do so again, but here he unreservedly revealed his full attitude and how, along with protecting the trails, he conceived his duty. On February 26 Connor reported to San Francisco that troop discipline was excellent, but instruction in military exercises was not so effective as he would like.[15] From San Francisco on February 28 General Wright told Harding that far from removing the troops in Utah he was preparing to send reinforcements in the spring.[16]

The *Deseret News* and other Mormon sources continued to make insinuations against and even to denounce Governor Harding. The paper continued to follow the apparent policy of the Mormon Church. In January Brigham Young had put in the public notices that the "Deseret News is not and has not been an organ of mine, for, except matter accompanied with my name, I have only occasionally, and that too some time ago, known any more of the contents of the News, until after it is published, than I have the copy furnished to the compositors of the *New Ledger*."[17] Probably the statement was basically correct, but that the paper followed Church policy—therefore Brigham Young's policy—there can be no doubt. And at this time there was no opposition press in Salt Lake City.

One move by Governor Harding and Judges Waite and Drake early in 1863 particularly irritated the Mormons. They petitioned Congress for certain changes in the territorial government that would place more jurisdiction in the hands of federal officials rather than with the Mormons. A major change was that jurors would be selected by the U.S. marshal rather than by the local officials. Officers of the militia would be named by the governor. These moves would have considerably diluted Mormon control in courts and in the militia, and their possible implementation caused widespread consternation.[18]

The *Deseret News* took its usual sacrosanct and sarcastic tone on March 4, 1863, in regard to the federal officials:

It is never a pleasant task to publish the follies of men; where it can be done justly, we prefer to cover up the infirmities of humanity with the mantle of charity; but when wickedness is unmistakably manifest everywhere, and misrepresentation and falsehood are resorted to, in order to accomplish an evil purpose, we have no disposition to shrink from the telling of the truth. We have been studiously silent on the proceedings of some of the Federal officers, though we confess it has been hard at times to shrink from telling the truth. We have been accustomed to suffer wrongs, and probably have acquired too much patience for our own good.

The *News* went on to warn that "some men were building their own sepulchres. . . . For some time back, it has been very evident that the labors of Governor Harding and the Associate Justices were hostile to the interests of the people of Utah and the Governor particularly was straining every nerve to create difficulties." The paper took the same stand on Harding as it had before on Dawson, and complained, "it has been often a matter of doubt whether he was perfectly responsible for his actions."[19] In a long screed, the *News* characterized Harding: "He is a perfect compound of contradictions. We have hoped for reformation; but we have hoped in vain."[20]

The protest over Harding continued to rise, until finally a meeting was held in the Tabernacle in Salt Lake City on March 3, "for the purpose of investigating certain acts of several of the United States officials now in the territory," reported Mormon leader John Taylor, ". . . the time had come for certain documents to be placed before the people." Harding's offending message was read to the assemblage. The *News* noted that the audience "unmistakably indicated their uneasiness over the insult offered to their representatives. . . . There was one deep feeling of contempt manifest for its author."[21] The meeting was then read letters from Delegate to Congress Bernhisel and Senator-elect Hooper. One letter represented Harding as communicating with Vice-President Hannibal Hamlin in a way injurious to the Mormons. Hooper on January

27 wrote that "Governor Harding is, of course, doing all he can by letters against the people of Utah." The paper commented: "When the insinuation of the disloyalty of the people was read, there was a loud murmer of dissatisfaction throughout the audience."[22]

Taylor went on to proclaim the loyalty of the people of Utah. He added that, under conditions of civil war, "we had a right to look for a friend in our Governor who would, at least, fairly represent us, we have met a most insidious foe, who through base insinuations, misrepresentations, and falsehood, is seeking with all his power, privately and officially, not only to injure us before the government, but to sap the very foundations of our civil and religious liberty, he is, in fact, in the pursuit of his unhallowed course, seeking to promote anarchy and rebellion."[23]

Brigham Young then rose to deafening applause. According to the paper, Young said they had heard the governor's message and "would readily perceive that the bread was buttered, but there was poison underneath."[24] The text of the Church leader's address as found in the Brigham Young Letter Books is somewhat stronger than that in the *Deseret News*. Supposedly it is the correct text as reported by G. D. Watts. In writing to former Acting Governor Frank Fuller on this text, Young said, "In the remarks at the mass meeting I used some expressions rougher than is usual with me in public speaking, but you now have them as spoken, without qualification."[25] According to this account, Young said,

. . . there seems to be a secret influence existing, among a class that I do not know what others call but that I call Black-hearted Republicans, against the Pacific railroad and the overland mail route and telegraph line. . . . If a military government can be established in this Territory, it is universally believed that the people of Utah would not bear it. (Cries of "No") There [in Utah] it is expected that the telegraph wires would be severed, the mail be stopped, and free travel across the continent put an end to. This would appear to be the plan of some of the Black-hearted Republicans; and this fool down here [Harding] is probably openly in it. The Democrats do not wish to see this, neither does any true Republican want it; it is desired only by Black-hearted Republicans, rabid abolitionists, or negro worshippers. I have used the term Black-hearted, because they worship the image of that which is dark as midnight blackness. . . . A man or a thing, which ever term you prefer, some time ago came into Utah, pretending to be Governor, and he was received as such on his first appearance among us. . . . He stated that he had told the President of the United States that if the question of polygamy ever came up, he would have to stand in defense of it or deny the bible. . . . Said he, if the time ever comes when I am obnoxious to this people, and they do not wish my presence here, I shall leave the Territory (cries, "it is true, we heard him say so").[26]

Young continued his denunciation:

Whether these other two [the judges] are tools in his hands or not, I do not know. Whether they know any better is a matter of question with me; I do not think they are in possession of any better wisdom. It is supposed, if by any means this people can be driven to desperation, they will defend themselves, and this will prove their disloyalty to the General Government, create collition [sic], and break up all communications between the eastern and western portions of the country. . . . They are determined, apparently, to bring this about; it is not, however, for me to say whether this is their real intent or not. But there does appear to exist a secret influence to break asunder the western from the eastern portions of our country, and many of their doings point to this object. . . . They are trying to break up civil government in Utah and set up a military despotism, and woe be to that man who undertakes to introduce despotism in Utah; in such an attempt they will then learn who is Governor (great applause). . . . When once a military despotism is established, life and liberty would be at their mercy; and then for our juries to be selected from among strangers who have nothing in common with us, and the lives of our best citizens would be placed in jeopardy by those who value money more than life. When our civil, religious, and military rights are thus wrenched from us, what then remains (voices, "nothing"). Yes, something, service to despots, service to tyrants. If we would be just to ourselves, true to our country and to our friends, we will show it by giving an expression of our feelings with regard to having such men stay in our midst, and give the Governor the privilege of keeping his own promises; let them resign their offices and withdraw from this Territory. . . . I say let the nation remain happy and free, as it was previous to the present difficulties. . . . Let the Lord be God, and let us serve him and try to do his will and trust in him, and he will lead this people to victory and glory (cries of "Amen").[27]

Colonel Connor in a report to San Francisco on March 15 added comments of Brigham Young's at the March 3 meeting which he said were not reported by the *Deseret News*, although it is not clear where Connor got the quotations. The words are somewhat different from other accounts. Young reportedly repeated the statements that Joseph Smith "had told him that the South would rise against the North, and the North against the South, and that they would fight until both parties were destroyed, and for my part I give it godspeed, for they shed the blood of the prophet."[28]

Connor also quoted Young as saying of Governor Harding:

"This man, who is sent here to govern the Territory—man, did I say? Thing, I mean; a nigger worshiper. A black-hearted abolitionist is what he is and what he represents—and these two things I do utterly despise. He wants to have the telegraph torn down and the mail stopped and turned by the way of Panama. . . . Do you acknowledge this man Harding as your Governor?" (Voices: "No; you are our Governor.") "Yes," replied Brigham, "put him out. Harding and Drake and Waite must leave the Territory. If they will not resign, and if the President will not remove them, the people must attend to it. I will let him (Harding) know who is Governor. I am Governor. If he attempts to interfere with my affairs, woe! woe! unto him."

According to Connor, Young also said: "'Judges Drake and Waite are perfect fools and tools for the Governor.'"[29]

After Young had spoken, resolutions were presented to the meeting. It was asked "That we consider the attack made upon us, by his Excellency, Gov. Harding, wherein our loyalty is impugned as base, wicked, unjust and false; and he knew it to be so when uttered." The resolutions accused Harding of trying to set up a "military despotism." The attempt to control the selection of juries was "so base, unjust and tyrannical, as to deserve the contempt of all freemen." They accused Judges Waite and Drake of being subversive and of perverting justice. One resolution charged that "a serious attack has been made upon the liberties of this people, and . . . it not only affects us as a Territory; but it is a direct assault upon the Republican principles, in our own nation, and throughout the world; and that we cannot either tamely submit to be disfranchised ourselves; nor witness, without protest, the assassin's dagger plunged into the very vitals of our national institutions."[30] The resolutions called for a committee to be appointed by the meeting to call on Harding, Waite, and Drake to request them to resign and leave the Territory, and also requested the President of the United States to remove the men and "to appoint good men in their stead."[31] When the vote was called, "the building rang with a glorious 'Aye' for their adoption." A petition to Lincoln containing most of the resolutions and asking him to remove the officials was also framed.[32]

It was clear that this unprecedented move had the support of most of the people of Utah. Other meetings in similar vein were held elsewhere in the Territory.[33] On the other hand, a counter-petition signed by Connor and many of his officers urged President Lincoln to retain Harding and the judges.[34] Colonel Connor wired the army in San Francisco on the day of the Mormon mass meeting: "Excited meeting of Mormons held to-day in Tabernacle; appointed committee; asked Governor Harding and Federal Judges Waite and Drake, the only Federal officers here who dare to do their duty, to resign. Have no fears for me."[35] As was his wont, Connor, sensing a crisis, kept San Francisco well informed. On March 5 he wired that "Brigham removed ordnance and ordnance stores from territorial arsenal and guard of fifty men around his residence last night; do not purpose to trouble him; he fears I will."[36]

Also on March 5 Brigham Young wrote to George Cannon in Liverpool: "The few troops on the bench keep very quiet and to themselves; it is presumable that a plenty to do in the States will prevent the carrying out of the original design in their being here, at least for the present, for the purport of despatches indicates that they will have use for the few here and many more, in other places than Utah." Young indicated that he believed the main reason for the federal troops in Utah was to persecute the Mormons.[37] The Mormon leader continued to Cannon: "Gov. Harding and Judges Waite and Drake have been doing their utmost to stir up strife and mischief between Utah and the general Government, proof thereof having come to hand, on the 3rd inst. a mass meeting of some 3000 convened in and around the tabernacle to take action on their course."[38] Young described the meeting and the resolutions, and then said:

The committee, on the following morning, called upon Gov. Harding who received them courteously, but said he would not resign and leave until removed by President Lincoln. Judge Drake was present, and upon being asked whether he accepted the notification of the committee, he delivered himself of a short, virulent tirade. . . . The petition for removal was, in a few hours, signed by a double column of names almost three rods long. That number could have been increased to nearly the entire population of the Territory, but it was deemed sufficient.[39]

Colonel Connor wrote a lengthy and detailed report on March 15, giving his account of the meeting of the committee with the governor and judges. The reason for Mormon opposition, he suggested, was that the federal officials were pushing a bill in Congress inimical to the Mormons. But Connor felt the real reason was because "those gentlemen do not choose to become the tools and creatures of Brigham Young, and follow in the footsteps of ex-Governor Cumming, the present Chief Justice Kinney, and the present Secretary of State, Frank Fuller." The general felt Kinney and Fuller "disgrace their commissions and the Government they represent."[40] Connor also charged that in Kinney's court no conviction could be held against a Mormon unless Brigham Young sanctioned it.[41]

In the same report Connor described what happened when the Mormon committee waited upon the governor and presented the resolutions of the March 3 meeting, calling for his resignation. Harding replied to the committee, at least in substance, as Connor put it,

You may go back and tell your constituents that I will not resign my office of Governor, and that I will not leave this Territory until it shall please the President to send me away. I came here a messenger of peace and good will to your people, but I confess that my opinions about many things have changed. But I also came, sirs, to discharge my duties honestly and faithfully to my Government, and I will do it to the last. It is in your power to do me personal violence, to shed my blood . . . but this will not deter me from my purpose. . . . I will not cowardly desert my post. I may be in danger by staying, but my mind is fixed, I desire to have no trouble. I am anxious to live and again meet my family, but if necessary an administrator can settle my affairs. . . . I, too, will prophesy if one drop of my blood is shed by your ministers of vengeance while I am in the discharge of my duty, it will be avenged, and not one stone or adobe in your city will remain upon another. Your allegations in this paper are false, without the shadow of truth.[42]

Judges Drake and Waite also turned down the demand for their resignations. Drake said he understood Brigham Young "called me a fool and the tool of the Governor." The committee admitted that. Drake, warming up, said, "Go back to Brigham Young, your master, that embodiment of sin and shame and disgust, and tell him that I neither fear him, nor love him, nor hate him, but that I utterly dispise him; tell him, whose tools and tricksters you are, that I did not come here by his permission, and that I will not go away at his desire or by his directions . . . don't you ever dare to speak to me again." Waite was brief and less fiery, but he also turned down the committee.[43]

The *Deseret News* told a somewhat different story of the committee to the officials. The committee, according to this report, said that Governor Harding received them courteously

but upon being informed of the purport of our visit, both himself and Judge Drake, who was in the Governor's office, emphatically refused to comply with the wishes of the people, notwithstanding the Governor had repeatedly stated that he would leave whenever he learned that his acts and course were not agreeable to the people. Upon being informed that, if he was not satisfied that the action of the Mass Meeting expressed the feelings of the people, he could have the expression of the whole Territory, he replied, "I am aware of that, but that would make no difference."[44]

For the moment the issue was in deadlock. The officials would not and did not resign, and the Mormons continued their opposition, often virtually ignoring the governor and the two judges.

At this time Brigham Young was asked, as he was so often, about the stand of the Mormons. The inquiry came from a Colonel J. M. Rosse, who said he had been engaged by various parties to represent to the President of the United States causes of complaints against Young and the people of Utah by some federal officials. Rosse asked Young certain questions and the Mormon leader replied,

First you say it is alleged that I as well as the people of Utah are disloyal to the Government of the U.S. In answer to that accusation I will answer in one brief sentence—If I rightly understand the term disloyalty, the allegation is *utterly and absolutely false.* But if I do not rightly understand the term and a devotion to and love for my country constitutes disloyalty then I as well as the people are disloyal. If a prompt response to the call of my country during the Mexican War by the sending of over 500 of our young men to help bear aloft in triumph our flag, whilst we were yet wanderers in the desert plains, constitutes disloyalty, I as well as the people have been disloyal in the past. If a prompt response to the call of our acting-Governor, and a subsequent call by the President of the U.S. in April last, for men to protect the Overland Mail constitutes disloyalty, I as well as the people are disloyal. If a present readiness at all times and under all circumstances to aid and assist in protecting the honor and glory of our common country constitutes disloyalty, I as well as the people are thoroughly disloyal; but if the above acts referred to are evidences of loyalty, then no part of the U.S. contains a more loyal and devoted people than are the people of Utah. Let me add, were it not clear to every intelligent mind, I might show a thousand reasons why the people should be loyal and I defy the man, however acute, to show one single reason why we should be disloyal. Second, you say it is alleged that the laws of the U.S. cannot be executed in the Territory, because of my opposition either directly or indirectly as the head of the Mormon Church. . . . I will say that I have never, directly or indirectly, thrown any impediment in the way of the execution of the laws of the U.S.; and further, that, so far as my influence and powers extend, shall at all times be at the service of the civil authorities to assist in the execution of the laws; and I believe that I can speak for the inhabitants of this whole Territory, [that they] will sustain the Constitution and laws of our Government to the uttermost, as we have ever done. In regard to the third allegation—that influential Mormons encourage the robbery and massacre of immigrants by the Indians—I have the means of knowledge that it is absolutely false. And now, as to the concluding allegation, that the hostile feeling of the people to the federal officials renders it necessary to maintain at this point a large military force, to enforce the laws and secure the personal safety of the federal officials here.—So far as the first part of this accusation is concerned, I can but repeat what I before stated, that, to the extent of my influence, any and every law for the government of the people of this Territory shall be executed without any hindrance whatever; and in regard to the personal safety of federal officials, I believe they are as safe from violence here as they would be in New York & Boston.[45]

Young, in this important missive, is somewhat contradictory. He plays down his actual influence in enforcing laws, and then says he can speak for the inhabitants and can assure their adherence to the laws, which was undoubtedly true. He does not discuss the flaunting of the anti-polygamy law, the major sticking point as to law enforcement. He also emphasizes Utah's readiness to aid in protecting the overland trails.

In an equally important discourse on March 8 at the Tabernacle entitled, "The Persecutions of the Saints.—Their Loyalty to the Constitution," Brigham Young said in part: "We are objectionable to our neighbors. We have a warfare. . . . We are accused of disloyalty, alienation, and apostasy from the Constitution of our Country. We were accused of being secessionists. I am, so help me God, and ever expect to be a secessionist from their wickedness, unrighteousness, dishonesty and unhallowed principles in a religious point of view; but am I or this people secessionists with regard to the glorious Constitution of our country? No." He pointed out again, as he did so often, the previous service of Mormon people to the country. "We have done everything that has been required of us. . . . But if the Government of the United States should now ask for a battalion of men to fight in the present battle-fields of the nation, while there is a camp of soldiers from abroad located within the corporate limits of this city, I would not ask one man to go; I would see them in hell first." He pointed out again that in 1862 Utah or Mormon troops had guarded the overland trails and had promptly responded.

But all this does not prove any loyalty to political tyrants. . . . We do not need any soldiers here from any other States or Territories to perform that service, neither does the Government, as they would know if they were wise. I will, comparatively speaking, take one plug of tobacco, a shirt and three cents' worth of paint, and save more lives and hinder more Indian depredations than they can by expending millions of dollars vested in an army to fight and kill the Indians. Feed and clothe them a little and you will save life; fight them, and you pave the way for the destruction of the innocent.[46]

Young went on to say, "We complain of the barbarity of the red man for killing innocent men, women, and children, especially for killing women and children. They are to blame for this. But remember that they are savages, and that it is an usage among them to kill the innocent for the acts of the guilty." He felt that the Mormons had got along with the Indians better than other groups had.[47]

Turning to other subjects in this long and revealing discourse, Young said,

The outside pressure now is that this people, called the Latter-day Saints, are secessionists in their feelings, and alien to the Constitution and institutions of our country. This is entirely false. There is not another people upon the face of the earth that could have borne what we have, and still remain as loyal to our brethren as we have been and are. They might be displeased with some of the acts of the administrators of the law, but not with the Constitutional laws and institutions of the Government. . . . The affections of the masses of American citizens,—both of the people in the North and in the South, are alienated from each other, and they are divided. We would it could be otherwise, but this is the result of the acts of leading politicians of our nation. When the people's affections are interwoven with a Republican government administered in all its purity, if the administrators act not in virtue and truth it is but natural that the people become disaffected with mal-administration, and divide and subdivide into parties, until the body politic is shivered to pieces. . . . What can we do? We can serve God, and mind our own business; keep our powder dry and be prepared for every emergency to which we may be exposed, and sustain the civil law to which we are subject.[48]

He referred to some of the state officers:

I would not give the ashes of a rye straw for any influence that our officials here, who are operating against this people, have in Washington. If their true characters were only known there, their influence would be devoid of weight in the mind of any right thinking men. I am in no way concerned about what they can do against us. I wish one course to be pursued by this people, and all the rest will be right. If they will walk faithfully in the path of their duty, in uprightness before God, clinging to right, and so conducting themselves that no being in the Heavens, on the earth, under the earth or in hell, can say in truth that they are guilty of any unjust or wicked action committed knowingly, all will be right. . . . It is God who rules. . . . We have our Constitutional laws and our Territorial laws; we are subject to these laws, and always expected to be for we love to be. . . . I stand for Constitutional law, and if any transgress, let them be tried by it, and if guilty, suffer its penalty.[49]

Then, going after the abolitionists, Young said,

The rank, rabid abolitionists, who I call black-hearted abolitionists, have set the whole national fabric on fire. Do you know this, Democrats? They have kindled the fire that is raging now from the north to the south, and from the south to the north. I am no abolitionist, neither am I a proslavery man; I hate some of their principles and especially some of their conduct, as I do the gates of hell. The Southerners hate the negroes, and the Northerners worship them; this is all the difference between slaveholders and abolitionists. I would like the President of the United States and all the world to hear this. Shall I tell you the law of God in regard to the African race? If the white man who belongs to the chosen seed mixes his blood with the seed of Cain, the penalty, under the law of God, is death on the spot. . . . The nations of the earth have transgressed every law that God has given, they have changed the ordinances and broken every covenant made with the fathers, and they are like a hungry man that dreameth that he eateth, and he awaketh and behold he is empty. . . . I say to all men and all women, submit to God, to his ordinances, and to His rule; and cease your quarreling, and stay the shedding of each others blood.[50]

Turning to polygamy, Young reasoned,

If the government of the United States, in Congress assembled, had the right to pass an anti-polygamy bill, they had also the right to pass a law that slaves should not be abused as they have been; they had also a right to make a law that negroes should be used like human beings, and not worse than dumb brutes. For their abuse of that race, the whites will be cursed, unless they repent. . . . If I could have been influenced by private injury to choose one side in preference to the other, I should certainly be against the pro-slavery side of the question, for it was pro-slavery men that pointed the bayonet at me and my brethren in Missouri, and said, "Damn you we will kill you." I have not much love for them. . . . I would cause them to repent, if I could, and make them good men and a good community. . . . Now, as we are accused of secession, my counsel to this congregation is to secede, what from? From the Constitution of the United States? No. Well then, what from? From sin and the practice thereof.[51]

The torrent of words on both sides did not abate nor did the provocative actions, though these were relatively trivial. Distrust was the watchword. There was, however, some excitement in early March. Connor wired San Francisco on March 8: "Mormons hard at work making cartridges; a guard of 300 men at Brigham's nightly; don't understand what he is about; suppose he fears I will arrest him. I am quite safe."[52] On March 9 Connor wired to his Pacific Department headquarters that "Brigham just raised national colors on his house and called his people to arms. They are responding and rushing to his home. He is trying to frighten somebody or is frightened himself."[53] The raising of the flag as a signal and the mobilization around Brigham Young's house apparently resulted from someone overhearing Connor and Judge Waite talking. The colonel was supposed to have said, "These three men must be surprised." The judge reportedly replied, "Colonel, you know your duty." In less than an hour, after the signal flag had been raised atop the Bee Hive House, about a thousand armed Mormons gathered around the Young residence and another thousand supposedly arrived soon thereafter.[54] As Stenhouse described it, "The city was in commotion, and rifles, lead, and powder, were brought out of their hiding-places. On the inside of the high walls surrounding Brigham's premises, scaffolding was hastily erected in order to enable the militia to fire down upon the passing volunteers. The houses on the route which occupied a commanding position where an attack could be made upon the troops were taken possession of, the small cannon were brought out, and the brethren prepared to protect the Prophet."[55]

There was no truth to the story that the army intended to arrest Brigham Young and his counsellors. Connor and Waite had been talking about another matter. But the Mormon leaders took no chances. They mounted a telescope on top of Young's residence and watched Camp Douglas carefully. For several weeks there were armed men around Young and his mansion and the signals were kept ready to summon the citizens day and night.[56] The troops at Camp Douglas seem to have been quite circumspect during this temporary and unnecessary crisis.

It was obvious that there were not enough soldiers at Camp Douglas to overawe the Mormons. Stenhouse wrote, "To know that they 'could use them up any morning before breakfast,' and yet be forced to tolerate their presence on the brow of a hill, like a watch-tower, was irritating to the Prophet's mind."[57] Young, nervous over the federal presence, was susceptible to any rumor. The citizens believed that their response had intimidated Connor and that he would now make a dash at night to seize the Prophet and carry him off to the States. Connor, of course, never had such orders and, despite his views and his intrepidity, would never have decided on such an action on his own. News, more or less accurate, of this latest furor in Utah soon reached the nation's press, with California papers making much of it.[58]

Connor sent San Francisco more details on March 10: "Flag yesterday was the first raised by Brigham in this Territory. Was a signal to his people, who assembled armed to number of 1,500; two pieces of cannon. They are determined to have trouble, and are trying to provoke me to bring it on, but they will fail. They swear I shall not be re-enforced, and if attempted will cut them off in detail and attack me. I am not giving any cause of offence."[59]

General Wright in San Francisco kept Washington well posted with succinct reports. On March 11 he wired to Adjutant General Thomas: "Excitement at Salt Lake. Brigham Young raised national colors on his house and called his people to arms. Colonel Connor and troops cool and waiting events. He will telegraph direct to you if anything important takes place."[60] In turn Wright told Connor the same day: "Be prudent and cautious. Hold your troops well in hand. A day of retribution will come."[61] Connor sent another message on March 12 at 9 P.M.: "Brigham had called in his men and then subsequently dismissed the Mormon guards," but there were patrols nightly around Young's house.[62]

General Wright summarized the situation to Washington on March 14: "Within the last ten days affairs in Utah have assumed a threatening aspect."[63] After receiving Wright's report, General Halleck, as general-in-chief, sent a message that the Secretary of War had authorized the raising of additional troops for Utah, California, or Nevada, and had ordered Wright to prepare to reinforce Connor.[64] Yet there was no outright action—only words and posturing on both sides. It was obvious that the issues had been more clearly drawn by the speeches, resolutions, and comments during the winter and spring of 1863.

Governor Harding was also writing messages. On March 13 he wrote to Secretary of State Seward, "I deem it to be my duty to forewarn the President against any arranging that may have for its object the withdrawal of the present military force now here, as well as witholding reinforcement which have been anticipated from California." Persons unacquainted with the intrigues in Utah, according to Harding, could not understand the situation. If the President should remove the federal troops and place protection in the hands of Brigham Young, he would be strengthening the purpose of the Mormon leader for mischief. "It is folly to say that these people under the religious influence of Brigham Young and other leaders are loyal to the Government of the United States." Harding charged that Young was "secretly pushing forward" his own purposes.[65]

Colonel Connor on March 15 sent one of his verbose, detailed, and sharply critical messages to San Francisco. Included in this epistle was his full account of the March 3 Tabernacle meeting. The raising of the flag on March 9 Connor believed to be a signal rather than a gesture "of patriotism or for any loyal purpose." A similar incident occurred March 12. Connor said the only excuse was that Young feared the federals would arrest him for uttering treasonable sentiments. Connor felt that this was not the real reason, for there was nothing in the colonel's utterances or actions that could have given Young that idea.[66] Connor offered his own opinion of the flag incidents:

The courtesy we have given is returned with abuse. They rail at us in their sermons in which we are also classed with cut-throats and gamblers, our Government cursed and vilified in their public speeches and meetings, and those of their people who supply this camp with vegetables, eggs, butter, and produce are proscribed and shamefully abused for extending such favors. The late armed display was a mere ruse to frighten the proscribed Federal officers from the Territory; or else they desire to have a conflict with the Government, and are endeavoring to provoke me into inaugurating it. The latter I believe to be the real motive, however Brigham Young may try to disguise the fact.[67]

Connor then told how, for some weeks past, the people, under orders from Brigham Young, had been engaged in preparing ammunition and artillery and the foundry had been reportedly used for casting "cannon balls." Connor added, "They also loudly assert that I shall not be re-enforced. . . ."[68]

In another vein, Connor complained,

The law against polygamy is a dead letter on the statute books. Brigham Young has lately violated it, and boasts that he will have as many wives as he desires, and advises his people to pursue the same course. American citizens (who are not Mormons) can not hold real estate in the Territory, and those who undertake to do so are abused and threatened, their property stolen or confiscated by the Mormon courts upon a charge manufactured for the occasion. I have applications daily from people of the Mormon faith who desire to leave the Territory, and who say they cannot do so without protection from me, as they fear they would be arrested, their property taken from them on some trumped up charge, and probably their lives taken.[69]

Connor no doubt exaggerated in some of his statements, but he was not through: "Yesterday morning Brigham Young started to the northern settlements, with a guard of 150 mounted men. Previous to starting they were drawn up in front of his residence, and as the Governor's son, who is also his private secretary, was passing, some of them shouted 'three cheers for Ex-Governor Harding [Cumming], and long life to Jeff. Davis.' Companies are drilled daily and exercised in target practice." Connor reported that he had contemplated another expedition against the Indians when the weather grew warmer, but "in consequence of the hostile attitude of the Mormons I will be compelled to forego such duty for the season." The commander repeated that his troops should be removed if not reinforced; "My command is in no immediate danger, but if the present preparations of the Mormons should continue I will be compelled for the preservation of my command to strike at the heads of the church, which I can do with safety, for their being once in my power their followers will not dare touch me; but if I remain in my present position (although a strong one) for them to attack me, I am lost, as they have about 5,000 capable of bearing arms and cannon of heavier caliber than mine."[70]

Despite his worries, Connor soon had his reward. On March 29 the fiery little colonel informed San Francisco that he had the following dispatch from General-in-Chief Halleck: "I congratulate you and your command on their heroic conduct and brilliant victory on Bear River. You are this day appointed a brigadier-general."[71] This gave the men on the bench confidence that they were not forgotten and gave Connor further ammunition in his struggle with the Mormons. The night of March 29 the citizens of the Salt Lake area were aroused by the sound of cannon from Camp Douglas. The Mormon signal cannon sounded. Hastily clothes were donned, arms seized, and the Mormons rushed to Young's residence, sure an attack was coming. The noise of arms fire from Camp Douglas was accompanied by the sound of martial music. It was just another false alarm. The soldiers were serenading their newly promoted general with band music and the firing of cannon.[72] Nevertheless, it showed the tenseness and almost comic-opera quality of the confrontation in Salt Lake City.

General Wright on March 30 sent Connor's lengthy March 15 communication to Washington with the comments:

The astounding developments exhibited in these documents demand serious consideration and prompt action to enforce obedience to our laws and to sustain and support the officers of the General Government in the proper discharge of their duties. Although the excitement at Great Salt Lake City, brought about by the unreasonable acts of Brigham Young and his adherents, has somewhat subsided, yet I am fully satisfied that they only wait for a favorable opportunity to strike a blow against the Union. . . . The good order and strict discipline enforced by Colonel Connor have left the people of the city without any cause of complaint on account of the proximity of the troops, but they have doubtless great apprehensions that their odious institutions, so repugnant to civilized society, may receive a check by the presence of a large body of loyal men sworn to maintain the laws and authority of the United States.[73]

There is no doubt the federal authorities were concerned. While it was obvious that the issue of the civilian authorities in Utah Territory was becoming intertwined with the presence of the military, and that both were in virtual conflict with the Mormons, there were repercussions in Washington as well. The continuing issue of statehood became unavoidably enmeshed with the other problems.

Delegate Bernhisel continued during the winter and spring of 1863 to labor for the admission of Utah as a state, but with negligible results. Bernhisel had told Brigham Young on January 9 that the Senate Committee on Territories had ended its work for the session without any resolution of the Utah question. As before, Bernhisel felt the major objection to admission was polygamy "and that the prejudice against that, of a majority of the members of the committee is strong and deep rooted."[74]

As to the House Committee on Territories, Bernhisel told Brigham Young on January 16 that the committee reported a bill with a provision that Utah Territory should call a convention in July to amend the constitution and abolish polygamy and that this amendment is irrevocable and irrepealable. Bernhisel said he told the committee that the conditions were degrading and that he did not think the people of Utah would agree to such an amendment. By this time Harding's December message to the legislature was well known in Washington and Bernhisel felt this message had an adverse influence with the House Committee on Territories as to admission.[75]

Reporting continuously, Bernhisel on January 22 wrote that Vice-President Hamlin had received a copy of the governor's objectionable speech and a letter from Harding complaining that it had been suppressed. Bernhisel told Young that the letter "lays the blame of its suppression to your charges." As we have seen, the Committee on Territories of the Senate had resolved to inquire into the question of the speech not having been printed. Bernhisel said he told the committee, "Our people are loyal to the constitution and Union if however there should be any manifestation of disloyalty even on the part of a few of our people, our enemies would take advantage of it, and it would prevent us from obtaining any appropriations or favors from the government, and would effectually prevent the admission of our Territory into the Union." [76]

The Senate Committee on Territories, meeting again, decided in the negative as to admission. [77] In the House, Representative James M. Ashley of Ohio tried to get a bill through the committee to admit Utah with slavery and polygamy both prohibited. Bernhisel objected and the committee refused to agree on a bill or to report a measure back to the House. Other bills in 1863 provided for popular election of probate judges in Utah, and George W. Julian of Indiana introduced a measure to counteract polygamy by granting suffrage to women. Nothing came of either measure. [78]

Utah Senator-elect William Hooper was also reporting to Brigham Young. He felt the Senate Committee on Territories had only "*pretended* to have the question of an Enabling Act for Utah under consideration, but if considered, I think the verdict is foreshadowed." [79] Hooper looked for nothing good from the committee for Utah except perhaps for profits for army contractors and the like. [80] Hooper, however, did have an interview with President Lincoln. Writing from New York on March 30, he told how he had laid the wishes of the people before the President and had asked for the removal of Governor Harding and the judges. Hooper wrote that Lincoln "wanted to know what or if any objection to Gov. Harding did not grow out of his trying to be Governor and leaving control to Brigham Young. I explained matters at once & fully as I could for the brief period I had but am confident he is so biased or prejudiced in his mind that nothing I could have said would have moved him." [81]

Hooper and Bernhisel kept the reports coming. On April 27 Hooper wrote Young that he had been told there would be a movement of more federal troops from California to Salt Lake City and also from Denver to Utah. [82] Bernhisel meanwhile reported that as of February 29 the Senate Committee on Territories would take no further action.[83] He also reported on March 9 that Seward "utterly refuses to do anything in regard to the removal of Harding. . . . If Harding is removed a strong effort will be made to promise the appointment of Mr. Superintendent Doty who we think is the most available person whose name we can present."[84]

Bernhisel also managed to see Lincoln during the spring of 1863, and wrote: "In regard to the Governor and the two judges, he said matters had come to a pause, a stand still, that there was no immediate danger of an outbreak, and therefore he thought it was best to let things alone, that he had heard a great deal about the difficulties in Utah, that he wanted more information. . . . In regard to the troops among other things I said that the people were anxious to avoid a collision. He said that was right. The President has concluded to adopt for the present the let alone policy, relative to our affairs."[85]

By mid-June Hooper, strangely enough, was more optimistic about Mormon affairs relative to the federal government. He wrote to Brigham Young that he was not seriously discouraged: "We never saw so good a disposition and spirit prevailing here towards us as there exists now. We have been received warmly and kindly by men of all parties and from many we have received expressions of sympathy and hope of success in our undertaking. Some few of the Members openly avow their willingness to vote for our admission, but many of them are very cautious about committing themselves."[86]

The situation in Utah itself was a bit quieter by the end of March, but nothing had been settled as far as the Mormons were concerned, either as to the federal officials or the army. As spring arrived, Brigham Young, as always, was greatly interested in the emigration of Mormons to Utah, many of them from abroad.[87] He admitted that things in Salt Lake were a little calmer. In writing Bernhisel on March 23, he said,

The worse than uselessness of the location of Col. Connor . . . within the limits of the city has been most signally demonstrated, if it needed any proof more than was self evident, for through machinations of Harding, Waite and Drake, there was strong indications of a collision between the citizens and soldiers. Fortunately the breeze blew over quietly, but such a location for troops is the height of nonsense, aside from the constant chance of disturbance either through accident or design, when classes so distinct as citizens and soldiers are in such close proximity. Why does not Mr. Stanton see that they are soon ordered where they can be of some use. . . .[88]

He added that Harding and the judges "had better be removed at once." He hoped Seward would remove the officials and send the troops elsewhere, "for we are ready and willing to protect all within our borders at a far cheaper rate than imported troops can."[89]

Thus neither side was retreating from its position or altering its demands. One incident that might well have triggered overt activity was passed by without undue agitation. On March 10 an affidavit was made before Chief Justice Kinney charging Brigham Young with violating the federal anti-polygamy act by taking another wife. Judge Kinney issued the writ and it was given to the U.S. marshal, who served it upon Young with a posse. Immediately Young appeared at the State House before Judge Kinney with two or three friends. The judge held the defendant in bail for $2,000 for appearance at the next term of court. The case never came to trial, and undoubtedly was meant only as a test.[90]

One eyewitness was to relate years later that Judge Waite was determined to get at polygamy and claimed that the judge wanted Connor to make a military arrest of Young.[91] This witness believed that bloodshed was avoided because Young was arrested on a civil warrant and not by the soldiers. The author, Edward Steptoe, claimed that Waite had issued an arrest warrant to be served by the troops and that the Mormons rose at this news in response to the distress flag. Steptoe recounted that he suggested that the civil authorities arrest Young and it was so done, and that the troops returned to camp and the citizens dispersed. The truth of this story is difficult to determine, but from internal evidence it could well have at least partial validity.[92]

The *Deseret News* characteristically commented that for a number of days it had been contemplated to issue writs against President Young. The paper did say there had been an unusual stir at Camp Douglas with "the most ample preparations made for the purpose of making a descent with an armed force upon the President. . . . It was vainly and foolishly supposed that he would resist of the service of a writ. . . . Persons desiring collision were anxious to make the pretext of an armed military force in executing the process as the excuse for gratifying their wicked purposes. But in this they have been disappointed." The paper declared that no one had more earnestly taught submission to the law of the land than had President Young. Yet the anti-polygamy law had been openly flaunted.[93]

Young had some pithy comments on his arrest. After explaining the Harding case to his son, now in Liverpool, Young wrote on March 26:

Said officials, more or less countenanced and aided by Col. Connor, continued their meddlesome and mischievous ways. Judge Kinney, upon complaint, issued a writ causing me to appear before him and answer to a charge of bigamy. The writ was serviced by U.S. Marshal Gibbs, to which I promptly responded and after examination was bound over to appear for trial at the March term in 1864. Since then the hue and cry about testing the operation of the anti-polygamy bill . . . has considerably abated, and Harding, Connor & Co. are at present quite crestfallen and apparently at a loss what to try next. It is probable that their efforts to create trouble will prove futile, and that they and their like will disappear as the grass grows.[94]

Young wrote much the same thing to Elder Dwight Eveleth in San Francisco the same day. He did praise the orderly processes of the court. "It is quite likely, as you remark, that government is too busy at present to give much heed to the representations, lies and slanders concocted here by some three or four persons so very insignificant wherever they are known even though holding Federal offices. . . . Peace we have, and present appearances and movements bid fair for its continuance."[95] Also on March 26 Young wrote in like vein to Hooper in New York City, referring to the federal officials. He hoped that "President Lincoln will soon remove them, and fill their places with good men or none."[96]

Yet Young kept up his lines of influence with non-Mormons such as the stage-line operator Ben Holladay. Professing that all the people of Utah wanted was peace and the privilege of exercising their own rights as American citizens, he claimed it was necessary to "eliminate" Governor Harding and the two judges who he felt were plotting against the enjoyment of those rights. He reiterated the willingness of the Mormons to protect the mail and telegraph and to do it cheaper than the federal troops. Why, he asked, were the troops within Utah's borders? "The reason appears obvious to us; and the recent hair's breadth avoidance of a collision between citizens and soldiers, consequent upon 'Harding' & co's cowardice pointedly proves the folly of ordering within our borders troops from abroad."[97]

So, as spring unfolded into summer, the positions of both the Mormon Church and the federals, civil and military, remained at odds. Yet words had not so far come to blows.

NOTES

1. Brigham Young Letter Books, Church Archives, Jan. 26, 1863.
2. *Ibid.*
3. *Ibid.*, Feb. 21, 1863.
4. Journal History, Dec. 11, 1862, p. 1043.
5. Journal History, Dec. 15, 1862.
6. Utah Territorial Papers, U.S. Department of State, Record Group 59, National Archives.
7. O.R., vol. L, pt. 2, pp. 314–15.
8. *Ibid.*
9. *Ibid.*, pp. 318–20, to Dept. of the Pacific Hdq.
10. *Ibid.*
11. *Ibid.*
12. *Ibid.*
13. *Ibid.*
14. *Ibid.*
15. *Ibid.*, pp. 325–27.
16. *Ibid.*, pp. 330–31.
17. *Deseret News*, Jan. 28, 1863.
18. Gustive O. Larson, *The "Americanization" of Utah for Statehood* (San Marino, Cal.: Huntington Library, 1971), p. 30 for summation; see also Tullidge, *History of Salt Lake City*, p. 300.
19. *Deseret News*, Mar. 4, 1863.
20. *Ibid.*
21. *Ibid.*
22. *Ibid.*
23. *Ibid.*
24. *Ibid.*
25. Brigham Young Letter Books, undated, about the end of March, Church Archives.
26. *Ibid.*, speech of Mar. 3, 1863, in undated letter, sent to Frank Fuller about end of March, 1863.
27. *Ibid.*

28. *O.R.*, vol. L, pt. 2, p. 371.

29. *Ibid.*

30. *Deseret News*, Mar. 4, 1863.

31. *Ibid.*

32. *Ibid.*

33. *Deseret News*, Mar. 11, 1863.

34. Stenhouse, *Rocky Mountain Saints*, p. 604; Tullidge, *History of Salt Lake City*, p. 325.

35. *O.R.*, vol. L, pt. 2, p. 334.

36. *Ibid.*, p. 340.

37. Brigham Young Letter Books, Church Archives.

38. *Ibid.*

39. *Ibid.*

40. *O.R.*, vol. L, pt. 2, p. 370, Mar. 15, 1863.

41. *Ibid.*, p. 371.

42. *Ibid.*, p. 372; Waite, *Mormon Prophet*, p. 97.

43. *O.R.*, vol. L, pt. 2, pp. 373–74; Waite, *Mormon Prophet*, pp. 98–99.

44. *Deseret News*, Mar. 11, 1863.

45. Brigham Young Letter Books, Church Archives, Mar. 7, 1863.

46. *Journal of Discourses*, vol. X, pp. 105–7.

47. *Ibid.*, p. 107.

48. *Ibid.*, pp. 108–9.

49. *Ibid.*, pp. 109–10.

50. *Ibid.*, p. 110.

51. *Ibid.*, pp. 110–11.

52. *O.R.*, vol. L, pt. 2, p. 342.

53. *Ibid.*

54. Stenhouse, *Rocky Mountain Saints*, p. 604; Rogers, *Soldiers*, pp. 79–80, quoted from *Millennial Star*, May 9, 1863.

55. Stenhouse, *Rocky Mountain Saints*, p. 604.

56. *Ibid.*, pp. 604–5.

57. *Ibid.*, p. 606.

58. Whitney, *History of Utah*, p. 99.

59. *O.R.*, vol. L, pt. 2, p. 344.

60. *Ibid.*, p. 345.

61. *Ibid.*

62. *Ibid.*, pp. 350–51.

63. *Ibid.*

64. *Ibid.*, p. 357.

65. Utah Territorial Papers, U.S. Department of State, Record Group 59, National Archives.

66. *O.R.*, vol. L, pt. 2, p. 371.

67. *Ibid.*

68. *Ibid.*

69. *Ibid.*, pp. 371–72.

70. *Ibid.*

71. *Ibid.*, p. 369.
72. Stenhouse, *Rocky Mountain Saints*, pp. 608–9.
73. O.R., vol. L, pt. 2, pp. 369–70.
74. Bernhisel Papers.
75. *Ibid.*
76. *Ibid.*
77. *Ibid.*, Jan. 22, 1863.
78. Howard R. Lamar, *The Far Southwest* (New Haven, Conn.: Yale University Press, 1966), p. 366.
79. William Hooper Letters, Church Archives, Feb. 23, 1863.
80. *Ibid.*
81. *Ibid.*, Mar. 30, 1863.
82. *Ibid.*, Apr. 27, 1863.
83. Bernhisel Papers.
84. *Ibid.*
85. *Ibid.*, May 1, 1863.
86. William Hooper Letters. Church Archives.
87. Brigham Young Letter Books, Church Archives, to Joseph Hobart of New Orleans, Mar. 23, 1863.
88. *Ibid.*
89. *Ibid.*
90. *Deseret News*, Mar. 11, 1863; Tullidge, *History of Salt Lake City*, pp. 313, 316.
91. Edward Steptoe, "An Unwritten Page of Utah's History: How Brigham Young Was Arrested for Polygamy," *Overland Monthly*, 2nd ser., vol. 28 (Dec., 1896), 677–78.
92. *Ibid.*, p. 679.
93. *Deseret News*, Mar. 11, 1863.
94. Brigham Young Letter Books, Church Archives.
95. *Ibid.*
96. *Ibid.*
97. *Ibid.*, Apr. 4, 1863.

CHAPTER

IX

Indians and Governors

Melting snows and refreshing tinges of green on the arid landscape were not the only signs of spring in the Wasatch Mountains in 1863. Reports, both founded and unfounded, of accelerated Indian depredations or expected depredations began to come in. And it appeared that the army in Utah was anxious to continue its policy of containment of the Indians which was started in the engagement at Bear River in January. Connor decided to take action against the renewed Indian troubles, most of which were now reported to be south and west of Salt Lake City on or near the Overland Trail. Apparently he felt he could afford to weaken the garrison in the city to carry out this plan.

It was Connor's view that Goshute Indians had been raiding the Overland Mail Route to the west. These Indians had spent the winter in the Mormon settlements of the Tooele Valley quite close to Salt Lake City, and Connor was convinced that the Indians were "encouraged and instigated . . . by Mormons."[1] On March 26 he sent twenty-five men of Company A, Second California Volunteer Cavalry under Lieutenant Anthony Ethier to look for the marauding Indians. After five days of fruitless searching, crossing the Cedar Mountains several times, they started back toward Camp Douglas. Upon reaching Camp Crittenden, they saw "some Indians coming out of Trough Cañon." The horses being very much tired and sore-footed, Ethier commandeered a mail coach from William S. Wallace, the Overland Mail Company agent, into which piled thirteen soldiers. Along with eight men mounted on the soundest horses, they set out in pursuit of the Indians. They overtook them at Cedar Fork, which afforded the Indians a natural defensive position. "The Mormons," Ethier reported, "through treachery, I suppose, and wishing to see my party destroyed, gave me false reports as to the position of the Indians and also in regard to their numbers." The lieutenant's small force advanced toward the area where he was sure the Indians were lying in wait, though all he could see were two chiefs on horseback, "riding the war circle." Acting on his own judgment rather than the intelligence he had received from the Mormons, he attacked, only to receive a "withering fire" from a direction he least expected, and he was compelled to give way. Regrouping, the troops attacked again, but could see no Indians and, continuing to receive a "severe fire from an unseen foe," they withdrew. Ethier claimed that Mormons stood near where his horses were, within 100 yards of the Indians, and yet not a shot was fired at them. He also held that he saw a Mormon in conference with an Indian.[2]

There was another expedition from Camp Douglas April 2–6, to Spanish Fork, southeast of Cedar City. This time Captain George F. Price was in command with a complement of fifty-three, though he was joined at Cedar Fort by Ethier's men. The combined force went after the Indians who had fought Ethier several days before, searching the country around Goshen and Spanish Fork. The Mormons there said they had seen no Indians for ten days, but Price's scouts reported late in the day on April 4 that the Indians had entered Spanish Fork Canyon. "'Boots and Saddles,' and 'to horse' were immediately sounded, taking the men away from supper, and in less than five minutes . . . the entire detachment . . . was en route to the cañon, four miles from camp."[3]

Captain Price found the Indians "in considerable force, numbering in sight between forty and fifty, being posted on both sides of the cañon, a large stream of water (Spanish Fork) separating us from the south side." The Indians opened fire as the soldiers entered the canyon. Using flanking parties, the troops forced the Indians to retreat up the canyon, "until they finally broke into a run under fire." Price ordered his men to return to camp as it was nearly dark. During the return march fighting continued. Next morning he again sent flanking movements up the narrow, rugged, rocky canyon, and there was sporadic firing from the few Indians they encountered. Nearly out of rations and with horses in an extremely jaded condition, they proceeded to Provo and then on the 6th returned to Camp Douglas, after having traveled 165 miles.[4]

Yet a third expedition was carried out from Camp Douglas to Spanish Fork Canyon April 11–20 with two skirmishes on the 12th and the 15th. In a long report, Colonel George S. Evans of the Second California Volunteer Cavalry described the action. In the town of Pleasant Grove the advance party of Lieutenant Francis Honeyman had been attacked by Indians. Honeyman had a howitzer in an adobe house and the Indians surrounded him. He fired two shots from the howitzer, but it cracked the walls of the building so badly that the gun could not be used further. Honeyman had only five men with him but they withstood a sharp attack. No one was hit, but the door, windows, stovepipe, pans, plates, and most other things in the house were riddled.[5]

Colonel Evans said this occurred in the town

in the face and eyes of a population of several hundred people calling themselves civilized and American citizens—God save the mark! Right in the heart of a Mormon town, where there were not less than 100 or 150 white men (Mormons), in the broad daylight 75 or 100 savages attack and attempt to murder six American citizens and do carry off mules, harness, and other Government property, and not a hand is lifted to assist or protect them or to prevent the stealing of the Government property; but on the contrary they stand around the street corners and on top of their houses and hay stacks complacently looking on, apparently well pleased at the prospect of six Gentiles (soldiers) being murdered. They actually assisted the Indians in catching the Government mules that had effected their escape from the corral, and from their natural fear of the redskins were endeavoring to keep beyond their reach.[6]

Honeyman, as reported by Evans, felt he had sufficient evidence that the Indians were informed by the Mormons of his presence "and that it was a contrived and partnership arrangement between some of the Mormons to murder his little party, take the property, and divide the spoils."[7]

On April 13 Connor wired San Francisco of the Honeyman affair: "Unless speedily re-enforced with cavalry the overland mail will be broken up and the emigrant route will be impassable. The Indians, urged on by the Mormons, are congregating for that purpose. Five of my men had a fight with 100 Indians yesterday in a Mormon town, and not a Mormon would help them."[8]

On April 13 Colonel Evans sent out scouts. He felt the Mormons had misled him as to where the Indians had gone. The force went through Provo toward Spanish Fork. Evans dressed a soldier as a citizen, enabling him to pass himself off as a Mormon. He found that a Mormon had gone into Spanish Fork Canyon to notify the Indians of the troops' approach, their number, and other details. Evans pulled a ruse, letting it out that he was going to spend the night south of Provo. But about midnight on April 14 the soldiers quietly slipped away toward the mouth of the canyon, which they reached at daybreak on April 15.[9]

Evans put out flankers, the typical way of approaching Indians in such a position. Through a heavy rain the federals moved forward. About 5 A.M. on April 15 the Indians opened fire. Lieutenant Honeyman had the howitzer on the spur of a mountain and dropped shells among the main group of Indians. The principal body of troops also advanced. The Indians began to withdraw and the federal orders were "forward" and "charge." There was a running fight, the troops chasing the Indians fourteen miles up the canyon, "scattering him like quails." The horses were giving out, and it was a long road back, so recall was ordered. About thirty warriors had been killed, including, supposedly, their chief, and many more were captured. Lieutenant F. A. Peel was killed and two sergeants wounded.[10] All in all, this was a foray typical of the small expeditions Connor's men had to carry out. The officers in charge of these actions, to a man, felt that the Mormons, instead of cooperating in punishing the Indians, encouraged them.

Connor reported on April 9: "From the evidence before me I am well satisfied that the Mormons are the real instigators of the late raid. Brigham Young has sent commissioners to Washington for the purpose, I am told, of proposing to the Government to take charge of the overland mail and emigrant route in this Territory for half the amount it costs at present, provided the troops are withdrawn. And also to use their influence with the President to have the Governor and Judges Waite and Drake removed."[11]

Connor had no fear of further difficulties with the Mormons, he said, until the commissioners returned, but if the Mormon mission were unsuccessful, "then I have every reason to fear there will be trouble, as they are determined that the laws shall not be executed, and the three officers named are as equally determined that the laws shall be enforced." If the troops were to be withdrawn, he reiterated, the Mormons were aware that the three federal officers would have to leave as well, "as their lives would not be safe one hour after the withdrawal of the troops if they remained. The object of Brigham in encouraging Indian raids at present is, undoubtedly, to induce the Government to withdraw the troops from this post and have them stationed at different points on the mail line. They also wish to impress upon the Government the idea that his people can protect the line better than troops can, and there is no doubt but he can, as the Indians are completely under his control and do just as he tells them."[12]

Connor asked for reinforcements to give him a total of 3,000 men and for at least five more guns. He then added, as he did so often, ". . . this people are at heart disloyal, and are only waiting a favorable opportunity to demonstrate the fact."[13] Overland Mail Company Agent Wallace at Fort Crittenden endorsed Connor's opinion and said that in the Indian raids of March there was "treachery" on the part of the Mormons.[14]

Meanwhile Brigham Young continued his unabating criticism of the federal officials. Writing to a Church leader on April 3, Young was bitterly critical of Governor Harding for having pardoned six Morrisites convicted of murder in the court of Chief Justice Kinney: Young said Bernhisel had written him that the conduct of Governor Harding would be investigated in Washington, and if he had acted improperly he would be removed, but if his conduct be deemed proper Harding would be kept in office. To Young, "If his 'conduct' should be decided to be proper, it would be rather difficult to define what would be deemed improper." However, Harding and his "clique" had remained quiet as far as outward operations were concerned, wrote Young.[15]

The *Deseret News* in mid-April continued its vituperative attacks on the governor. In its pages Harding was accused of "contemptible, diabolical acts and proceedings done and performed by him in derogation of law and the administration of justice, and if not in violation of his official oath, a palpable breach of the trust imposed by his appointment."[16]

Connor meanwhile wrote to San Francisco that he had a dispatch from General Halleck suggesting that he might be able to raise companies in Utah or out of emigrant trains. Connor felt that it would be impossible to form a company from emigrants, as they "are inflicted with the gold fever, and the Mormons are too disloyal to be trusted with arms, even if they would enlist, which I doubt." Of course, most of the Mormon men already had arms, as did the militia. He did propose making use of the Morrisite apostates. He suggested that a company of Morrisites man a post on the Overland Emigrant Trail about 150 miles north of Salt Lake City in Idaho Territory where the Beaverhead Mines route intersected that from the east to California and Oregon. Another of Connor's objects was to form an anti-Mormon settlement and have a refuge for those who wished to leave the Church: "I consider the policy of establishing such a settlement of loyal people in close proximity to the Mormons of great benefit and importance to the Government for many reasons."[17] The Morrisites, Connor added, were industrious but very poor, as "the Mormons have stripped them of almost everything they possessed." If enlisted and settled with the help of the army, they could farm and be more financially independent.[18] Connor was clearly trying to devise ways to add to the anti-Mormon population and thus water down the power of the Church.

On April 28 he again asked headquarters for reinforcements, as the Indians were reportedly congregating near Mormon settlements south of Camp Douglas "with a view of depredating on the overland mail and emigrant routes, and are incited and encouraged in their hellish work by Brigham Young, by whose direction they are also supplied with food, and by his people with ammunition, which I have no means of preventing, nor can I strike at them before they get stronger, as in order to reach them I have to pass through Mormon settlements, and the Mormons notify the Indians of my approach, when they scatter to their inaccessible mountain retreats and thus avoid me."[19]

Connor said the Overland Mail Company agents were opposed to having more troops in Utah, but he could only surmise why.

. . . nothing can be proved here against a Mormon, or one of their Gentile Favorites. I deem it a duty I owe to my command to notify the Government through the general commanding of the danger to which they are exposed from the treachery, fanaticism, and disloyalty of this people in case of a serious reverse to our arms in the East. I have also serious fears in consequence of my small command being necessarily scattered over a large extent of territory, of being overpowered in detail by the hordes of Indians now congregating under Mormon auspices, and who my spies inform me are to be joined by Mormons disguised as Indians. Brigham Young has complete control of the Indians of the Territory, and could, if he chose, prevent the horrors that will soon be enacted on the overland route, and which with the force at my command I am powerless to prevent.

Again Connor stated that if he was not to be reinforced, he would recommend that Brigham Young's offer to protect the mail and emigrant routes for money be accepted and Connor's command removed.[20]

Wright told Washington on April 30 that things were quiet at the moment on the routes, that he was trying to throw forward reinforcements, but was having great difficulty in raising men and means. Soldiers were hard to get owing to the high price of labor and the inducements of the mines, plus the rapid depreciation of currency.[21] On May 6 General Wright gave orders for Connor to raise one or more companies in Utah if they would enlist for three years or the duration of the war.[22]

From May 5 to 30, a different sort of expedition from Camp Douglas headed for Soda Springs on Bear River in Idaho Territory. Connor reported that Company H of the Third Infantry under Captain Henry M. Black left Camp Douglas going north via Box Elder, Bear River, the Cache and Marsh valleys to a point near the great bend of Bear River known as Soda Springs. The purpose was to set up a new post for protection of overland emigration to Oregon, California, and the new Bannock City mines in future Montana.[23]

With this expedition were a number of Morrisites whom Connor called in his report seceders from the Mormon Church. He felt removal was the only solution for these people, and he provided transportation for those who did not have their own. In all, there were 160 persons comprising some 53 families. On May 6 Connor himself moved out with Company H of the Second Cavalry California Volunteers and overtook the main train. By easy march they moved north along Great Salt Lake. Connor took the cavalry on a different route from the main party north of Brigham City. By

May 13 Connor was at Snake River Ferry 200 miles from Camp Douglas. He found the area rich with luxuriant vegetation.[24]

Connor was accompanied by James Doty, superintendent of Indian affairs for Utah. Connor and Doty had various conferences with the Shoshones or Snakes at Snake River Ferry. The Indians "were informed that the troops had been sent to this region to protect good Indians and whites, and equally to punish bad Indians and bad white men; that it was my determination to visit the most summary punishment, even to extermination, on Indians who committed depredations upon the lives and property of emigrants or settlers." The conference was satisfactory, Connor thought, and the show of force useful. He went into a long description of the area and the investigations of trails they made. When the infantry and settlers arrived, a suitable location was chosen on the north bank of Bear River for the new community of Soda Springs. Connor and his force returned to Camp Douglas, obviously satisfied with their explorations and with setting up the new community without fighting Indians.[25]

Back in Salt Lake City the *Deseret News* reported that about two hundred of the "scapegraces who have been hanging around Camp Douglas all winter, went North" with Connor's command "and we hope the balance of the Camp followers will soon imitate their example." The paper also reported that a minor, one Agnes Lowry, who had allegedly been abducted from her husband, had been awarded to her mother and not to her husband Ward Pack of Bountiful. Judge Drake had made the ruling, obviously in support of the anti-polygamy law.[26]

Brigham Young on May 27 wrote to Secretary Fuller that he had word Harding was out and Indian Commissioner James Duane Doty had been appointed governor of Utah. Young also told Fuller, who would probably be acting governor, that "Affairs here are peaceful with a good prospect of their continuing for a time longer, and promise of abundant crops of fruit and other products."[27] Of course, Connor did not consider things so peaceful. On May 30 Young wrote Bishop Cannon in Liverpool that if Harding were really removed, ". . . it is evident that the enemies of truth in the States have concluded that they are not ready to commence open war upon the other 'twin relic' but it is by no means an indication that their feelings toward us are any better, for beyond doubt, they are more bitter than in any previous period. It is altogether probable that the work on hand will so keep them busy that we will have quiet for a time longer. This removal is favorable ... as a precedent for similar obnoxious cases in future. ..."[28] Young crowed a bit over the apparently accurately reported departure of Harding. On June 3 he wrote to his son in Liverpool: "... it is certain that the backbone of opposition and strife-stirring slander at home is broken, and there is no apparent prospect of their being able to create any disturbance here at an earlier date than next year at the soonest."[29]

As to Connor, Young wrote Elder John W. Young on June 13, "Connor is still here, a Brigadier without a Brigade or the prospect of one, and is said to be anxious to get away, with the expectation of soon being gratified by being recalled or ordered to more active service and a wider field. Under these circumstances the mischievous clique, in such full feather not long ago, is entirely broken, and I presume despair of being able to carry out any of their evil plans."[30] Of course Connor was not removed, despite the wishes of the Mormon president and, no doubt, most of his followers.

Taking a philosophical approach, although not a new one, Brigham Young said in the Bowery May 31:

Had the rulers of our nation known how to sustain the Union to an everlasting continuance, this knowledge would have been beyond price. Had they possessed wisdom to have maintained the nation in its true character, in all its liberal institutions built upon the Constitution and Declaration of Rights, the Government would have continued inviolate in truth and purity and power. ... True knowledge would have enabled them easily to accomplish all this. ... Teach the people true knowledge, and they will govern themselves. ... Through their oneness, the Latter-day Saints have become a terror to the enemies of truth.[31]

In his usual doom-predicting manner, Brigham Young, again in the Bowery on June 14, asked, "What object was there, we might ask, for inaugurating the present war that is spreading dismay through our once happy land? Is it to kill off the African Race? No; but ostensibly to give freedom to millions that are bound, and in doing this they did not know that they would lay the foundation for their own destruction as well as that of the object of their pursuit. Those whose minds are opened to see and understand the purposes of the Most High are made happy in a timely deliverance from approaching evil."[32]

Always free and persistent with his advice, Young gave some to the California emigrants on July 8 in the Public Square: "Instead of being secluded, we find ourselves in the great national highway. We must be known, and we could not be in a better situation to be known than where we are. . . . The spirit of our politics is peace. If we could have our choice, it would be to continually walk in the path of peace; and had we the power, we would direct the feet of all men to walk in the same path." The present situation of the country, he said, was lamentable and disastrous. Mankind did not understand itself or the designs of its Creator. "War is instigated by wickedness—it is the consequence of a nation's sin."[33]

He told the emigrants that they would have no trouble with the Indians "if you will do right. I have always told the traveling public that it is much cheaper to feed the Indians than to fight them." He said a little bread, meat, sugar, tobacco, or a little of anything would make them your friends. This would be better than making enemies. "I am satisfied that among the red men of the mountains and the forest you can find as many good, honest persons as among the Anglo-Saxon race." Young believed the Indian innocently followed the traditions and customs of his race and that it was customary for him to steal and shed the blood of enemies.[34]

In San Francisco, meanwhile, General Wright was still endeavoring to get more troops for Connor. He was trying to obtain men from the acting governor of Nevada and also planned to send Connor a battalion of the Third California Infantry.[35]

On June 3 the *Deseret News* reported that it was rumored that the hated Governor Harding had been removed by Lincoln and that the new governor would be either Superintendent of Indian Affairs J. Duane Doty, or one Baron S. Doty. The editor was grateful to Lincoln "for the removal of what they considered a great nuisance." The same issue of the *News* complained about troops riding promiscuously through the streets of Salt Lake City. It also announced the new Tabernacle foundations were mostly in place and some of the columns raised.

Both Young and the *Deseret News* had been correct. Harding had been deposed as governor and James Duane Doty appointed to replace him. On June 17 the *Deseret News* made the welcome announcement that former Governor Harding had departed. Apparently trying to appease both the Mormons and the Radical Republicans, Lincoln had made Harding chief justice of Colorado Territory. He also removed Secretary Frank Fuller and the popular Chief Justice John F. Kinney. The new Utah secretary was Amos Reed, the son of John Reed, of Colesville, Broome County, New York, who had defended Joseph Smith in 1830 during his trial in that city. The younger Reed had for a brief period been a resident of Utah and clerk of the Indian superintendency under Doty and was known as a conservative.[36]

Apparently Brigham Young felt Judge Kinney's removal was because the judge was considered pro-Mormon.[37] While firm evidence is lacking, it would appear that the Lincoln administration was compromising by making a clean sweep of the main officials. Harding had not approved of the roles of Fuller and Kinney. When back in Washington in July, he wrote to Secretary of State Seward about the question of Fuller's removal. According to Harding, Fuller had been absent from his post since April 1 and he charged that Fuller had obtained consent from the President under false pretenses. Supposedly Fuller desired to visit once more his aged, blind father who was dying. But, according to Harding, Fuller instead engaged in various mining speculations farther west. There had been other absences as well. Harding openly accused Fuller of malfeasance in office. He did not want Fuller to receive the salary of some $1,000 which Harding said Fuller had never earned. Harding did recommend Amos Reed for the secretary's post.[38]

The *Deseret News* on June 24 supported Chief Justice John F. Kinney, a Gentile, as delegate to Congress. Kinney had been on friendly terms with the Mormons, certainly in comparison with Connor, Dawson, Harding, and Judges Waite and Drake. The paper also applauded the appointment of Doty as governor. His commission had been received at the Salt Lake City Post Office while he was on his trip north with Connor.

James Duane Doty, no longer young, had already had a long and controversial career. He was born in Salem, New York, in 1799 of a colonial English family. After a secondary education he read law and was practicing law at Detroit in Michigan Territory by 1819. He became involved in politics at an early date and was clerk of the supreme court of the Territory and of the Territorial Council.

In 1820 he went with General Lewis Cass, as secretary, on a tour of the Great Lakes and the Mississippi River. Judge of the judicial district of Northern Michigan, Doty in 1823 settled at Green Bay, then in Michigan Territory. In this vast district he traveled widely. He developed a sizeable group of friends and admirers, and had many contacts with trading firms in the area. His resignation as judge was supposedly requested of him, and in 1832 he explored the upper Mississippi Valley region, seeking out sites for towns, mills, and wharves. He was described as being a compulsive speculator. He surveyed military roads in Wisconsin for the army and was a member of the legislative council of Michigan. He was instrumental in dividing Michigan Territory and in laying out the state capital at Madison, Wisconsin. In 1839 he was elected delegate in Congress for Wisconsin and was reelected in 1840. In 1841 President Tyler named Doty governor of Wisconsin Territory, a post he held until 1844, except for a short break.

Some of his activities seem to have been somewhat irregular, particularly those in land speculation and building. He had a running fight with the territorial legislature. On the other hand, many of the activities that brought him criticism were based on his speculations. There was no proof of dishonesty, but it does seem that Doty combined politics, government, and personal affairs. Later he was a member of the first constitutional convention of Wisconsin, and for two terms, 1849–53, represented the new state in Congress. First he was a Democrat, then a Whig, and even later a Republican. It was as a Republican that Doty was named superintendent of Indian affairs in Utah Territory. It is said that Doty was a perceptive lawyer, well-read and cultured. He had a vast and colorful experience in the West and in frontier development and politics.[39] In Utah he managed to steer a central course and was generally respected by the Mormons, yet he worked quite ably with the Indians and the army. Doty brought a respite in the continuing feud between the Mormons and the territorial governor. In accepting the governorship of Utah Territory, Doty on June 19 wrote Indian Commissioner Dole that as the "condition of the Indian Affairs in this quarter seems to require the service of a Superintendent at this time, I have therefore determined to continue to perform its duties until a successor is appointed, or I am otherwise instructed."[40]

Connor kept up his negotiations with the Indians, despite his often repeated worries over the Mormons. His policy toward the Indians was becoming one of trying, often successfully, to make treaties as well as to protect the trails by force. He almost seems to have engaged in competition with the Mormons to better relations with the Indians. After meeting with the Shoshones near Fort Hall and at Fort Bridger, he wrote on June 10: "They say they are tired of fighting and want to be at peace. . . . The fight of last winter is telling on them. There are two small bands at large yet, who are hostile. They number about 100 men. Troops are now in pursuit of them, and I hope soon to destroy them. I have no fears for the safety of the emigration to the Bannock mines. . . . On the whole I consider the Indian troubles in my district very near at an end."[41]

Governor and still Indian Superintendent Doty wrote the commissioner of Indian affairs on June 20, 1863, that he was meeting with the Shoshones at Fort Bridger and that "Many of these Indians have been hostile and have committed depredations upon the persons & property of emigrants and settlers, but now express a strong desire for peace." He felt treaties could be made with about a third of the Shoshones, but it was impossible to assemble the whole tribe.[42]

As to the Utes, Doty wrote on June 26 that he and General Connor had met with Little Soldier, chief of the Weber Utes who had been hostile for some months. Little Soldier met with them near Salt Lake City and said he wished to make a firm and lasting peace and promised to remain at peace with the whites. He had also sent word to other Ute bands to come in and make peace. Doty concluded: "I have now strong hopes that hostilities on the part of the Utes will cease."[43] But on June 11 Connor wrote to San Francisco that a powerful tribe of Southern Utes had commenced hostilities, killing the driver of a coach and an employee of the mail company twenty-five miles west of Salt Lake City. "Rumor says 1,600 of them in Mormon settlements south on way to attack me and destroy overland mail. The Snake Indians, with the exception of two small bands, are peaceable and have given up stolen property, Goshutes still troublesome. My force much scattered; should be doubled at once. I am surrounded by enemies, white and red."[44]

On June 12 troops of the Second Cavalry were ordered by the Headquarters of the Army of the Pacific to Salt Lake City. Others of the same regiment were to leave Fort Churchill.[45] On the same day Connor went direct to Halleck by wire: "A powerful tribe, the Southern Utes, are threatening the overland stage, east and west. My forces are inadequate to its protection. Have received no re-enforcements from California. Could a regiment of cavalry be sent from Denver?"[46] Although he was optimistic as to his peace negotiations, at the same time Connor proved more apprehensive of Indian attacks than was usual for him.

Brigham Young stepped directly into the Indian problem by writing an important letter to various chiefs on June 15: "We have been informed that you have determined to take up the war hatchet, and to kill the whites who are peaceably traveling across the country; and we learn with sorrow that some Indians and for all we know some of your men, have not only attacked the western mail line and killed some of the drivers, but that you intend also to attack the Eastern mail coaches, and destroy the telegraph lines and make war upon the whites generally." Young was sorry to hear this and added, "We hope you will not do so, but cease to molest the mails and telegraph wires and let the travellers pass this way in peace and unmolested. We have fed you for many years and given you clothing and always been your friends and treated you kindly; but we cannot feed you and be friends to you unless you stop making war on the whites, and cease to interfere with the mail coaches and immigrants, and let the white man and their property alone. If you feel mad it is not good, and you had better go away somewhere far away from the mail route until you feel good again, and feel kind and friendly and peaceable as you used to do before you made war." But if the Indians were determined to make war upon the whites, "you may be assured sudden vengeance will follow you and you will be chastised in a terrible manner, and no doubt many if not all of you will be killed, for such conduct can not and will not be endured. You may think the whites have wronged you. This is no excuse for you. It is better to suffer wrong than to do wrong. I have always been your friend and have endeavored to do you good, and *you must* abide *my command*."[47] A very strange letter, particularly the conclusion wherein he demands that the Indians obey the bidding of Brigham Young. The rationale behind this is hard to fathom. He does not ask the Indians to obey the laws or authority of the United States, but that of Brigham Young! There is no evidence that this letter did any particular good.

From brief reports it appears there was a skirmish near Government Springs on June 20 when an expedition from Fort Bridger under Captain Lewis captured fifty of San Pitch's band of Indians. Ten Indians were reported killed. Connor also noted more gathering of the Utes in "settlements south in large numbers, and threatening destruction to soldiers and overland mail. Have only sixty men for duty at Camp Douglas."[48] It seems that such a small complement at Camp Douglas was lower than usual, but he had been sending out various parties to protect the trails.

Typical of the numerous, but often fatal, incidents was one at Canyon Station on June 23. Four soldiers had been guarding the stage station; two had gone as a guard to the water car. The other two went hunting, leaving the station unprotected. Indians attacked the water car, killing a Corporal Hervey and wounding the private with him. The two men who had gone hunting were also killed. As a result, the infantry force along the road was soon strengthened.[49]

While Connor had been continually bombarding Army Headquarters in San Francisco, and thereby Washington, with spirited, very full, and often laborious reports, in the summer of 1863 he became even more prolific. One would have to study all these messages in detail to get the full impact, but they make for repetitious and sometimes tiresome reading.

Connor's report of June 24 is clearly one of his most trenchant. Perhaps he is excessive on many points, but his sincerity cannot be doubted. As his sojourn in Utah lengthened, so did the frequency and vehemence of his outspoken diatribes. That his reports were somewhat injudicious cannot be denied, as were some of the words coming from the other side. "The authority of the Church is here recognized as supreme—above and beyond constitutions, laws, or regulations of the civil authorities . . . but in its practical works is superior to and transcends all authority emanating from whatever source." Connor was indeed exaggerating and was grossly unhistorical when he wrote:

The world has never seen a despotism so complete, so limitless, so transcendent, controlling not alone the outward and internal civil polity of the Territory, but entering into all the details of everyday life and the minutiae of the domestic economy of each individual, as exhibited in the construction of the Mormon Church. . . . Of that church Brigham Young is the acknowledged head and recognized despot. Upon his will alone depend as well the acts of public officials as the course, temper, and feeling of the humblest member of his flock. Fanaticism can go no further than it has in this case.[50]

To Connor, the "consequence is that the rightful authority of the United States is exercised only by sufferance, and peace and a doubtful quiet maintained only upon the slender thread of one man's will or whim." He felt that in dealing with the people even in trivial matters, he was "but dealing with their supreme monarch." At any time, he felt, Young could embargo the sale of anything to Connor's command, and all acts, words, and deeds of all Gentiles reached his ear. There was, according to Connor, an extended system of espionage "that no secret military movement against hostile Indians can be undertaken without the latter being possessed of the number, time of starting, direction, equipments, &c."[51]

The situation was intolerable, the general believed, with "striking and undutiable evidences of hatred to the Government, disloyalty to the Union and affiliation and sympathy with treason in the East and savage massacre and plunder all around and about us." Connor found it difficult to restrain his indignation at the "harangues" of the Mormon leaders each Sabbath and with what he termed "flippant expressions of disloyalty and vulgar threats against the Union." He said "mock tears and sneering lamentations" greeted each reverse to federal arms. The government was deemed impotent and the destruction of the Constitution and the Union sure, as prophesied by Joseph Smith. The whole people were being "educated" in this vein, according to the general. Everything was taught as subservience to the head of the Church. He did admit that the Mormons showed no regard for the South and even displayed a repugnance to slavery, but he felt the Confederacy received some support because "it is regarded as the appointed means of destroying the Government."[52]

In this same June 24 report, Connor enlarged on his previous statements that Brigham Young "has an immense influence over the savages." He said he had proof for believing that recent raids on the Overland Mail "were incited by white Mormons, and not

improbably under the direct orders of the head of the Church."
But even if this were not true, the Mormons beyond doubt aided
the Indians materially. He went into considerable detail about how
the Indians collected in or near southern Mormon settlements,
passed through towns, and were fed and supplied and encouraged
by the residents. These Indians supposedly boasted they would kill
emigrants and break up the overland mails. They even threatened
to attack Camp Douglas. He said the chiefs were in touch with
Brigham Young. He stressed his view that it was "likewise significant of Mormon complicity that the savages seldom or never molest the Mormons or steal their stock, but pass through their settlements and by their defenseless ranches content with the aid the
Mormons volunteer to give them."

Further, Connor charged that no intimation of Indian movements was ever sent to army headquarters by the Mormons. He
called this course relative to the Indians "insidious and damnable"
on the part of Brigham Young. As to the army, Connor felt "That
the presence of the military in this Territory is unwelcome to the
heirarchy of Brigham Young cannot be doubted. It has to a great
extent abridged his power, limited his dictation, and secured protection to those whose persecutions cried aloud to Heaven." The
army also had released from "bondage" hundreds of those "deluded" by Mormonism and who wished to get out, according to
the general.[53]

He believed that if Young could get the army to leave by offering
to protect the Overland Mail Route better and cheaper, Young
would be protecting his own power. He felt Young could cause the
Indians to desist from attacks, and would do so if the army left.
But in that case Connor believed the emigrants would be at the
mercy of the Indians. He concluded his epistle by saying that his
present force was grossly inadequate to protect the overland, the
telegraph lines, and the various emigrant roads, let alone to cope
with resistance to the laws "or the outbreak of armed treason lia-
ble to occur on any serious reverse to our arms in the East, or at
any attempt on the part of the authorities to enforce laws conflicting with the tenets of the Mormon Church or inimical to any of
their practices," subjects which Connor had harped upon repeatedly in the past.[54]

This is one of Connor's longest, strongest, and most exhaustive communiqués about the Mormons. While over the years most historians have used something of Connor's vituperations, only a study of all of them reveals the full impact of his violent views. The relations of Connor and his men with the Mormon Church and Brigham Young were at an impasse in the summer of 1863, but not a silent impasse. It is remarkable, with all the expressed ill feeling on both sides, that more overt conflicts did not occur between the two factions.

In contrast to the fiery Connor, Young wrote to his son in Liverpool June 24, "Up to the present, since Harding's departure . . . the transient persons within our borders are very quiet in their operations here, and so far as I learn, despair of being able to cause much disturbance for some time to come. Those who would injure us find there is plenty of work for them to attend to outside our borders." Young also quoted Brother Stenhouse's report to the effect that President Lincoln had "expressed a hearty readiness to let us alone if we would let them alone. If he sticks to his statement there will be quiet times in Utah during his administration, for we are certainly not only ready and willing to let them alone, but are and ever have been anxious to give them all the good in our power, so far as they would receive good at our hands."[55] In the summer of 1863, most of Young's surviving correspondence involves Church business, with very little concerning the war, the troops in Utah, or unwelcome governors.

Young's reference to Lincoln's statement was amplified in his letter of June 25 to Elder Cannon, "We have ever been anxious to let them alone further than preaching to them the gospel and doing them good when they would permit us, and if they will cease interfering with us unjustly and unlawfully, as the President has promised, why of course they will have no pretext nor chance for collision during his rule."[56]

The generally accepted story is that when Lincoln was asked by Stenhouse about the policy he intended to pursue in regard to the Mormons, he replied, "'I propose to let them alone.'" He was said to have illustrated the statement with one of his stories, in which he compared the Mormons to a knotty green hemlock log on a farm on the frontier. The log was too heavy to remove, so the farmer decided to plow around it.[57] In a fuller version, Lincoln is quoted as saying: "Stenhouse, when I was a boy on the farm in

Illinois there was a great deal of timber on the farms which we had to clear away. Occasionally we would come to a log which had fallen down. It was too hard to split, too wet to burn and too heavy to move, so we ploughed around it. That's what I intend to do with the Mormons. You go back and tell Brigham Young that if he will let me alone I will let him alone." [58] While the details and the exact words Lincoln spoke are not certain, it seems clear that the President did say something of the sort regarding Brigham Young and the Mormons.

To reinforce his own statements, General Connor forwarded to San Francisco two letters relative to Indian raids and the reception of the Indians by the Mormons. Major P. A. Gallagher of the Third California Volunteer Infantry had written from Fort Ruby, Nevada Territory, June 25, 1863, that he had stopped a train of emigrants, "mostly rebels, and a great many of them former soldiers in Price's army." By "Price's army" he meant former soldiers who had fought with Sterling Price in Missouri and Arkansas, either as Confederates or as pro-Missouri sympathizers. Reports of the presence of veterans of Price's forces were rife in the mountain West and probably were to a great extent exaggerated. Gallagher further said he had obtained a letter of one Phoebe Westwood, who wrote from Fort Crittenden that at Salt Creek she had seen the scalps of two men killed by Indians. "The bishop [Mormon] down there treated the Indians with tobacco and ordered the people to feed them, and it made me so mad that I pitched into them and told them what I thought of them, and then I felt better." [59]

On June 30, 1863, Connor's District of Utah had present for duty 47 officers and 857 men, an aggregate of 1,065, with present and absent 1,226, and 6 field guns. [60] They were stationed widely: at Camp Douglas, Fort Bridger, Fort Ruby, Nevada Territory, Fort Churchill, Nevada Territory, Camp Connor, Idaho Territory, with various commands en route. [61]

On July 18 Connor penned another of his long, substantial, and illuminating reports, this time mostly on Indian relations. It was in the main devoted to the negotiations and treaties with the various tribes, but he could not resist repeating some of his denunciations of the Mormons. First he related how he had received overtures from the Southern Utes. Connor felt he had better talk, considering the inadequacy of his command as well "as from motives of

prudence and humanity." Some weeks earlier he had induced the
Utes of Little Soldier to confer. The understanding was that Little
Soldier should give up all his stolen government stock and the
army would give him thirteen Indian ponies. Connor and Doty,
also acting as superintendent of Indian affairs, located this band in
West Mountain Valley, about twenty-five miles west of Salt Lake
City. Connor believed, probably correctly, that the agreement with
the aggressive Little Soldier undoubtedly would influence other
tribes favorably. He was aware that this understanding contra-
dicted the Mormon propaganda which alleged that Connor intended to exterminate the Indians.[62]

On July 14, Connor and Doty met with the Southern Utes. After
the chiefs had expressed some apprehensions, Connor claimed, he
was able to dissuade them from the idea that the army wanted to
fight or exterminate them. Doty distributed presents and food and
the chiefs pledged themselves to peace. Connor felt the Utes would
be the last to break the peace.[63]

The general then related his making of a treaty at Fort Bridger
on June 5 with the Snakes or Shoshone. He held that the several
bands of Shoshone were once more united under the peaceful
Chief Washakie. Furthermore, the famous chief Pocatello had also
sued for peace. There were only a few hostile Goshutes, probably
no more than 100 braves, he reported. Two companies of the Second Cavalry under Captain S. P. Smith had been sent to drive
them off. Perhaps too optimistically, Connor added, "I may therefore confidently report the end of Indian difficulties on the Overland Stage Line and within this district, from the Snake River, on
the north, to Arizona, on the south, and from Green River to Carson Valley."[64]

Connor reiterated that his force was too meager to do much
more than guard the stage road from Indian attacks. "Without the
most criminal conduct on the part of bad white men no apprehen-
sion need be entertained of future trouble with either the Snake or
Ute tribe." For any other purpose than suppressing Indian problems his force "is manifestly and ridiculously inadequate, and its
presence here, no matter how circumspect and prudent we may be,
is necessarily but a source of irritation to a people who regard us
as trespassers and enemies no less than as armed representatives of
a Government they have always hated, and which I fear they are

now learning to despise." If a strong hand was to be taken with the Mormons, with suppression of "the evil deeds of this peculiar people," and laws enforced, the command must be materially reenforced. "If this is not the intention of the government the California Volunteers should be withdrawn to California."[65]

"Unable as we are effectually to overawe or suppress continued exhibitions of enmity and hatred, and violation of law, our feebleness to cope successfully with the Mormons being as well known to them as to ourselves, the presence of our small force here but tends to irritate and provoke those difficulties which it is certainly desirable to avoid until the Government shall be prepared to assume other relations toward the people of this Territory and the autocrat of the Church."[66]

Connor reported an immense emigration crossing the plains and mountains that summer of 1863. He estimated, with characteristic overstatement, that four-fifths were "loudly and notoriously disloyal to the Government and bent on the destruction of the Union." He was concerned with the possible growth of anti-Union sentiments on the Pacific Coast as a result of this supposedly disloyal emigration.[67] This protracted message did not represent a change in Connor's viewpoints, but rather a new emphasis in degree. He continued to pressure the government to make up its mind what, if anything, to do about the Mormons.

General Wright sent Connor's July 31 letter to Washington and repeated Connor's views on the Indians. He was sure that with the proper reenforcement the Overland Mail Route would be perfectly safe. He suggested removing the garrison at Salt Lake, not to California, but to old Camp Floyd or Crittenden, with the district headquarters still at Salt Lake City. He added, "I shall not withdraw the troops from Utah. The presence of the force now there is indispensable for the protection of the Overland Mail Route and the general safety of the country."[68]

On July 30 Governor Doty wired that a treaty had been made by Doty and Connor at Box Elder with the bands of the Shoshones, including Pocatello, San Pitch, and Sagwich. The treaty entered into at Fort Bridger with Shoshones was also mentioned.[69] By October General Benjamin Alvord at Fort Vancouver in Washington Territory was able to wire to Washington: "Owing to the pacification effected by General Connor and Governor Doty of Utah, the Snake Indians upon that route have been very quiet this summer."[70]

NOTES

1. O.R., vol. L, pt. 1, pp. 198–99.
2. *Ibid.*, pp. 200–201.
3. *Ibid.*, pp. 201–3.
4. *Ibid.*
5. *Ibid.*, pp. 204–5.
6. *Ibid.*, pp. 205–6.
7. *Ibid.*
8. O.R., vol. L, pt. 2, p. 391.
9. O.R., vol. L, pt. 1, pp. 206–7.
10. *Ibid.*, pp. 207–8.
11. *Ibid.*, pp. 198–99.
12. *Ibid.*
13. *Ibid.*
14. *Ibid.*, p. 199.
15. Brigham Young Letter Books, Church Archives, Apr. 3, 1863, Brigham Young to H. S. Eldredge in New York.
16. *Deseret News*, Apr. 18, 1863.
17. O.R., vol. L, pt. 2, pp. 410–11, Apr. 22, 1863.
18. *Ibid.*
19. *Ibid.*, p. 415.
20. *Ibid.*
21. *Ibid.*, pp. 416–17.
22. *Ibid.*, p. 427.
23. O.R., vol. L, pt. 1, p. 226.
24. *Ibid.*, pp. 226–27.
25. *Ibid.*, pp. 226–29.
26. *Deseret News*, May 6, 1863.
27. Brigham Young Letter Books, Church Archives.
28. *Ibid.*
29. *Ibid.*
30. *Ibid.*
31. *Journal of Discourses*, vol. X, pp. 189–90.
32. *Ibid.*, p. 209.
33. *Ibid.*, pp. 229–30.
34. *Ibid.*
35. O.R., vol. L, pt. 2, p. 430.
36. Whitney, *History of Utah*, p. 104.

37. Stenhouse, *Rocky Mountain Saints*, p. 609.

38. Letters of Application and Recommendation, U.S. Dept. of State, Record Group 59, National Archives, Harding to Seward, July 25, 1863.

39. *Dictionary of American Biography*, vol. V, pp. 390–91; *National Cyclopaedia of American Biography*, vol. V, p. 72; *Biographical Directory of the American Congress*, 1774–1961, p. 824.

40. Letters Received, U.S. Dept. of the Interior, Office of Indian Affairs, Record Group 75, National Archives.

41. *O.R.*, vol. L, pt. 2, p. 479.

42. Letters Received, U.S. Dept. of the Interior, Office of Indian Affairs, Record Group 75, National Archives.

43. *Ibid.*

44. *O.R.*, vol. L, pt. 2, p. 481.

45. *Ibid.*

46. *Ibid.*

47. Brigham Young Letter Books, Church Archives.

48. *O.R.*, vol. L, pt. 1, p. 229.

49. *Ibid.*, p. 230.

50. *O.R.*, vol. L, pt. 2, p. 492.

51. *Ibid.*, pp. 492–93.

52. *Ibid.*, p. 493.

53. *Ibid.*, pp. 493–94.

54. *Ibid.*, p. 495.

55. Brigham Young Letter Books, Church Archives.

56. Tullidge, *History of Salt Lake City*, p. 325.

57. Whitney, *History of Utah*, p. 24.

58. Larson, "Utah and the Civil War," p. 67, quoting from Richard D. Poll, "The Mormon Question, 1850–1865: A Study in Politics and Public Opinion" (Ph.D. diss., University of California, 1948). See also Hubbard, "Abraham Lincoln," and Nibley, *Brigham Young*, p. 369.

59. *O.R.*, vol. L, pt. 2, pp. 499–500.

60. *Ibid.*, p. 505.

61. *Ibid.*, p. 507.

62. *Ibid.*, pp. 527–28.

63. *Ibid.*, p. 528.

64. *Ibid.*, pp. 528–29.

65. *Ibid.*, pp. 529–30.

66. *Ibid.*

67. *Ibid.*, pp. 530–31.

68. *Ibid.*, p. 545.

69. *O.R.*, vol. L, pt. 1, pp. 219–20.

70. *Ibid.*, p. 157.

CHAPTER

X

A New Approach

☆

In Salt Lake City on July 4, 1863, there was the customary patriotic celebration, while forest fires were raging up Big Cottonwood Canyon. In a day or two Utah would know of the momentous Union victories at Gettysburg and Vicksburg.

On that day in Salt Lake City there was an author, Fitz Hugh Ludlow, who was on his way to San Francisco with the celebrated painter of the West, Albert Bierstadt. Ludlow, in his early twenties, was a perceptive observer, albeit a rather florid writer in the overblown style of the day. A literary "bohemian" from New York, his major claim to fame was his best-selling book *The Hasheesh Eater*. He was soon to publish books and articles about his western trip.[1] "Though Mormondom is disloyal to the core," he wrote, "it still patronizes the Fourth of July, at least in its phase of festivity, omitting the patriotism of our Eastern celebration, substituting 'Utah' for 'Union' in the Buncombe speeches."[2]

Ludlow saw Brigham Young at the Fourth of July ball, and the Mormon leader earned the author's grudging respect. He wrote that Young was sitting in the theater dress circle "looking down on the dancers with an air of mingled hearty kindness and feudal ownership. I could excuse the latter, for Utah belongs to him of right. He may justly say of it, 'Is it not the great Babylon which I have built?' His sole executive tact and personal fascination are the key-stone of the entire arch of Mormon society. While he remains, eighty thousand (and increasing) of the most heterogene-

197

ous souls that could be swept together from the by-ways of Christianity will continue building into a coherent nationality."[3] Ludlow felt, "The instant he crumbles, Mormondom and Mormonism will fall to pieces at once, irreparably." In this he was completely wrong, but it was an opinion shared by many. Further describing Young, he wrote, "His individual magnetism, his executive tact, his native benevolence, are all immense; I regard him as Louis Napoleon, *plus* a heart; but these advantages would avail him little with the dead-in-earnest fanatics who rule Utah under him, and the entirely persuaded fanatics whom they rule, were not his qualities all coordinated in this one,—*absolute sincerity of belief and motive.*"[4]

His character sketch continued, "Brigham Young is the furthest removed on earth from a hypocrite; he is that grand, yet awful sight in human nature, a man who has brought the loftiest Christian self-devotion to the altar of the Devil." Ludlow described Young as looking very distinguished at the ball in the customary suit of solemn black, but that his daily homespun "detracts nothing from the feeling, when in his presence, that you are beholding a most remarkable man." The writer labeled him the greatest businessman on the continent. "The hand of the church holds the souls of the saints by inevitable pursestrings. . . . Over all these matters Brigham Young has supreme command."[5]

On the other hand, the young author hyperbolized that Brigham Young's power was "the most despotic known to mankind." He was criticial of Mormondom's "licentious marriage-institutions" and held that Brigham Young's life was "all one great theoretical mistake." Ludlow quoted Young in conversation at the ball: "You find us trying to live peaceably. A sojourn with people thus minded must be a great relief to you, who come from a land where brother hath lifted hand against brother, and you hear the confused noise of the warrior perpetually ringing in your ears." Ludlow detected in Young's words a "latent crow over that 'perished Union' which was the favorite theme of every saint I met in Utah."[6]

On August 3 Judge Kinney received every vote cast, as far as is known, for Utah territorial delegate to Congress. On August 7 John Titus of Pennsylvania arrived to succeed Kinney as judge. Kinney left August 29 for Washington.[7] For the rest of 1863, according to the *Deseret News*, events seemed to have been less hectic, and its pages contained more national and even international news than its previous copious local reports. Elias Smith retired as editor in September and Albert Carrington was listed as editor, with T. B. H. Stenhouse to "assist in editorial labors."[8]

The new territorial delegate, Judge John Fitch Kinney, had long experience in law and with the Mormons. He was born in New Haven, Oswego County, New York, in 1816, was admitted to the bar in 1837 and practiced in Marysville and Mount Vernon, Ohio, and Lee County, Iowa. He was secretary of the Iowa State Council in 1845–46, and served as a prosecuting attorney and then judge of the Iowa Supreme Court from 1847 to 1854. President Pierce appointed Kinney chief justice of the supreme court of Utah Territory in 1854 and he served until 1857 before returning to private practice in Nebraska. President Buchanan appointed Kinney to be chief justice in Utah again, in 1860. It was during this term that Kinney appeared to work particularly well with the Mormons, sometimes being criticized by others for being too pro-Mormon. He served as delegate in the U.S. Congress from 1863 to March of 1865, and was not a candidate for reelection. After more private practice, Kinney became a commissioner to the Indians and an Indian agent. He died in Salt Lake City in 1902.[9]

In August General Wright was able to tell Washington that "the Indian difficulties in the Territory have been brought at last to a happy termination, and that a good feeling exists between the troops and inhabitants, promising peace and quiet in the country." Wright had changed his mind about moving the troops to Fort Crittenden and told Washington the command was to remain at Camp Douglas. Two more companies at Fort Churchill would move soon toward Salt Lake City.[10]

Governor Doty on August 9 wrote General Wright that he had visited some of the Goshute Indians in Tooele Valley and had found that they wanted peace, protesting that "they are friendly to the whites and are afraid the soldiers will kill them. This is the condition in which I desire to see all the tribes in this Territory. They now realize the fact that the Americans are the masters of this country, and it is my purpose to make them continue to feel and to acknowledge it. Without this there can be no permanent peace here and no security upon the routes of travel. This has been mainly accomplished by the vigor and bravery of the troops under your command."[11]

Doty urged continuing occupation of Soda Springs, Fort Bridger, and Fort Ruby, with frequent excursions by cavalry along the roads east and west of these points and north and south of Salt Lake City. "Your troops have displaced the Mormon power over these Indians, and it is of great importance to Government at this moment that it be kept where it is for a year or two at least. This city is the seat of all power in this country, and the only point from which the authority of the Government over the Indians or people can be, I think, successfully maintained. But it is only in case of hostilities by the Indians or open resistance to the laws and the judiciary that the soldiery can be usefully employed here."[12] The Governor continued:

At present there appears to be no danger of a collision between the troops at Camp Douglas and the inhabitants of this town. Several of our most respected citizens were apprehensive at one time that seizures of citizens would be attempted without due authority, but it is now believed their fears were groundless, or if not, that the crisis has passed, and the inhabitants and troops are now associating together upon the most friendly terms. There are reasons which cannot now be given why it is supposed Brigham Young does not desire the presence of troops either here or at any place in the Territory; but I think it would be a detriment to the public service if this post should be abandoned at present, and until there shall appear a manifest occasion for it. If a collision occurs between the civil officers of the United States and the Mormons this is the place where it must occur, and where those officers will require instant protection and assistance. I presume you are aware that a military organization exists among these people in this city and in every settlement, which, it is understood, is provided expressly to be used to maintain the Mormon authority whenever it shall conflict with that of the United States. While I do not think such a conflict is likely now to occur, yet prudence and duty require that we should be prepared for it at the right point. The sword is not the weapon, as I conceive, with which to correct errors of either morals or religion, and I am sure, General, that you no more than myself would wish to see it so employed; but it may well be used to resist the attacks of fanatics upon the constituted authorities of our country engaged in the performance of their duty.[13]

The governor concluded that he was fully aware of the difficulties of the position "by the fate of my predecessors and the knowledge acquired during my residence here. Many of these difficulties arise from the mistaken notion that the interests of this people and those of the Government are at variance. I think they are not, and that they can possibly become reconciled by one who seeks for peace, which, as heretofore, is my mission." Doty also recommended that no more troops be sent to Salt Lake City but he suggested that a new post be established in the Uintah Valley.[14]

The fact that the federal Indian policy, supported ably by General Wright, was paying off, at least in part, is clear in many ways. The appointment of Doty was certainly a factor, as was the pacification policy of Connor and the army. Thus the Mormon strategy of feeding and supplying the Indians and of friendliness toward them was no longer quite as effective as it had been. There seemed to be an amelioration of strained relations all around.

In the issue of September 23, the *Deseret News* reported the arrival of various troops from Fort Churchill, Fort Ruby, and Sacramento. The printed voice of the Mormons had a much less strident tone than heretofore, although Brigham Young still had pungent things to say. Yet even he seemed more content in the fall of 1863. To Elder Warren S. Snow in Liverpool on September 1 he wrote: "I am informed that the new Governor J. D. Doty, professes that he will confine his official acts to the legitimate duties of his office, and if he carries out his profession we will have no disturbance from that quarter. Ex-Chief Justice Kinney, our present Delegate to Congress, left on the stage for the states on the 29th ult." Young wrote much the same to Cannon, also in Liverpool on September 11, "Present appearances indicate that, through prudence, strict attention to our own affairs and doing right we will continue to enjoy the favor of Heaven that the plans of the wicked in regard to the Saints in Utah will continue to be thwarted, at least for the present."[15]

In a major address in the Bowery October 6, the Mormon leader asked what was the cause of the waste of life and treasury now going on in the East. "To tell it in a plain truthful way, one portion of the country wishes to raise their negroes or black slaves, and the other portion wish to free them, and, apparently, to almost worship them. Well, raise and worship them, who cares? I should never fight one moment about it, for the cause of human improvement is not in the least advanced by the dreadful war which now convulses our unhappy country."[16]

Young felt the Civil War would not really free the slaves but would be a detriment to them. "Many of the blacks are treated worse than we treat our dumb brutes; and men will be called to judgment . . . and they will receive the condemnation of a guilty conscience, by the just Judge whose attributes are justice and truth. Treat the slaves kindly and let them live, for Ham must be the servant of servants until the curse is removed." [17] The decrees of the Almighty cannot be cast off. Young mourned the terrible losses in the war which he felt were "all to gratify the caprice of a few," whether abolitionists, slaveholders, religious bigots, or political aspirants. The people are "wasting away each other and it seems as though they will not be satisfied until they have brought universal destruction and desolation upon the whole country." [18]

In a second address to the Semi-Annual Conference of the Church the same October 6, Young questioned whether the general government sustained a wicked plan to break up and disturb the peace of "this people." He wondered if the non-Mormons, and mainly the army, were in Utah to protect the mail and telegraph lines or "to discover, if possible, rich diggings in our immediate vicinity, with a view to flood the country with just such a population as they desire, to destroy, if possible, the identity of the 'Mormon' community and every truth and virtue that remains." [19] Young obviously already understood at least a possible result of the newly raised cry of gold in Utah and one reason for the promotion of mining by non-Mormons, especially soldiers. "I can tell you what they have in their hearts, and I know what passes in their secret councils. Blood and murder are in their hearts, and they wish to extend the work of destruction over the whole face of the land, until there cannot be found a single spot where the Angel of peace can repose." [20]

Mormon policy had always been opposed to most mining and especially the search for precious metals because of its supposed corrupting influences. Again in the Bowery at the conference, Young warned that God would not make them rich by opening gold mines: "If he makes us rich, he will make us rich in the same way that he became rich, by faithful labor, ceaseless perseverance and constant exertion and industry." He wanted not gold or silver but to build the Temple and finish the new Tabernacle and

send the gospel to the nations, and gather home the poor. . . . We want riches but we do not want them in the shape of gold. . . . It is a fearful deception which all the world labors under, and many of this people too, who profess to be not of the world, that gold is wealth. . . . Should this feeling become universal on the discovery of gold mines in our immediate vicinity, nakedness, starvation, utter destruction and annihilation would be the inevitable lot of this people. Instead of its bringing to us wealth and independence, it would weld upon our necks chains of slavery, groveling dependence and utter overthrow.[21]

Gold and silver, according to Young, were the least wants of the Mormons. They wanted an abundance of wheat and flour, wine, oil, choice fruits, silk, wool, cotton, flax, vegetables, and the products of the flocks and herds. They did want the coal and iron concealed in the mountains as well as the lumber and rock. "The colossal wealth of the world is founded upon and sustained by the common staples of Life. . . . It behooves us, brethren and sisters, to live near to God and honor our profession, rather than to become insane after gold and paper money." As to the war: "I care for the North and the South more than I do for gold, and I would do a great deal, if I had the power, to ameliorate the condition of suffering thousands. . . . I care enough for them to pray that the righteous men may hold the reins of government, and that wicked, tyrannical despotism may be wiped away from the land; that the Lord would raise up men to rule who have hearts in them, who care for the comfort and happiness of mankind and let there be a reign of righteousness."[22]

Although there had been reports of precious ores being found in Utah by the Bingham Brothers in the late 1840s, mines had not been developed until George B. Ogilvie and others discovered silver ores in Bingham Canyon in mid-September, 1863. There are some conflicting stories of the find, as is usual in such events. It is sometimes also credited to a picnic party of officers and men in the canyon, at which one of the ladies, who knew something about minerals, discovered a loose piece of gold ore. Knowledge of this find was immediately taken to Connor.[23]

On November 2 Young told the new territorial delegate Kinney, now in Washington, that the federal troops and money used in Utah were needed elsewhere. He said there was no "compensating benefit" to their presence in Utah. He expected that if the troops were not removed by spring there would be petitions for their removal, "for, aside from their uselessness where they are, they are a serious injury to and infringement upon the rights of quite a number of citizens, by both spoiling the water and churning it in the time of irrigation, and wasting the timber already scarce . . . and the mountains in this vicinity have been an almost continuous sheet of flames the past season. This has to be endured without much complaint, but how long it may continue to be so patiently endured, when there is no reason for it, I am not prepared to say." This letter to Kinney was undoubtedly meant as instructions to the delegate.[24]

Young was still writing frequently to the Church leaders in Liverpool. To Cannon on November 30:

The troops and others at Camp Douglas remain very quiet, the Lord having thus far thwarted their evil designs. At present the great majority of them are in the mountains getting out wood for camp use. Their past plans have failed, they at present are trying to induce an influx of outsiders by inflated misrepresentations of rich gold and silver deposits in Utah's mountains, awaiting discovery and development (I think they will wait a good while.) But the new discoveries in the Territories of Washington, Idaho, Nevada, Colorado, New Mexico, and Arizona bid fair to out blow them, which again results in bad disappointment in their fond expectations, and tends to hasten their departure without having accomplished the purpose for which they were sent here.[25]

By the "purpose" of the troops Young, of course, meant they were, in his view, sent to control or even destroy the Mormons.

A few days later, on December 3, Young wrote Delegate Kinney asking to be kept posted on what was going on in Washington. He recounted with some joy the soldiers' trouble getting wood in the mountains, where several had been injured. "Past plans having failed, the present one seems to be to raise a hue and cry about gold and silver in Utah, thinking thereby to induce an influx of strangers next season. But their prospects are so slim here while the prospects are so glittering and tangible at many places outside our borders, that their present plans will doubtless fall harmless like the others, and they will soon find themselves entirely played out."[26]

Governor Doty addressed the Utah Territorial Legislature in November, 1863, and in considerably different tones than had Harding in December, 1862. "It affords me great pleasure to be able to announce to you the termination of hostilities and depredations by the Indians, and the conclusion of treaties of peace with all the bands occupying the territory and the southern part of Idaho." He praised the "loyalty of the people . . . and the efficiency, energy and courage of the California volunteers in our midst." He suggested a revision of the laws of the Territory, but because of the expense and difficulty in accomplishing this, he did not recommend it at the present time.[27]

Brigham Young had been correct in his assessment in the fall of 1863 that General Connor was taking a new approach in dealing with the Mormons. In one of his verbose reports to San Francisco, on October 26, Connor wrote:

I need hardly repeat that it has been my constant endeavor to maintain amicable relations with the people, and avoid conflict so far as was compatible with the strict and proper fulfillment of the obligations resting upon me, fully understanding that it was no part of my business to interfere with the religious tenets or even the illegal practices of this peculiar people except when called upon by the civil authorities. The open declaration of hostility to the Government on the part of their public men, and their bold, continued, and unceasing teachings of disloyalty have time and again tended to produce excitements leading to collision, which have only been avoided by the most temperate and moderate course of the officers and men of my command. Until such time, therefore, as the Government, in the interest of humanity and the vindication of its offended dignity and laws, shall inaugurate by force an observance of its recorded laws, and come to the relief of a people oppressed and downtrodden by a most galling church tyranny, my own course has been plainly marked by the dictates of policy and the manifest necessity of the case. Entertaining the opinion that Mormonism as preached and practiced in this Territory is not only subversive of morals, in conflict with the civilization of the present age, and oppressive on the people, but also deeply and boldly in contravention of the laws and best interests of the nation, I have sought by every proper means in my power to arrest its progress and prevent its spread.[28]

In this outspoken statement Connor suggested that there were but two ways of striking at the root of Mormonism and "annihilating its baneful influence." One was by adequate military force acting under martial law and "punishing with a strong hand every infraction of law or loyalty." The other (which had been divined by Brigham Young) was by "inviting into the Territory large numbers of Gentiles to live among and dwell with the people." He realized that the military force policy was at the time impracticable, unworkable, and frowned upon by Washington. But his other idea,

if practicable, is perhaps in any event the wiser course. With these remarks I desire to inform the department commander that I have considered the discovery of gold, silver, and other valuable minerals in the Territory of the highest importance, and as presenting the only prospect of bringing hither such a population as is desirable as possible. The discovery of such mines would unquestionably induce an immigration to the Territory of a hardy, industrious, and enterprising population as could not but result in the happiest effects, and in my opinion presents the only sure means of settling peaceably the Mormon question. Their presence and intercourse with the people already here would greatly tend to disabuse the mind of the latter of the false, frivolous, yet dangerous and constant, teachings of the leaders, that the Government is their enemy and persecutor for opinion's sake . . . these doctrines are continually being preached to them until the mass of the people believe that the Government instead of desiring their welfare seeks their destruction. To the end, then, that the inducements to come hither may be presented to the teeming populations of the East and West, seeking new fields of exploration and prosperity, I have looked upon the discovery of mines in the Territory as in the highest degree important—first to this people and secondly to the Government, for the reasons stated.[29]

Connor went on with his ingenious scheme of watering down the Mormon population and Mormon power:

Having reasons to believe that the Territory is full of mineral wealth, I have instructed commanders of posts and detachments to permit the men of their commands to prospect the country in the vicinity of their respective posts, whenever such course would not interfere with their military duties, and to furnish every proper facility for the discovery and opening of mines of gold, silver, and other minerals. The results so far have exceeded my most sanguine expectations. Already reliable reports reach me of the discovery of rich gold, silver, and copper mines in almost every direction, and that by spring one of the largest and most hopeful fields of mining operations will be opened to the hardy and adventurous of our people. Both gold quartz and silver leads have been discovered at Egan Cañon, about 200 miles west of this city, are believed to contain rich mines of precious metals. The mountains in the immediate vicinity are being explored and prospected, and I have reason to believe with successful results. Already, within a distance of from twenty-five to fifty miles of this city, in the East and West mountains, mines have been discovered yielding, with imperfect tests, rich indications of silver, and largely charged with lead and copper ores. The work is still going on, and I have little doubt that rich veins of silver, and probably gold, will be discovered in almost every direction, and still near to Great Salt Lake City. I may also mention that near Camp Connor, 150 miles north of this place, large deposits of salt, sulphur, and extensive beds of coal have been found, while the springs adjoining the camp yield immense deposits of the carbonate of soda, which will one day, I have no doubt, be of very considerable commercial value. If I be not mistaken in these anticipations, I have no reason to doubt that the Mormon question will at an early day be finally settled by peaceable means, without the increased expenditure of a dollar by Government, or, still more important, without the loss of a single soldier in conflict. I have every confidence, therefore, in being able to accomplish this desirable result without the aid of another soldier in addition to those already under my command, notwithstanding the obstacles sought to be thrown in my way by the Mormon leaders, who see in the present policy the sure downfall of their most odious church system of tyranny. I have no fear for the future and believe the dawn is breaking upon this deluded people, even though their elders and bishops, and chief priests may escape the personal punishment their sins against law and crimes against humanity and the Government so richly merit.[30]

As it turned out, Connor was too optimistic about these reports of precious ore finds, but at any rate he had taken a novel tack for a military operation.

On October 27 Connor reported to San Francisco that he and Doty had concluded a "final" treaty of peace with the last remaining band of Shoshones and that on the 12th another treaty was made in Tooele Valley by the deputy superintendent and a staff officer with 250 Goshutes.[31] With obvious pride Connor stated,

I have the honor to report the settlement of terms of peace with all the Indians within this military district from the Snake River on the north to the lower settlements of Utah, and from the Rocky Mountains on the east to Reese River on the west, a region heretofore constantly infested by roving bands of savages, and desolated by their horrid barbarities on passing emigrants for a long series of years. For the first time in the history of the country it may now be truly announced that the great emigrant roads through the Territory may be safely traversed by single persons without danger to life or property or fear of molestation by Indians. . . . I have the pleasure, therefore, to report that through the indomitable bravery, activity, and willingly endured hardships of the California column under my command, the Indian country within this district is freed from hostile savages, and travel through it by unarmed persons, emigrants, miners, or others is perfectly safe and exempt from the dangers heretofore besetting them on every hand.

And he felt this state of things would continue.[32] Wright sent this message along to Washington.[33]

Connor took still another approach in November. The *Union Vedette* newspaper, which published until November 27, 1867, was started by and controlled by the officers and men at Camp Douglas and, of course, General Connor. The first editor was Captain Charles H. Hempstead, who served until December of 1864. It was an obvious effort to provide an opposing voice to that of the Mormon-controlled *Deseret News*. In its first issue the *Vedette* admitted it was not a commercial venture. The publication was bold, sarcastic, and obviously partisan, but no more so than most papers of its day. Through telegraphic dispatches it did bring to its public a quantity of war news.[34]

The new journalistic venture announced editorially in its first issue of November 20, 1863, a very clear policy. It was regrettable that relations between the mass of the people and the military in Utah had not been cordial or amicable. There were many misrepresentations, which it characterized as largely "trash." "The efforts of evil disposed persons to bring about conflict in this Territory, between the military and the civil inhabitants—the appeals of ambitious, crafty, designing men, to wean the people from the Government, that their own ends may be subserved—who constantly vilify and abuse the officers of the best Government with which this or any other people was ever blessed—it will be our duty to expose." The *Vedette* wordily proclaimed the United States

the freest, greatest, and most paternal Government on earth. . . . The teachings which border on treason, if indeed they fill not the full measure of iniquity, the whisperings of some and the defiant speech of others appealing to the passions, prejudices, and religious fervor of the multitude, seeking to wean them from their loyalty to the Nation, we trust and believe have found no deep abiding place in the mind and heart of the great mass of the people of Utah. . . . For those bold, bad, men—if such there be—who to compass their own ends, seek to mislead the multitude as to the intentions and wishes of the Government and its representatives, civil and military, in Utah, we have little respect and far less care; but for the mass of the people who we know to be honest and sincere, though mistaken and, it may be, prejudiced, we have both.

The paper claimed that the army had not come to make war on the people or to intrude on their everyday life: the primary object was to protect the trails and the telegraph. It was the desire of the military to live in peace, but "respect for the Government and the institutions of the land should be voluntarily accorded by one and all, high and low, and toleration for disloyal sneers is no part of the duty of the true citizen, whether official or otherwise. . . . Our first duty is to the Nation, whose preservation and advancement every good citizen holds near his heart."[35]

The *Vedette* naturally carried a good deal of news of Camp Douglas, theater notices, orders from General Connor, and other useful information, as well as considerable news from California.

An enticing and persuasive circular from Genral Connor relative to mining appeared in the first issue, ". . . strongest evidence that the mountains and canyons in the Territory of Utah abound in rich veins of gold, silver, copper, and other minerals, for the purpose of opening up the country to a new, hardy and industrious population, deems it important that prospecting for minerals should not only be untrammelled and unrestricted, but fostered by every proper means." Miners and prospectors would receive the protection of the military. "The mountains and their now hidden mineral wealth, are the sole property of the Nation, whose beneficient policy has ever been to extend the broadest privileges to her citizens, and with open hand, invite all to seek, prospect and possess the wonderful riches of our widespread domain." Furthermore, soldiers would be allowed to prospect when it did not interfere with their military duties.[36]

Mining continued to be promoted strenuously in the *Vedette*. On December 4 it reported, "The city is filled with strange faces. There is a continued incoming and outgoing of miners to and from the Bannock region. . . . Many, we learn, propose resting here till the spring opens, but with ready hands are preparing to prospect the gulches in this vicinity and further south." The issue of November 18 reported a meeting of miners to set up by-laws for the Wasatch Mountain District.

On December 18 the *Vedette* printed the message of Acting Governor Amos Reed, Doty being out of the territory, announcing "the termination of hostilities and depredations by the Indians," and, for this "we are indebted to the loyalty of the people and the valor of our brave troops at the East, and to the efficiency, energy and courage of the California Volunteers in our midst." Reed also emphasized the development of mining and expressed considerable optimism as to its possibilities. He said mining operations would require new laws from the legislature, and he called for a revision of the territorial laws, changes in the Indian reservation lands, and, in general, advocated throwing land open to occupation. But he termed the past year one of general good health and of unusual prosperity.[37]

As of December 31, 1863, Connor had 42 officers and 920 men present for duty, with present and absent 1,307, and 9 guns.[38] The situation vis-à-vis the army and the Saints had changed markedly since the beginning of the year. The issues that rankled were still there, but were now sublimated. The fighting was over for a while, the Indians were reasonably peaceable for the moment, and the political antagonism of soldiers and Mormons was at least apparently quiescent. The military was engrossed in a new and tantalizing endeavor—the search for minerals—and the press and army correspondence reflected a far less tense situation in general on both sides.

NOTES

1. William Mulder and A. Russell Mortensen, eds., *Among the Mormons, History Accounts by Contemporary Observers* (New York: Knopf, 1958), pp. 347–48.
2. Fitz Hugh Ludlow, "Among the Mormons," *Atlantic Monthly*, 13 (Jan.–June, 1864), 484.
3. *Ibid.*, p. 485.
4. *Ibid.*
5. *Ibid.*, pp. 486–87.
6. *Ibid.*
7. *Deseret News*, July 8, 15, Aug. 5, 26, Sept. 2, 1863.
8. *Ibid.*, Sept. 23, 1863.
9. *Biographical Directory of the American Congress*, p. 1169.
10. O.R., vol. L, pt. 2, p. 582.

11. *Ibid.*, p. 583.

12. *Ibid.*

13. *Ibid.*, pp. 583–84.

14. *Ibid.*

15. Brigham Young Letter Books, Church Archives.

16. *Journal of Discourses*, vol. X, pp. 250–51.

17. *Ibid.*

18. *Ibid.*

19. *Journal of Discourses*, vol. X, p. 254.

20. *Ibid.*, pp. 255–56.

21. *Ibid.*, pp. 266–71.

22. *Ibid.*, pp. 271–73.

23. Stenhouse, *Rocky Mountain Saints*, pp. 712–14; Leonard J. Arrington, *Great Basin Kingdom, an Economic History of the Latter-day Saints* (Cambridge, Mass.: Harvard University Press, 1958), pp. 201–2. For a brief summary of mining see also S. George Ellsworth, *Utah's Heritage* (Santa Barbara, Cal.: Peregrine Smith, 1972), p. 262ff.

24. Brigham Young Letter Books, Church Archives.

25. *Ibid.*

26. *Ibid.*

27. *Deseret News*, Dec. 16, 1863.

28. O.R., vol. L, pt. 2, pp. 655–56.

29. *Ibid.*

30. *Ibid.*, pp. 655–57.

31. *Ibid.*, p. 658.

32. *Ibid.*, pp. 658–59.

33. *Ibid.*, p. 668.

34. For a detailed history of the paper see Lyman C. Pedersen, Jr., "The Daily Union Vedette: A Military Voice on the Mormon Frontier," *Utah Historical Quarterly*, 42 (Winter, 1974), 40–47.

35. *Union Vedette*, Nov. 20, 1863.

36. *Ibid.*

37. *Union Vedette*, Dec. 18, 1863, and printed copy of Governor's Message in Utah Territorial Papers, U.S. Dept. of State, Record Group 59, National Archives.

38. O.R., vol. L, pt. 2, p. 711.

CHAPTER

XI

Gold in the Mountains?

☆

"GOLD! GOLD! GOLD! . . . GOLD IN THE MOUNTAINS! GOLD
IN THE ROCKS!! GOLD IN THE SANDS!!! GOLD IN THE STREAMS!!!!
GOLD IN THE CELLARS!!!!! GOLD IN THE STREETS!!!!!! GOLD IN
THE GUTTER!!!!!!! GOLD EVERYWHERE!!!!!!!!" heralded the *Deseret
News* of March 2, 1864.

But stop, we wish the public to know things as they are. In sober earnest
and truth, where is all this Gold? We presume, from what we hear, that it
is still tolerably plenty in California, very plenty in Washington, Idaho,
and Arizona Territories, and there is some in Colorado and Nevada Territories. But so far as Utah is concerned, after sifting all reports up
to present date, it is only in the hands of Madam Rumor, who is lavish-
ing her blandishments and loudly blowing her trumpet to deceive the
thoughtless into a waste of time and means. To some this may seem too
broad a statement, but where in all Utah's borders is there a single gold
mine being worked, or ever has been? Many of a certain class have
hunted, ransacked, tried to buy information, etc., etc., but where in Utah
is there either surface gulch, vein, or any description of gold diggins. Nowhere, unless the lean discoveries of gold in Egan Canyon are inside of
our western boundary. . . . But are there minerals in Utah? Yes, salt, coal
and iron, the most useful of all in a newly settled region, and some lead,
copper, and manganese.

Diametrically opposite was the voice of the new *Union Vedette*.
In an editorial on November 27, 1863, the army paper in "The
Mines of Utah—A Word to Our Farmers," announced, "The light
is dawning on the people of Utah! The day of prosperity, so long

deferred, is breaking and the unmentioned though cherished hope, whose fulfillment has for years been withheld, we believe is about being realized. The discovery of mines of precious metals near these great valleys and at the very hearthstone of this people, opens a wide field in the prospect of a near future of prosperity and increased wealth." The paper predicted that thousands seeking employment and wealth and new forms of investment for capital would come into the mountains of Utah.

The indications of the existence of silver, lead, copper, and in some places of gold, not far distant from this city, grow every day in number and importance; and when the opening of spring shall melt away the winter's snows, prospecting for these metals will receive a new impetus and, we are convinced, be attended with the most practical and successful results. . . . We would remind the farmers that those who will probably come hither with the early spring in search of the glittering ore, will look to these valleys for food, and it behooves him to prepare for the increased demand for the staples of life.

On the first day of 1864, the *Union Vedette* noted,

Brigham Young boasts he can see more gold and silver from the door of his house than would equal the whole currency of the world. These mines are not allowed to be opened! In 1849 we heard Brigham say: "If any body comes here discovering gold and distracting my people, as the Lord liveth, I'll cut that man's throat." If Brigham ever said it, we guess he has changed his mind about opening mines in Utah. The work is going bravely on and Brigham is too wise and foreseeing to even attempt to check the onward movement. . . . The opening of mines will now enrich and not impoverish or destroy them.

The *Vedette* was also concerned with the depreciation of Treasury notes which "has worked a great injustice upon the California Volunteers."

Thus a new conflict, at least of opinion, was rising between Connor and his troops and the Mormons. Both sides clearly overstated, owing to their poles-apart positions on mining in Utah—as on most everything else. The Church downplayed and basically feared the influence of mining for precious metals. Connor, clearly, was pushing mining to water down the Mormon influence. There is no doubt that he was over-optimistic, for precious metals in Utah never proved to be in great abundance, although the area was rich in other minerals.

Former Judge Kinney, as territorial delegate in Washington, undoubtedly reflected the view of the Mormons, although he was a Gentile, when on January 4, 1864, he wrote General Halleck and the War Department urging that the federal troops be withdrawn from Salt Lake City, and strongly defended the loyalty of the Mormons.[1]

Kinney wrote that the purpose of the federal troops in Utah was understood to be to protect emigration, the overland mail, and the telegraph. Kinney felt "the necessity for the troops in Utah does not now exist." Peace with the Indians prevailed, travel was safe. "This being the case, I cannot but believe that the object of the expedition has been fully accomplished." The removal of Connor's command "would very much accommodate the people I have the honor to represent." The delegate went on to say that the army used part of the farm crop which had been short, and the camp had contaminated the stream depended on by the inhabitants of the city. Also, the presence of the camp had shut off some livestock range.[2]

Kinney declared that Connor had expressed to him a wish to be sent east to fight, and added, firmly, "I know that the people of Utah are loyal to the Constitution and Government of the United States." He claimed that no one while he was judge refused to take the oath of loyalty: "I am aware that converse opinions impugning the loyalty of the people have been freely expressed and circulated, but such opinions are only entertained by corrupt, weak, or mistaken, or ignorant minds."[3] Did he include Connor in this view?

The *Union Vedette* was quick with comment on Kinney's letter, which leaked out:

Mr. Kinney's position among the Mormon population has never been more clearly defined, and some folks have regarded it as being decidedly equivocal. He was a long time Federal judge of the Territory, and for a while ranked as a Gentile. By some process, however, which has never been explained but which is probably pretty well understood by most people, the good folks hereabout woke up one morning and found that Bro. Kinney had been unanimously nominated for Congress, by somebody; and on another bright morning it was further announced that he had been duly elected with like unanimity. Like all new converts to either political or semi-religious faith, the delegate proceeds to show his devotion by the most extraordinary and radical course.[4]

General Wright in San Francisco also received a copy of Kinney's missive and recommended not only that Camp Douglas be maintained, but that it be strongly reinforced, for he had "but little faith in the loyalty of the Mormons."[5]

Connor, as was natural with him, replied at length to Kinney's letter. On February 15 he wrote Halleck that Camp Douglas was on public domain at least two miles from the nearest house and not in the city. "I recognized the supreme authority of the United States as existing here, however little it may be respected by the leaders or masses of the people."[6] He protested that the alleged annoyance to citizens by pollution of a stream was "greatly exaggerated" and felt the camp had to be located near the city "in the immediate vicinity of the headquarters of Brigham Young and his attendant nest of traitors."[7]

As to the delegate's letter, Connor wrote:

Mr. Kinney overstates the fact very considerably when he dwells on the loyalty and peacefulness of the people of Utah. They are bound down by a system of church tyranny more complete than that which held the bondsmen of ancient Rome in early days or now enthralls Africa's sons on the cotton fields of the South. The world has never seen a system of bondage, abject slavery, espionage, and constant, unremitting tyranny in the most trivial relations of life more galling than that [with] which Brigham Young oppresses the people in the name of religion. His teachings and those of his elders all tend to impress disloyalty upon the minds of his subjects and antagonism toward the Government, in which he recognizes neither authority over him nor goodness in itself.[8]

The longer Connor stayed in Utah, the more extreme became his language in describing the Mormons. But that was in part true on both sides, for the invective flew thick and the similes waxed more colorful.

Connor wrote of what he thought were Brigham Young's "outbursts of bold-faced treason." "Even now he and his chosen apostles, the minions of himself and the teachers of the people, can hardly conceal their inborn treason or repress the traitorous words which fill their hearts and break upon the ear in ill-concealed sneers and covert insinuations against the Government which fosters and protects them in their iniquities." He quoted from Young's sermon in the Bowery on October 6, 1863, a somewhat lurid portion not in the *Journal of Discourses*: " 'As for those who Abraham Lincoln has sent here, if they meddle with our domestic affairs I will send them to hell across lots, and as for those apostates running around here, they will probably fall down and their bowels will gush out, or they will bleed somewhere else.' " [9]

Connor called this sermon "innate treason, villainous hatred of the Government, and extreme vulgarity." To Connor the people were "ignorant and deluded" by the Mormon leaders. He felt the troops were the only reason the "wiley, traitorous, and treacherous leaders" had been suppressed for a time. Utah was a land of "polygamy, treason and kindred crimes," despite Kinney's statement. [10]

To remove the troops would be injurious to the government and would abandon thousands of citizens suffering "bondage" under the Mormons, Connor argued. He further said that often troops in the field could not buy forage or supplies from the Mormons. "The hypocrisy of claiming either loyalty or peacefulness for such a people is too palpable to require further comment," he felt. [11] Connor enclosed with his letter one of February 5 from twenty-six citizens—apparently mostly miners—of Franklin, north of Salt Lake City, quoting some of the anti-government statements supposedly made by the Mormons there. "It is a constant stream of burlesque against the Government and you and your soldiers," they wrote, and gave as examples statements such as " 'Thank God the buzzards are picking the bones of the U.S. Army,' " and references to the army as a " 'set of vagabond hirelings,' " who would soon be forced to leave Utah. [12]

Thus, while somewhat sublimated compared to early 1863, the rankling issues still remained. Connor's evidence is strong, in his view, but so is that of Kinney and the Mormons in their views. Definitions in such a supercharged atmosphere are obviously being used in different ways by both sides.

In a January 26 debate on confiscated property in the national House of Representatives, Fernando Wood, former mayor of New York City, who was at least a peace Democrat if not a Copperhead, commenting on proposed confiscation of Confederate property, characterized the Mormons as "profligate outcasts, who have been always hostile to your moral and political institutions." [13]

The following day Utah Territorial Delegate Kinney rose to take exception to Wood's dragging in the Mormons in his remarks on confiscation. Kinney accused Wood of "known sympathy with the rebels" and stated the reason Wood attacked the Mormons was "because the people of Utah are loyal to the Government, and have no sympathy with Rebels." He objected vehemently to the word "outcasts" and reiterated the loyalty of the people of Utah. He added that they "have never been in rebellion against this Government. They have not, as the gentleman from New York has, any sympathy with rebels." Kinney even suggested expelling Fernando Wood from the House. This met with some laughter. Wood, of course, was incensed at Kinney's remarks and denied his alleged disloyalty. It was, in short, a rather acrimonious debate.[14]

The *Union Vedette* continued to raise its voice in constant conflict with the *Deseret News* and the Mormon Church. It can never be known how many Mormon readers the *Vedette* had, but its message did not seem to be more than a slight irritant to the Mormon population. Quite naturally the *Vedette* kept playing up past Indian depredations and the need for the presence of the army. The issue of January 14 asked the public to contrast the present peaceful and happy condition of the people, under the protection of the army, with the situation of a year or two before. "The people of the settlements pursue their vocations in peace and quiet; prosperity smiles upon the land; the presence of the troops opens up to them a ready market for their produce; their flocks and herds roam without molestation through the valleys, and the mountains are giving up their rich stores of mineral wealth." This was somewhat overstating it, but conditions had improved, though passions and opinions, including those of the *Vedette*, still were often extreme.

The *Vedette* had become a daily paper on January 5, 1864. Now it was able to run more war news from the East, very often carrying "Yesterday's Dispatches." It also gave extensive coverage to the Utah Territorial Legislature. There was somewhat less opinion, but still a copious amount, often hidden in "news." However, in the new format the *Vedette* had become more of a "news" paper than it had originally been. Among its columns it covered the consideration by the legislature of an unsuccessful measure to force

Camp Douglas to move.[15] It told that the great comic lecturer Artemus Ward, a favorite of Lincoln's, was in Salt Lake City, but was seriously ill.[16]

On February 6 the *Vedette* announced the arrest of a "Judge" A. P. Smith who had been banished from Bannock, Montana Territory, by vigilantes and arrested under Connor's orders for being a "notorious and loud spoken secessionist, whose peculiar delight was to render noisy homage to Jeff. Davis, and cast contumely on 'Lincoln's hirelings,' [the army] when safe opportunity offered." Smith was released under condition that he left the Territory within a week and took the oath of allegiance.[17]

The *Vedette*'s slogan was "A Champion brave, alert and strong. . . . To aid the right, oppose the wrong." Two thousand people heard a recovered Artemus Ward give his lecture on February 8. Also printed in the pages of the *Vedette* were numerous complaints of inferior mail service.[18] But more important than the local news was a spirited defense of General Connor in the *Vedette* of February 10: "He approaches his subject in plain old Saxon words and says just what he means and means what he says, so clearly expressed that 'he who runs may read, and the wayfaring man, though a fool, understand.'" Neither General Connor nor Brigham Young was especially noted for his subtleties; both placed things pretty well on the line.

The *Vedette* continued February 10 to extoll the mining possibilities of the region: "There is the strongest reason to believe that the mountains of Utah abound in precious metals, and it is the wish of Gen. Connor and the interest as well of the people as of the government, that this mineral wealth should be early developed." The paper asserted that it had been the cherished policy of the Mormon Church to prevent discovery and working of the mines, but times were changing. Utah, because of being geographically on the great highway of the nation, and because of the believed mineral wealth, was "about to be transformed." The "great, busy Gentile world is coming to its doors from the East and the West. Isolation, once its favorite and cherished creed, can no longer be either its policy or its destiny, the dream of an independent, religio-political government if ever indulged in by the leaders of the Mormon church, is fast being dissipated . . . and the Territory, once a wilderness and a desert, is awaking to a new life." The *Vedette* put forth that the people were beginning to realize the new order and accommodate themselves to it. It was thought that the people saw the new economic opportunities as did the leaders of the Church. They all would, the paper predicted, "accept the fate—the happy fate—which progress presents to them. . . ." As to threats against the miners, the *Vedette* hoped these did not emanate from Church leaders, but, no matter what, the paper wanted to warn the people against the threats. The people should "repudiate those teachers as false prophets and unsafe guides."

One of the apparent threats against the miners occurred when the Territorial Legislature passed a mining act. This created a superintendent of mines who had the power to supervise all claims, locate them, set the extent of each mining district, establish boundaries of each claim and assess value for taxes. It also provided a 20 percent per annum tax on the assessed value of claims. Acting Governor Reed vetoed the act, feeling it would cut down on Utah mining development.[19]

On February 19 the *Vedette* took issue, probably inaccurately, with those who claimed that Connor's order inviting miners to come to Utah was a part of the conflict between the Mormons and the army. "We can discover no evidence of an unfriendly intent in it; but, on the contrary, the tone of the document is pacific, and such as the Mormons can take no reasonable exception to; nor are they likely to do so, unless the impression should be conveyed to their minds by outside interpretations that the order is intended to cover something not apparent on the surface."

Property prices were on the rise, according to the *Vedette*, having more than doubled during the previous few months and many permanent and substantial buildings were being built.[20] On March 2 the *Vedette* was of the opinion that the election of city officials in Salt Lake City was being railroaded; "somebody" was nominated by "somebody," "somebody" cast ballots and "somebody" was duly declared elected.

Brigham Young meanwhile was keeping Delegate Kinney posted and instructed. On February 3 he wrote, "The occupants of Camp Douglas continue to be very quiet, and in the main apparently not interfering in matters outside their camp, though there is more or less mingling between a certain class of residents and some of the sojourners on the Bench, of course of a character not very improving in its tendency to either party." [21]

He felt part of the quietude was because the army was having difficulty filling their larder. They had, he wrote, rejected the bids put in by Bishop Sharp when they advertised for supplies. But one of their accepted contractors failed, and so Brigham Young had requested Bishop Sharp to supply them with flour. "Depending upon us for flour very naturally . . . is in effect to put them in the channel of tolerably good behavior." Young continued to wonder how, with the great cost of the war, the government and the President could account for the expense of quartering troops in a peaceful and loyal city. He obviously suggested to Kinney that the subject of the troops was a proper one for the Joint Committee on the Conduct of the War. "If frauds, swindling, malfeasance in office, etc., etc., which are bleeding the Treasury at a fearful rate, are fit subjects of inquiry, then surely a leak so large and more than useless should be exposed to the public, that also may be speedily corrected in connection with other palpable abuses." [22]

As to mining, Young said that despite the hue and cry and hunting high and low "by the diggers on the Bench," as he now called the soldiers at Camp Douglas, he had yet to learn of a single particle of gold found within Utah's borders. He wanted the delegate still to work for statehood for Deseret: "God reigns, borrow no trouble, and only do your best." [23] Again to Delegate Kinney the Mormon president wrote, almost gleefully, on February 17 regarding the search for gold: "The diggers on the Bench have not yet found it, nor are they likely to, which, with their depending upon us for their daily bread, continues to keep them very quiet." [24]

For his part, General Connor on March 1 issued a circular complaining that there had been numerous complaints "that certain residents of Utah Territory indulge in threats and menaces against miners and others desirous of prospecting for precious metals, and the latter [are] asking what, if any protection will be accorded to those coming hither to develop the mineral resources of the country." Connor announced that all citizens of the United States and those who wished to become citizens "are freely invited by public law and national policy to come hither to enrich themselves and advance the general welfare from out the public store. . . . The mines are thrown open to the hardy and industrious, and it is an-nounced that they will receive the amplest protection in life, prop-erty, and rights against aggression from whatever sources, Indian or white." Once more Connor proclaimed the supposed mineral wealth of the Utah mountains, and declared that gold, silver, iron, copper, lead, and coal were to be found in almost every direction and in sufficient quantity to bring rich results to miners.[25] If vio-lence were offered or attempted against the miners in pursuit of their lawful occupation, Connor continued, the offenders would be tried as public enemies and punished. Likewise, the miners must not interfere with the vested rights of the people of the Terri-tory. Although troops had been sent to protect citizens from Indi-ans, they were also "present to preserve public peace, secure to all the inestimable blessings of liberty, and preserve intact the honor, dignity, and rights of the citizen vested by a free Constitution."[26]

Brigham Young reached the peak of his sarcasm and condemna-tion of General Connor that spring of 1864 when he wrote Dele-gate Kinney an amazing letter on March 7. After mentioning that the paper mill was running again and complimenting Kinney for responding to criticism of Utah and the Mormons, Young said, ". . . your interview with Secretary Stanton must have been quite amusing, but after all maybe the Secretary and General Wright imagined that the infringement of Camp Douglas upon the rights of citizens as to water, &c., is more than counterbalanced by the expenditure of greenbacks for the support of the diggers on the bench. If so, and if an extravagant expenditure of means and a reckless waste of human life, for little or no benefit are the subjects sought to be attained, then indeed is the General a very fitting commander."[27]

Young pointed out that by rejecting Mormon bids to supply flour, Connor was paying much more. He also censured Connor at Bear River: ". . . did not his conduct . . . prove his recklessness of human life?" And now a new tack: has not Connor's conduct ". . . so alienated the feelings of his command, that only some half dozen, at latest date, have responded to his solicitation to re-enlist?" Young concluded,

Now if Secretary Stanton and General Wright wish the funds of the Trea-sury squandered in high prices paid to residents in Utah, far from the seat of war, and wish a large body of troops kept inactive when they are so much needed elsewhere, it is no marvel that they do not remove the General and his diggers to where they and their cost may be of use to the country in this her hour of trial. Not that the General could probably be of much use any-where, for I am informed that he is so ignorant and oppressive that even the privates despise him, but those are, perhaps, in the estimation of the Secretary and General Wright, recommendations for his being retained here. All this plays into our hand—we are making money out of it. And I am told that as to their being loyal, some of his soldiers go so far as to hurrah for Jeff. Davis and indulge in other suspicious acts and proclivities, but perhaps that is all right in their case.[28]

There is no evidence that Connor's soldiers in any number were disloyal or that they had any especial dislike for their commander. Obviously, Connor's small command would not have made any appreciable difference in any of the major theaters of the war.

Young apprised Kinney of various local matters and again praised his conduct. Admission of Deseret still rested "with the mind of Him who directs the affairs of the children of men." While awaiting the result, Utah people would continue to observe the Constitution "and all good, wholesome and Constitutional laws, and shall endeavor, from time to time, as the Lord may open the way, to guide affairs to His honor and glory and consequent well-being of the human family."[29] It is interesting that Young wrote of the observance of all "good, wholesome and Constitutional laws" and apparently reserved to himself the decision as to which met his criteria.

In the same letter Young suspected that his mail was being opened and read, but he did not say by whom. He then repeated a favorite theme:

After all the hue and cry by the Bench diggers and others, up to date there are no gold diggings being worked in Utah, unless, perhaps the small discoveries in Egan Cañon prove to be within our borders; but from all accounts they are not likely to prove of sufficient extent or richness to be very exciting. The lead mine in the West Mountains is not proving very rich in silver, and only $27 to the ton being reported of its best assay, which will not pay for digging up the dirt and bringing it out; judging from their slack operations, it is creating no excitement, and that is the only mining in the Territory, that I have heard of, wherein they so much as claim getting even silver. Under these circumstances all designing to come here to dig for gold have been advised, in the "News," to bring their breadstuff, bacon and groceries with them, or the chances are that they may suffer through lack of food.[30]

Delegate Kinney spoke again in the House of Representatives on March 17. After a long, wordy description of the status of territories in general, with a good deal of historical background, he covered the founding of Utah and the vicissitudes the Territory had gone through. He recounted what the citizens of Utah had created in their once barren valleys. Kinney claimed that Utah had not been afflicted with the Indian wars other territories had because of the "peaceful, wise, and conciliatory policy pursued by Brigham Young."[31]

The purpose of Kinney's verbose address was to urge the passage of an act enabling Utah to become a state. He protested what he called discrimination against Utah after fourteen years as a territory. He claimed that the people of the area whose

whole heart beats in unison with the Constitution and Government, and who, if admitted, will be represented in Congress by those who will vie with the foremost in sustaining your nationality, I ask that you do not turn them coldly away and for the third time reject their petition and prayer. We come to you in friendship and in love. We offer you our devotion, our industry, our enterprise, our wealth, our humble counsels in the affairs of the nation in this the darkest hour of our country's history. . . . We offer you one hundred thousand people who can truthfully boast that in all their settlements is not to be found a drinking saloon, a billiard table, or a bowling alley, and who with pride point you to their cities, their churches, their school houses, their manufactures, their farms and possessions as evidence of their achievements and results of their industry. Will you accept the offering?[32]

Young continued his frequent letters to Kinney, which were really instructions, not from the governor but from the civilian Church leader. He told Kinney on March 19,

As to the Indian reservations, please amuse yourself and manage with them as you choose, for in reality I know of no one that cares much of anything about them, especially in the Uinta reservation. . . . But in all this, and in all they do about the public domain in Utah you will find a general, constant and persistent feeling to withhold from us the pre-emption rights so properly extended to encourage and foster settlers in other Territories, and that justice in land matters which has been so properly and generally conceded to others.[33]

Young wrote that Kinney undoubtedly understood there was "a disposition to clutch at a straw by way of excuse to keep us out of our rights." As to admission, Kinney was free to remind the President that the government had failed to put down polygamy by force and that the government was now trying to put down the other "twin relic," slavery. Young told Kinney he could pledge to them that when the administration had outlawed slavery and restored the Union as it was, the Mormons would agree to abolish polygamy. A rather strange statement by Young, and a promise he was not to keep, though perhaps his excuse would have been "the Union as it was."[34]

Young was still crowing over the lack of success of the "diggers on the bench" and claimed they could not make the people believe in their mining yarns. Miners who had wintered in Utah had already left for mines to the north and west. "So results that plan they built so much upon, and so will, doubtless fritter out all their plans for evil to Israel, and they themselves pass quietly and chagrined out of our Territory." Young was still obviously engaging in wishful thinking regarding the departure of the soldiers: Connor was an equal match in stubbornness to the Church leader.[35] In the same vein to Kinney, Young wrote on March 30 that he expected the troops to leave: "The plan for which they were sent here having failed, and their humbugging representations of gold discoveries in Utah being so easily seen through as to have comparatively no attention paid to them," they would no doubt be recalled to where they would be more useful.[36]

On April 11 Young told Kinney that the *Vedette* was lying with "palpable and baseless falsehood," regarding Young's words and actions in Utah.[37] It is dubious whether either the *Vedette* or the *Deseret News* was engaged in printing absolute falsehoods, but the two papers continued to battle in print, espousing the principles of their wide-apart constituents and backers. Looking wherever it could for gossip, the *Vedette* on March 21 railed about liquor. The paper was concerned over "whiskey alley" as it claimed the main street of Salt Lake City to be, and charged that much of the profit from liquor sales was pocketed by high officials of the city and Church, despite the Mormon stand against drinking. Any story connected with polygamy was exploited in the *Vedette*'s pages.[38]

As spring progressed, the *Vedette* was expecting an "immense influx of immigration early in the summer, from the East and from the West," to Utah and Montana.[39] Governor Doty did indeed write Seward on April 16, 1864, that he needed more help, such as a clerk and a messenger, as the miners were arriving in greatly increased numbers.[40] Adding variety to its "news" the *Vedette* occasionally found apostate Mormons to support in its pages. But its main aim that spring was to extoll the mineral possibilities of Utah, frequently and over-zealously. By March 30 the paper proclaimed once again,

that the entire Territory abounds in mineral wealth has been made by repeated analysis of specimens brought in by various prospecting parties in different parts of the Territory, so manifest as to be now beyond a peradventure. That miners and the attendant influx of population will swarm over the face of the country during the ensuing season, is as certain as that effect follows cause. . . . The days of isolation from any but the most meagre communications with the outside world are happily past, and the time fast approaching when we shall here in Utah be forced by circumstances to recognize fully and fairly our dependence not only upon the Government of which we do and must form an integral part, but also our amenability to the well established opinions of Christendom at large; and lest the disruption of prejudices implanted by unreasoning and quasi religious partisanship might be so sudden as to become dangerous, [it is] manifestly the duty of such as have influences in the community . . . to give heed to the signs of the times as well as to prepare the minds of the people thereafter.[41]

General Connor was continuing his own campaign to open up Utah. By the end of March he suggested to Army Headquarters in San Francisco that he was convinced of the necessity and importance of opening all-weather routes southward to the Colorado River via Fort Mojave, Arizona Territory, near what is now Needles, California. The department commander approved of Connor's proposal.[42] Therefore, Captain George F. Price carried out a lengthy expedition from May 9 to June 22 from Fort Crittenden to Fort Mojave, with a force of two officers, sixty-one men, and four six-mule teams, plus sixty-four government horses. At first the trip went well, the soldiers pausing to build a monument to the victims of the Mountain Meadows Massacre. But from Mountain Meadows onward the livestock began to fail. Soon half the men were barefoot and the animals were in forlorn condition. Fortunately, there was no trouble with Indians. Nevertheless, Price outlined for Connor a possible route. Yet, in the long run, little came of this proposed trail.[43]

With the advent of spring there seemed to be less direct conflict between the Mormons and the army or Gentiles, with the emphasis more on mines and transportation. The *Union Vedette* on April 4 proclaimed editorially:

We stand forth in this Territory, fully committed to and openly and fearlessly espousing the cause of the Union against rebellion and treason. . . . This is the first part of our mission; the second and main one being to show the people of this Territory in what direction lie their real and veritable interests; to arouse them from a certain listlessness and apathy which seems to have seized them, while neighboring and much younger Territories have far outstripped us, both in political influence and in material wealth and its attendant prosperity.

Interesting here is the *Vedette*'s failure to mention the army's role in protecting the trails, supposedly the main objective of the federal forces.

In April, however, the *Vedette* did take some notice of the Indian problem again and yet spent much space in derogation of almost anything Mormon. The editor, after a trip to Provo, wrote of

the character of the people and the peculiar institutions whereby they are governed. When we say "governed" we mean it, in its broadest, longest, most exaggerated sense. Never have we seen a community more docile, tractable and obedient to the behests of those appointed to rule over them—not by free suffrage, but by trust . . . the danger and evil of the system lies in the proneness of human nature to wrong and injustice. Could the people be assured that their leaders in whom they place such implicit trust are always actuated by pure motives . . . all might be well. But it is the evil in men's nature that makes the system in vogue so dangerous. And it is to this that we object most strenuously, and against the wrongful acts of men high in authority, we enter our solemn protest.[44]

In the same issue the *Vedette* reported that the Mormon military force was in readiness and guards were posted in various settlements. "We deem it proper to assure the people, that somebody is wantonly trifling with their credulity, and playing upon them. The people, honest, straightforward and sincere, have naught to fear from either the troops or the law. . . . Those who seek to raise up ill feelings against the soldiers who are here for their protection, or against the government which shields and blesses them, are bad men seeking their own interests and not those of the people."

A day later, on April 7, the *Union Vedette* printed what everyone knew: that as to polygamy and the anti-polygamy law, "There is ample evidence that this law is being violated throughout this Territory, if not daily, at least so frequently as to bring the reproach on the people that they are not a law abiding community. Thus it happens, that the wrongful acts of inconsiderate persons under the counsel and dictation of bad men, injure the reputation of the entire people, and give color to the charge which is blazoned to the world that all set at defiance the laws of their country, which fosters, guards, protects and blesses them." But, it was hoped in the near future that "blind obedience to evil counsellors" would end.

The *Vedette* accused the Mormon leaders of trying still to sow and cultivate distrust and fear of the army. Both sides should and could live in amity, except for the influence of the Mormon leaders. "You may expect evil counsels from them—but be ye not deceived," the paper advised the people. The government was their best friend, not those who "sowed discord."[45]

On a recent spring Church meeting, the *Vedette* commented, April 11, that it was strange and remarkable "during the entire session of the Brighamites . . . we could detect no hearty or even simulated expression of regard for our country, or sympathy with the Government in its gigantic and holy struggle against the rebellion. On the contrary, not a few of the public speakers, men who are looked up to to guide public opinion . . . indulge in coarse ribaldry against the Federal Government, and even chuckled malignantly over the horrors of the terrible civil war raging at the East." But the paper did praise the address of Elder Orson Hyde, president of the Council of the Twelve Apostles. On the other hand, it quoted Brigham Young in the Tabernacle on April 8 as saying, "They are fighting in the East; let them fight and be d——d! They cannot get any assistance from Utah."

Continuing its "coverage" of the Mormon Conference, the *Vedette* commented on April 15 on a speech of Elder John Taylor: "The whole speech is simply a tirade of abuse against the Government at Washington, members of Congress and Uncle Sam." Then, quoting Taylor, "'Uncle Sam has been making more territories out of portions of Utah. He wants more States to come into the Union. What did I say? Union? I mean the confusion. (laughter) They don't want us to come into the confusion. We would not consider it a favor to come in. . . . There is not that political freedom existing anywhere in the United States, that there is in Utah. There, Abraham can put his finger on the telegraph wire and cause men to be arrested and put in prison without a trial. But he can't put men in prison here, without a trial.'"

As usual, the dialogue was not one sided. Brigham Young on April 16 wrote to H. B. Clawson in New York City that he hoped the new commander of the Department of the Pacific, Irvin McDowell, who had succeeded Wright, would ultimately make changes in Utah, "which will . . . relieve our neighborhood of the presence of an idle soldiery, by placing them in some position, where their greatest ambition may be fully and entirely gratified."[46] Young expressed the same thing to Delegate Kinney on April 23.

As to the sojourners on the Bench I presume so long as they attend strictly to their own affairs, they will be un-molested; as hitherto, notwithstanding their infringement, in merely stopping where they are, upon the rights of many citizens. It is quite possible that the influence which pulled the wires for the appointment of McDowell in place of Wright may also have the effect to remove the troops outside our borders, or at least away from proximity to our settlements. If that should fail, it is likely some contingency will soon arise that will require their services elsewhere. . . . So far as all parties, and really all persons are concerned, madness rules the hour, and they will not listen to wise council until they have passed through many seasons of deep sorrow and sore affliction.[47]

On May 15 in the Tabernacle, in one of his frequent discourses, Brigham Young took the familiar religious ground once more: "The war now raging in our nation is in the providence of God, as was told us years and years ago by the Prophet Joseph; and what we are now coming to was foreseen by him. . . . If they will turn unto the Lord and seek after Him, they will avert this terrible calamity, otherwise it cannot be averted. . . . The time is coming when your friends are going to write to you about coming here, for this is the only place where there will be peace. There will be war, famine, pestilence, and misery through the nations of the earth, and there will be no safety in any place but Zion. . . . This is the place of peace and safety." He urged the people to buy flour and raise wheat so that when the multitude came, Utah would be able to feed them. "It is distressing to see the condition our nation is in, but I cannot help it. . . . The only solution was for the people en masse to turn to God and cease to do wickedly." They also must cease persecuting "the honest and the truth-lover." [48]

Turning to more temporal matters, Young wrote Daniel Wells in Liverpool on June 9 that the surveying party for the Pacific railroad was making good progress in Weber Canyon east of Salt Lake City. The same day he wrote Hiram Clawson in New York City that the troops were scattered about the mountains and affairs were very quiet. He did add that the army had opened a recruiting office in the city, "but in a few days removed it to Camp, not a person, as far as I have heard, having called upon the recruiting officer. All their evil efforts continue to be thwarted, consequently home affairs continue in their accustomed peaceful channel." [49] Weather was good in early summer and the prospects for crops excellent. Cotton was reportedly doing well in southern Utah. [50]

This tranquil atmosphere was not entirely confirmed by the *Union Vedette*. Continuing its attacks on the "Teachings of the Tabernacle," the army paper on April 18 rebutted:

With a few (and a very few) honorable exceptions, the entire tone of the addresses and instructions uttered from the pulpit during the late Conference of the Brighamites . . . has been, where not actively hostile to the Government of the country, at least null in regard thereto, and apathetic as to the result of the great struggle in which we are now engaged for the maintenance of human rights, liberty, and a free government. Nay, some have even gone further, and indicated both by words, looks, and tones, a grim satisfaction in narrating the defeats and mishaps of our armies, and when the facts would not bear them out, have knowingly called fiction to their aid in the dismal attempt to decry our Government and the efforts we have been making to uphold and perpetuate it.

However, the *Vedette* did say that it felt (and that meant Connor and the army) that "The people are, in the main, sound in their loyalty to Government; their interests are directly at variance with those of their so-called leaders. . . ." [51] The paper asked and answered the question: if the people with their incessant toil and labor had not been under control of the Church, what would have been the results? "You are fully aware that the same amount of hard work and unwearied industry, would, under other auspices and in any other portion of our country, have secured you comparative affluence."[52]

Connor used the paper on April 21 to caution the soldiers as to their "course and bearing" toward the people of Utah. He had seen with

just pride that officers and men, during our sojourn here, have manifested a proper spirit, such as becomes soldiers of the nation, and have refrained, in general, from retaliatory measures of conduct under provocation. But the General is apprised that it is the object of teachings of many of the leaders of the people to wean them from their love of country, and instill in their hearts bitterness and hatred towards the soldiers as the representatives of the Government. Bad men have sought and still seek to educate the mass of their followers in constant lessons of antagonism towards Government, and lead them to the very verge of open handed treason by covert sneers or bold denunciations. That these efforts have not been followed by their legitimate, if not intended results, redounds to the credit of the people, aided by the straightforward bearing of the soldiers of this command.

He went on to say, however, that it was enjoined upon the soldiers to refrain on all occasions from interference in any shape with the rights of person, property, or liberty of the inhabitants of Utah. He was relying on the basic intelligence of the mass of the people to overcome "evil disposed persons."

The general contended that as to the private relations, domestic practices, and methods of belief or religion of the Mormons, "you have naught to do, in your capacity as soldiers of the Union. However contrary these may seem to us . . . it is not our province to reform by violent measures, but to protect all, so long as they violate not the Constitution and laws of the country, in manner subject to military laws." The soldiers were ordered to report to headquarters any cases of real or imagined wrongs by civil inhabitants.

The *Union Vedette* did take time to announce on April 23 the organization of a Union Baseball Club, but it is not known whom they played. The spring of 1864 also saw the resignation of Judge Waite. He expressed considerable disgust after he held a term of court during which there was not a single case. Waite had become decidedly anti-Mormon. Judge Drake remained on for a few years but felt he was in a hostile community.[53]

The *Vedette*'s words became somewhat more heated in an editorial of May 5:

Things have materially changed in Utah now, and no one need want the protection of Government in the enjoyment of his belief of whatsoever kind, nor is it now necessary to leave the country in order to rid one's self of the leeches and blood suckers who have preyed upon the vitals of this community . . . the strong likelihood is that the aforesaid vampires will be most likely, unless they very greatly change their course, to have to flee before that most fearful of vengeances, the concentrated and settled wrath of an entire outraged community . . . if anybody must leave, the persons to do so are those who have, all along, duped the people to their own scoundrelly advantage; whom pure shame ought to drive from the sight of those they have so meanly and so grossly abused, and on whom (if shame have no effect) the law will mayhap yet have an opportunity of seizing to make them disgorge their ill-gotten gains . . . we cannot consent to see a whole community imposed upon and lorded over, without show of law or right, by knavish imposters and their satellites.

Yet, despite the occasional vitriolic outbursts, the army mouthpiece became more nationally oriented and less concerned with attacking the Mormons. In late May and June this was perhaps the case because the editors had been away. In fact, on June 18 the *Vedette* reported a great change for the better in Utah. The paper said there was an "increasing feeling of loyalty that is manifested by the people," notwithstanding that "all the underhanded influences possible are brought to bear upon them to keep up and influence a spirit of hostility to the Government under which they live, which has protected them and will continue to do so. . . . Every sensible man knows that no Government but this would for a moment tolerate the disloyal utterances—the by-times quasi hostile attitude or the illegal or criminal practices which are here indulged in (Heaven save the mark) dignified by the name of religion."

NOTES

1. *O.R.*, vol. L, pt. 2, pp. 715–17.
2. *Ibid.*

3. *Ibid.*
4. *Union Vedette*, Jan. 14, 1864.
5. O.R., vol. L, pt. 2, p. 778, Mar. 5, 1864.
6. O.R., vol. L, pt. 2, pp. 748–49.
7. *Ibid.*, pp. 748–51.
8. *Ibid.*, p. 749.
9. *Ibid.*
10. *Ibid.*, pp. 749–50.
11. *Ibid.*, p. 750.
12. *Ibid.*, pp. 751–52.
13. *Congressional Globe*, 38th Cong., 1st sess., pt. I, Jan. 26, 1864, p. 353.
14. *Ibid.*, pp. 372–74.
15. *Union Vedette*, Jan. 7, 1864.
16. *Ibid.*, Jan. 20, 1864.
17. *Ibid.*, Feb. 6, 1864.
18. *Ibid.*, Feb. 10, 1864.
19. *Ibid.*, Jan. 21, 22, 1864.
20. *Ibid.*, Feb. 20, 1864.
21. Brigham Young Letter Books, Church Archives.
22. *Ibid.*
23. *Ibid.*
24. *Ibid.*
25. O.R., vol. L, pt. 2, pp. 774–75.
26. *Ibid.*
27. Brigham Young Letter Books, Church Archives.
28. *Ibid.*
29. *Ibid.*
30. *Ibid.*
31. *Congressional Globe*, 38th Cong., 1st sess., pt. II, pp. 1170–73. Also John F. Kinney, *Speech of Hon. John F. Kinney of Utah upon the Territories and the Settlement of Utah*, Mar. 17, 1864 (Washington, D.C., 1864).
32. *Ibid.*, p. 1173.
33. Brigham Young Letter Books, Church Archives.
34. *Ibid.*
35. *Ibid.*, Brigham Young to Church leaders in New York City, Mar. 28, 1864.
36. *Ibid.*
37. *Ibid.*
38. *Union Vedette*, Mar. 25, 1864.
39. *Ibid.*
40. Utah Territorial Papers, U.S. Dept. of State, Record Group 59, National Archives.
41. *Union Vedette*, Mar. 29, 1864.
42. O.R., vol. L, pt. 2, p. 803.
43. O.R., vol. L, pt. 1, pp. 355–60.
44. *Union Vedette*, Apr. 6, 1864.
45. *Ibid.*, Apr. 8, 1864.

46. Brigham Young Letter Books, Church Archives. Young knew this in April, 1864, although it had been apparently talked of for some time. McDowell was officially assigned May 21, 1864, as in *O.R.*, vol. L, pt. 2, p. 850, and assumed command July 1, *Ibid.*, p. 886.
47. Brigham Young Letter Books, Church Archives.
48. *Journal of Discourses*, vol. X, May 15, 1864, pp. 294–95.
49. Brigham Young Letter Books, Church Archives.
50. Brigham Young to Joseph A. Young, June 17, 1864, Brigham Young Letters, California File, Huntington Library, San Marino, Cal.
51. *Union Vedette*, Apr. 18, 1864.
52. *Ibid.*
53. Bancroft, *Utah*, p. 621.

CHAPTER

XII

The Impasse Continues

☆

By MID-1864 THERE WAS an accelerating interest in the national elections of that wartime year. Both the *Deseret News* and the *Union Vedette* were full of news of the nominating conventions, the candidates, and the election itself. A third newspaper appeared in Utah at this time, the *Daily Telegraph*, with T. B. H. Stenhouse, formerly of the *Deseret News*, as editor.[1] The new paper took over the coverage of daily dispatches and "news" for the most part, while the *Deseret News* now largely handled Church news and policy.[2] As usual there was wide interest in local government issues as well.

A convention of Utah citizens met in August to solve a difficult problem pertaining to trade. The convention worked out what they called an "equitable proportionate scale of prices" both for producer and consumer. On August 17 the *Deseret News* reported the setting up of a list of articles and prices in gold for Utah markets. Flour was put at $12 a hundred pounds, wheat $5 a bushel, and corn $4. This was, in reality, a form of price control.

Brigham Young, after much comment on Church business and internal administration of the Territory, wrote to his son, Elder Joseph A. Young, in New York City: "Uncle Sam's prospectors on the Bench are mostly scattered in the mountains in search of Gold and Silver, but so far as I can learn, with a result so meagre that they would soon quit, were it not that they are better paid and treated by Government, while as occupied, than while lying in camp."[3]

But the activities of the army, and especially Connor, were many. The general reported to San Francisco on July 1: "The policy pursued toward the Indians has had a most happy effect. . . . They fully understand that honesty and peace constitute their best and safest policy. In consequence every chief of any importance in the district has given in his adhesion with profuse promises of future good conduct." Indian chiefs had visited Camp Douglas over the winter and had been furnished provisions when the Indian Department was unable to do so. Connor continued:

So far, then, as Indian matters are concerned I have to report peace throughout the Territory, and except the continued and frequent violation of the anti-polygamic law of Congress by the Mormons, and a covert and deep-rooted hostility to the Government by the leaders, affairs in this Territory may be said to be wearing a cheerful aspect beyond any former period. . . . The peaceful and happy condition . . . has enabled me to pursue most vigorously the policy heretofore indicated of settling the Mormon question by peaceful means in the early development of the undoubtedly rich mineral wealth of the Territory.[4]

Whenever military affairs did not interfere, the soldiers at Camp Douglas were allowed to prospect the country and to open mines. Troops had been disposed so that the Mormons could not interfere. Connor felt

the country already feels the beneficial influences resulting from such a course. Miners and others, Gentiles, are flocking hither in considerable numbers, and the day is not far distant when a loyal Gentile population, acting in concert with the now oppressed but dissatisfied saints, will peacefully revolutionize the odious system of church domination which has so long bound down a deluded and ignorant community and threatened the peace and welfare of the people and country. . . . If from any cause the quota of troops in this Territory should be withdrawn or permitted to fall much below the number now here the result will be disastrous indeed.

If troops were withdrawn or reduced, Connor felt, the Indians, incited by "bad white men," might erupt again, and the old system of Church despotism would revive in tenfold vigor, and mining would be checked if not stopped entirely.[5]

By July Connor was reporting to the new commander in San Francisco. On July 1, 1864, Major General Irvin McDowell had assumed command of the Department of the Pacific, succeeding

George Wright. McDowell had had a long career in the army, though his exploits in high command in the earlier years of the Civil War had been far from spectacular. Born in Columbus, Ohio, in 1818, he graduated from West Point in 1838. He distinguished himself in the Mexican War and from 1848 on had served largely in staff posts, rising to the rank of major. Through the influence of Commanding General Winfield Scott, McDowell was named brigadier general of volunteers and is best remembered for his defeat in the Battle of First Bull Run or Manassas in July of 1861. A major general of volunteers in George B. McClellan's Peninsula Campaign, his troops were involved in the conflict between Washington and McClellan. With John Pope at Second Bull Run, McDowell was relieved of his command, but was later exonerated of various charges. He never again served in the field. Following his duty on the Pacific Coast and after the war, he headed other departments, eventually becoming major general of regulars. He retired in 1882 and died in San Francisco in 1895. McDowell cannot be said to have been a great soldier, although he had been rushed into command and had been unfortunate in many other ways. Serious and earnest, with no political axe to grind, he was never particularly popular. The Pacific Department command was obviously a mild form of exile for one of his rank during a raging Civil War. At any rate, Connor was to find a different attitude at the San Francisco Headquarters.[6]

On July 9 Connor informed San Francisco that there was a "persistent effort on the part of a few merchants and traders doing business in Great Salt Lake City to institute a forced change in the currency of the Territory, viz, from national Treasury notes to gold coin." Connor said his first thought was to arrest originators and crush "so unpatriotic and suicidal a policy." However, he now asked the department for specific instructions. The only currency of the Territory had been legal tender notes, for there was very little gold and silver coin in the Territory. Connor felt the change to gold coin would enormously depreciate the current value of the national currency. Also, it would "disseminate among a suspicious people the opinion that the Government was fast going to pieces, and its pledged securities little better than blank paper. The efforts of bad men among them to sneer at the importance of the Government and depreciate it in any manner would be furthered, and our

great nation become a byword and reproach among a deluded
community, already deeply inoculated with enmity and disloyalty
toward it." He felt that unless drastic measures were authorized "a
very few disloyal and greedy merchants, owing and neither feeling
any allegiance to nor regard for the nation, may consummate a
most disastrous stroke in the forcible change of the currency."[7]

On July 9 Connor changed his mind that the depreciation of the
currency move had been brought about by certain merchants.
Now, he said, "It has since been rendered patent to all the world
that the real origin of the movement was Brigham Young the traitor head of the Mormon Church and people. On last Sabbath in
the tabernacle one of the twelve apostles, the supple tool of Brigham Young, announced to the congregation the new policy, and
counseled (which is here equivalent to an order) a gold currency in
contradiction to that provided by the nation." As we have seen,
the *Deseret News* had pointed out that a convention had been
called to establish prices under the new policy.[8]

Connor complained that the day after this meeting flour rose
from $15 to $23 a hundred pounds and was still going up. He
quoted from the *Deseret News*, "'Mechanics, laborers, producers,
and all concerned will understand at a glance that we deem greenbacks the most uncertain in value of all the commodities in their
possession, and we trust will govern themselves accordingly, lest,
though retiring at night with pockets overflowing with currency,
they awake bankrupt.'" Connor also told of Stenhouse's *Telegraph*, which, according to the general, was "really an offshoot of
the church organ." This paper, said Connor, daily engaged in
"puffing up the movement, insidiously . . . advocating gold as the
basis of trade, barter, and commerce. The word has gone forth to
the people from the tabernacle, from the church organ, and its little coadjutor, while the high priest of iniquity and hypocrisy is per-
ambulating the Territory, instilling the poison into the popular ear
and striking a most fatal blow at the vital interests of the Territory,
as well as at the currency of the nation." Connor then rose to the
heights of his invective, calling Brigham Young "a man hardly second in disloyalty and even intent to Jeff. Davis himself." He asked
again for instructions.[9]

On July 12 Connor wrote to San Francisco that he had taken
matters into his own hands, as was his wont, and on July 9 had

established a provost guard in Great Salt Lake City itself. The motives that impelled this course were that

The people of this Territory, under the implicit guidance of Brigham Young, are steeped in disloyalty and omit no opportunity of making display of it and injuring the Government by every means in their power. The recent gold currency movement . . . has its origin in the disloyalty of the church authorities, and their determination to depreciate the national currency. Wherever the arch traitor Brigham Young has been recently among the settlements instilling his poison in the minds of the people, Treasury notes are depreciated to a mere tith of their value, and in not a few instances refused and repudiated altogether. I am in hopes that the establishment of a provost guard in the city, under the command of discreet officers, may be beneficial in its effect of checking, if not defeating altogether, the machinations of those bold, bad men. In addition to this, it has long been apparent that there was necessity for such guard to take care of soldiers visiting the city, and to prevent noisy demonstrations of disloyalty by emigrants passing through to California and Nevada.[10]

Connor kept up his bombardment of San Francisco headquarters. On July 13 he telegraphed, "Encouraged by the unfavorable news from the East, the Mormons are assuming a very hostile attitude. They have about 1,000 men under arms and are still assembling, and threaten to drive my provost guard from the city; alleged excuse for armed demonstration, the presence of the provost guard in the city. My command is much scattered, having only 300 men at this camp. If conflict takes place, which I will endeavor to avoid, can hold my position until re-enforced from neighboring Territories."[11] By unfavorable news from the East, Connor probably meant the Grant-Meade campaign in Virginia, which, after heavy casualties, had not succeeded in taking Richmond.

Brigham Young naturally had something to say about the provost guard. He wrote Daniel Wells in Liverpool on July 16, "A few days ago Bishop Sharp rented the store opposite the South Gate of the Temple Block to Capt. Stover, for the use of the Commissary Department, and on Sunday the 10th inst., while I was in Provo, a skeleton company of cavalry occupied it as Provost Guard. This move being entirely contrary to the purpose for which the building was rented and altogether uncalled for, caused a little excitement, which, however, allayed soon after my return."[12] Young did not seem too concerned. However, it was estimated that Young, who left Provo for Salt Lake City almost immediately, had a 200-man escort and by the time they reached the capital it had swelled to 500 and then to perhaps 5,000 armed men. These figures may be high, but at any rate the Mormons had again rallied to the call, though nothing overt occurred.[13] Probably Connor had made an injudicious move, for this was the first time he had really occupied even a small part of the city itself, although there were claims that at least a portion of Camp Douglas was in the city.

The *Union Vedette* on July 14 took the opposite view from Brigham Young:

The establishment of the Provost Guard in the city—a measure not only universal in every loyal community near which troops are stationed, but one the necessity of which has long been apparent—has created quite a ripple on the surface. Without knowing all the real facts in the case, or giving heed to the thousand and one rumors which fill the air, we strongly suspect that a few individuals are doing their utmost to create a most unnecessary and ill-advised excitement in the community . . . they will on a very little reflection see how ridiculous is their present course, and appreciate the position in which they are placing themselves.

The paper continued, ". . . we think we can see much improvement in the present over the past."[14]

On July 15 Assistant Adjutant General Richard C. Drum, the able staff officer of the Army of the Pacific, wired Connor in response to his request for instructions, "The major-general commanding the department [McDowell] approves of your determination to avoid a conflict with the Mormons. Do so by all means. Is there not some other cause than the mere presence of the guard in the city? Examine closely. Remove the guards and troops rather than their presence should cause a war."[15]

On July 16 Drum answered Connor's several communications in detail and with tact, obviously concerned over the situation in Utah. Drum wrote that "the major-general commanding directs me to say that he has every confidence in your discretion and good judgment, as he has in your zeal and ability, and is certain he will not have to appeal to these high qualities in vain. The condition of affairs at Salt Lake as reported by you is very critical, not only as regards your own command, but as regards this department and the whole country." The new departmental commander, through Drum, went on:

The question is, are we at this time, and as we are now situated, in a condition to undertake to carry on a war against the Mormons—for any cause whatever—if it can possibly be avoided; not whether there are not matters that require to be changed, bad government and worse morals to be corrected, and the authority of the National Government to be more thoroughly enforced; but can we not pass all these by for the present, at least, and thus avoid weakening the General Government, now taxed to its utmost and struggling for its very existence. . . . To send you the forces necessary to resist the Mormons, much more to assail them, would require more means and men than could be gathered together and sent to you from this coast; to send away those which could be had would leave it in the hands of the secessionists, and that at a time the inhabitants are looking with anxiety to the troubled and critical state of foreign affairs. A war with the Mormons would be the opportunity which our domestic enemies would not fail to improve, and it is not too much to say that at this time such a war would prove fatal to the Union cause in this department. Under these circumstances, the major-general considers that it is the course of true patriotism for you not to embark in any hostilities, nor suffer yourself to be drawn yourself into any course which will lead to hostilities. It is infinitely better that you should, under the present circumstances, avoid contact with them. The object of troops being at this time in Utah is to protect the overland route, and not to endeavor to correct the evil conduct, manifest as it is, of the inhabitants of the Territory. This undoubtedly will tax your forbearance and your prudence to the utmost, but the general trusts it will not do so in vain.[16]

McDowell, however, issued no specific instructions because of his distance from the Utah command, thus leaving operations and strategy to the feisty Irishman.

The same July 16, however, Connor wired San Francisco:

The excitement is fast abating; any indication of weakness or vacillation on my part would precipitate trouble. The presence of the provost guard was simply the excuse for the development of the innate and persistent disloyalty of the church leaders, who seek to force me into some position which will secure my removal and a consequent overthrow of my policy in Utah. The removal of the provost guard under the circumstances would be disastrous in the extreme. My opinion is decided that a firm front presented to their armed demonstrations will alone secure peace and counteract the machinations of the traitor leaders of this fanatical and deluded people.[17]

On July 19 McDowell took action through Drum and wired Connor to remove the provost guard in the city of Salt Lake. "The necessity for posting a guard in the city is not apparent to the commanding general, while on the other hand much dissatisfaction may result from such a movement."[18] This was the first time that the department had countermanded an action of Connor's. Drum wired again on July 20: "The major-general commanding desires me to say that he does not at this day deem it expedient to interfere by military force to regulate the currency in the District of Utah."[19]

Connor responded to McDowell on July 24:

The wishes of the commanding general will be strictly complied with. . . . For manifest reasons some of the acts performed by me or things done may at a distance appear a deviation from the peaceful policy which is at once my own aim and the desire of the general commanding, but I beg leave respectfully to assure you that these acts have been at times absolutely necessary to insure peace, and certainly always, in my judgment, calculated to promote it. The commanding general by this time, I presume, fully understands that in case of a foreign war the overland mail would stand in far more danger from the Mormons than from Indians or other foes. . . . The presence of the troops here, while giving no just cause of offense, and without infringing in the least upon the rights of any citizen, is potent to prevent difficulties and obstructions which would assuredly result in war. The exhibition of firmness and determination, accompanied by a display of force will, I am confident, secure peace and prevent complications.

He felt the additional troops he repeatedly asked for would enable him to do all that was necessary. "So long as my guns command the city as they do, and the force under my command is not too much reduced, I have no fear and will be responsible for the result. Brigham Young will not commence hostilities, I think, and I need hardly say that I will not inaugurate them so long as peace is possible without dishonor."[20]

Drum in San Francisco on July 27 told Connor he could leave a small police guard of less than a company in Great Salt Lake City for police purposes connected with the troops. This guard was not to have anything to do with the Mormon question. The companies of the Third Infantry at Fort Ruby were to be relieved by a company from Fort Churchill and could be drawn in by Connor. Four companies of cavalry now at Fort Churchill would be sent to Camp Douglas to replace troops being mustered out.[21]

In early August San Francisco was concerned over a mild outbreak of Indian troubles east of Salt Lake City. Connor replied the same day, August 5, that all had been settled by him recently at Fort Bridger and he did not expect any further problem.[22]

Late in the month Connor went on a trip outside of Camp Douglas, which included seeing to his various posts, to the Indians, and to mining. He reported that all was quiet at Camp Douglas and "The furnaces in Rush Valley are a decided success. Much rejoicing among miners. Brigham left for a six weeks' trip to the southern settlements this morning to subdue the growing spirit of resistance to his authority. Tocsin of his downfall is sounding." Of course the wishful-thinking Connor was far from correct about any imminent downfall of the Mormon leader.[23]

A group of citizens in Austin, Nevada, complained to Connor about the need for a military force in that town: "Copperheadism and secession are rampant in this city, and as it is the first place of any consequence reached by the emigrants, the numerical force of those opposed to the Government promises to be in the ascendant."[24] Connor forwarded the request to department headquarters, recommending a detachment of cavalry be stationed at or near Austin.[25]

By August 31 Brigham Young could write to Daniel Wells that the mining operations of the soldiers continued to prove a failure, "so far as their object in them is concerned, their efforts to create disturbances still proving futile, and the terms of many about to expire, with only here and there re-enlisting. We have been and still are in hopes that circumstances will ere long require their presence elsewhere, without their having been able to accomplish any of the evil designs they were sent here to carry out."[26]

The flap over the provost guard in the city had died down and, again, as in 1863, the flow of messages, the frenetic statements, and the tensions quieted somewhat. The Indians were reasonably inactive and there was a little less friction between the army and the Mormons.

Connor had even decided he needed no more troops from California, and in October San Francisco ordered him to raise four infantry companies in Utah.[27] General McDowell on October 3 told Governor Doty that he had received authority from Washington to raise forces in the Department of the Pacific. McDowell hoped this move would find no opposition in the community.[28]

The *Union Vedette* showed this lowering of tensions although the underlying irritants remained. A writer for the paper expressed his annoyance when, on August 9, he said he was refused admission to the Tabernacle for a convention of the people. "Have not the Gentiles (so-called) as much interest in our own affairs as the most devout and obedient Saint? . . . Why, except to keep up the infernal deception that all the world are enemies of the Mormons, for opinion's sake, and delude the ignorant into the belief that they are in constant danger?"

There was a row at a theater in Salt Lake City in mid-August when a party of drunken citizens reportedly taunted the military patrol. The city police threatened to put them all in the lockup. One Joseph Eldridge, after the play, proclaimed himself "a Jeff Davis man all the time." Soldiers, not of the guard or on duty, struck Eldridge over the head with their pistols. They finally succeeded in arresting him, but the crowd objected and Eldridge broke loose. A civilian mistaken for the fugitive was struck over the head and someone fired a shot which wounded one of the rioters. The episode obviously caused some hard feelings, and perhaps some bruised heads, but it never got dangerously out of hand.[29]

The *Vedette* on August 19 said the poor and destitute whites and some Indians received food and other supplies from the commissariat at the camp. The military patrol had arrested one Charles Blake for freely proclaiming himself a Jeff Davis follower and "other like treasonable talk." He was sent to Camp Douglas "to undergo the punishment and wholesome discipline there prescribed for blatant traitors." The *Vedette* on August 23 reported an increase in highway robberies in adjacent states and territories and the paper warned against any resort to lynch law.

The voice of the army continued its attack on the Mormons in late summer and fall of 1864. On August 25 it was of the opinion that

We daily see instances of men engaged in a course of talk and action which is apparently calculated, and even ingeniously shaped, for the purpose of bringing final ruin upon themselves. Now, there are at the present time, men in this Territory, and prominent ones, too, who are by their conduct, day by day, "heaping up to themselves wrath against the day of wrath," and we are the more astonished (we can hardly say grieved) at this, inasmuch as many of them are persons who should possess that ordinary common sense which would enable them to see the folly of their course, and the imbecility of all puny efforts they can make in this out of the way corner of God's creation, to control events transpiring in the great world outside, which lives, moves and transacts its business unmindable for the nonce, and oblivious of the bickering and squabbling—the spurious revelations and *soi-disant* counsel—the covert treason and open disregard of law, which manifest themselves in Utah. . . . So too, these blatant revilers of our country, ought, if they reflect at all, to know that even though not animadverted upon now, every one of their disloyal utterances, and every unpatriotic act is recorded against them, to be brought up in judgment at a proper time, when everything coming thus together at once, will cause their shaky and even now tottering edifice of imposture, delusion and treason, to crumble down about their ears.

Even as late as August 25, 1864, large numbers of emigrants continued to pass through Salt Lake City en route west. Many were from Missouri, while a lesser number came from Iowa, Illinois, and Michigan. An army captain, Eugene F. Ware, who was out on the Oregon Trail, was very interested in the Mormons. Watching the emigrant trains, "he marveled greatly that there should be a religion which could make absolute slaves out of people and that the slavery would be such a change of conditions as could be enjoyable." By this he meant that their condition as Mormons was superior to their previous station. He described the foreign emigrants as having "the features and appearance of being persons who had had an exceedingly hard lot in life." Furthermore, he said the Mormons paid no attention to the Indians and did not even want any army guard: "There was a sort of Masonic understanding of some kind between the Indians and the Mormons which we never understood."[30]

Occasionally the telegraph broke down, so that the *Vedette* could not print the war news, but this was not frequent. In the fall of 1864 increased Indian troubles east of Utah, though not in the Territory, were a cause of complaint, according to the paper: ". . . these miscreants have been too long allowed to wanton in murder and robbery. They must finally be wiped out—it can readily be done—might have been done ere now, and should no longer be postponed."[31]

By September 8, the *Vedette* was once more fulminating about Brigham Young: "Again in this community every body knows what the term 'the church' means, viz, solely, exclusively, absolutely and irremediably, Brigham Young. In him at once it exists, 'lives, moves, and has a being.' Authority, counsel, prophecy, spirituality, temporality, power, continuance, etc., etc., all center in his person."

As to the army, the *Vedette* announced on September 15 that it was well supplied

with provisions (no thanks to the ring leaders of covert treason in this city) and with augmented instead of diminished numbers, the troops of this District will remain, and it is believed to be the intention of the Government, that they shall remain until the exceeding loyalty of the people, and their strict obedience to all the rules of the moral and the behests of the civil law shall render the presence of troops utterly useless for any purpose of enforcing law . . . while they remain in this Territory no overt act of treason can be attempted, and if attempted will be most efficiently treated.

The army paper admitted to some pessimism about the mining question on September 30: "That gold has only been found in limited quantities throughout the Territory, is therefore to be regretted. In various parts of Utah, silver mines have been discovered, almost illimitable in extent, and from the peculiar character of the ore and its susceptibility of being worked, of exceeding value."[32]

The *Vedette* continued to carry stories of minor incidents of friction between the populace and the military. In a saloon on Second South Temple a man named Williams asked the fiddler to play "Dixie." A soldier struck Williams, who was drunk, and the man later died in his hotel room. In October the paper reported that the mails were disrupted again between St. Joseph and Denver by Indian depredations.[33]

On October 14 Connor wrote to San Francisco asking for a leave of absence to go to New York City on private business. "I deem it proper," he wrote, without an overabundance of modesty, "also to add that the policy inaugurated by me in the conduct of affairs in this district has worked so beneficially and its results are now so apparent, that I am satisfied that the granting of this request at this time would not be detrimental to the public service."[34] But Connor was turned down. Instead, he was ordered on October 16 to suppress Indian depredations between Salt Lake

City and Fort Kearny, Nebraska.[35] Halleck on the 18th wrote Connor that the order was not intended to transfer troops or to change commands except where parts of different commands acted together.[36]

On October 30 Connor told San Francisco of his usual aggressive plans. He had received a wire from Governor John Evans of Colorado Territory: "I am glad that you are coming. I have no doubt the Indians may be chastened during the winter, which they very much need. Bring all the force you can, then pursue, kill, and destroy them; until which we will have no permanent peace on the plains."[37] This was nearly a month before the notorious Sand Creek Massacre in Colorado. Connor proposed sending Companies L and M of the Second California Volunteer Cavalry on about November 4 toward Denver. Connor himself announced he was going to Denver by stage to gather information and examine the field. Should a winter campaign be feasible "with a fair probability of severely punishing the savages, of which I now entertain little doubt, I will make such arrangements and dispositions of the troops as may be necessary, and immediately return to this post by stage." He proposed to return to Denver later to take personal command of the expedition. "There is no doubt that until the savages eastward of Denver shall have been thoroughly defeated and severely punished no permanent peace can be hoped for; nor can their frequent raids upon the overland route be prevented by any number of troops at the disposal of the Government." He trusted that his plans would meet with approval.[38]

McDowell waited until December 17 and then wrote Connor that he did not see that Halleck's instructions directed him to leave his district for the purpose of an Indian campaign. Connor was simply to give protection to the trail east. General Curtis's forces far to the east could handle the situation there, and Connor was wise to halt at Fort Bridger. McDowell wanted to avoid a clash of authority, which he obviously felt had occurred, and wished Connor to consult with him if he got orders from elsewhere.[39]

That same day McDowell wrote the War Department a letter which indicated that he and Connor were apparently not on the best of terms. Writing in response to Connor's request for leave, McDowell now approved of such leave, but he also took the opportunity to question Connor's statement that "the present quiet which reigns throughout his district is due to his policy." McDowell felt Connor was mistaken, and "had he been allowed to pursue 'his policy' this department would have been involved in war with the Mormons. General Connor bears the reputation of being an excellent soldier, and his ready acquiescence in the instructions I had to give him, checking the policy he desired to follow, shows his reputation is merited; but I think it only right and prudent that it be well understood to what the quiet his district now enjoys is due, lest by an approval of his policy trouble may come." McDowell said he delayed on the application for leave because Connor had gone off to Colorado with the object of a winter campaign against the Indians. He felt that Connor should not have left his district and that his orders did not include an Indian campaign east of the Rockies, but only temporary protection of the overland route. McDowell clearly believed that Connor had exceeded his orders. In a sense McDowell went over the department commander's head and almost sighed with relief in granting Connor leave.[40] Toward the end of the year there were reports of Indians stealing horses around and in Utah, but the major Indian tension in Utah for the war years appeared to be over.[41]

The fall saw an ever more confident Brigham Young. With his usual sarcasm he wrote on October 27 to the bishops north of Salt Lake City that about 160 discharged soldiers were on their way to California: "Bishops have you any chickens, pigs, calves and sheep in your settlement? Have you any women? and are there are any children running around in your streets? Take care of flocks. Take care of your wards."[42]

In a long letter to Delegate Kinney on November 3, Brigham Young was of the opinion that the season had been favorable to the emigrants to Mormon Utah and that everything was peaceable in Salt Lake City. ". . . the people on the bench are attracting but little notice—their importance is and has been decreasing daily." He felt that Lincoln would be reelected, though he added ruefully: ". . . but what encouragement is there for yourself, or for any other lover of his country, to take part in politics under present circumstances and in the present condition of the parties? Wisdom has fled and folly and madness have taken possession of men instead, and the sober man—the true patriot, who would fain lift his voice in tones of solemn warning and remonstrances to his countrymen, is silenced by the clamor of contending factions." He commended Kinney's "abstinence" from party discussion. Young was, as he had been earlier, worried about the army using water needed by the city. He also stated that "we," meaning the Mormons, would be willing to move the camp to some other point at their expense and also were willing to protect the overland mail.[43] Later he pronounced a specimen of silver ore Connor's men brought in to be just lead, and rather poor grade lead at that.[44]

Other Church leaders continued to reiterate the well-worn prediction of disaster to the east. Elder John Taylor in the Tabernacle on December 11 emphasized that ". . . when the nation with which we are associated is shaken to its centre and crumbles to pieces (it is pretty well shaken now, notwithstanding what our President seems to say about it, that everything is very prosperous, and that we have more men now than before the war), notwithstanding all this, it is crumbling and falling, and it will continue to fall and to crumble, until it is no more, and by and by there will be an end of it. Not so with the Kingdom of God."[45]

The voice of the army was still somewhat strident in the fall and early winter of 1864. Regarding the desire of Utah Territory to be admitted as a state, the *Vedette* on November 16 lectured frankly on a familiar theme: "Those who raise the outcry . . . know full well that the trouble interfering with the admission of Utah is a very different one, and that is not only to be expected, but is simply and positively out of the question that any Territory shall knock and be admitted as a State which includes in the provisions of its Statutes, the institution of polygamy as a feature in its laws or Constitution, or practice." And in this the paper was undoubtedly correct.

Again on December 14 the *Vedette* took up the statehood subject:

They know as well as we, that so long as the recorded laws of the nation are hooted at, spit upon and daily violated, not only with impunity, but by Churchly direction and counsel, it would be a burning shame for Congress to confer sovereign powers on "this people." They know, too, that while their church leaders and Saintly hierarchies each Sabbath indulge in public harangues whose burthen is abuse of the Government, ribald sneers at the loyal North, and vulgar tirades against all that pertains to American institutions, it is the boldest hypocrisy for them even to ask to be admitted into the Union of the States. When Brigham Young shall have ceased to instill into his deluded followers opposition to the Government and hatred of our institutions; when his teachers and apostles shall refrain of discoursing disloyalty, when, in fine, the leaders of the people shall manifest a single spark of genuine regard for constitutional authority, then may Utah look for admission, but not till then. So long as the affairs of the people of this Territory are controlled by a semi-theological, anti-republican, oligarchical system, not only at variance with our institutions, but implicitly wielded by men who are the avowed and unrelenting enemies of the Government and the Union, Congress will not be wheedled into granting a sovereign power to the Territory of Utah.

The *Vedette* also predicted that the forthcoming Territorial Legislature would repeal laws it thought unjust and substitute new ones "in harmony with the new order of things which now exist[s] in this Territory. Laws are required which will extend to all persons residing here, equal and exact justice." [46]

Governor Doty, in sending his annual message of December 12 to the legislature, wrote Seward that he wanted it shown to the President. "I desire him to see it that he knows that I do not provoke difficulties with this people. There are three powers governing this country, the Mormon Church, the Military and the Civil. It is difficult to prevent collisions, but they are to be avoided, if possible." [47] In his message Doty pointed out that the legislative power and authority of a territory was vested in the governor and legislative assembly. He congratulated the Territory on the discovery of coal, iron, lead, copper, and precious metals, and commended the peaceful and friendly conduct of the Indians. He wanted reservations designated soon. [48] It was an innocuous address and typical of the patient Doty, who was aware of the Mormon desire for home rule and was at least tolerant of it.

In further explanation to Seward on January 28, 1865, Doty reviewed the work of the legislature, making it clear that the Church leadership controlled all civil and militia offices except those appointed by the U.S. President. He reiterated that there were three distinct governments in the Territory. "In the exercise of their several powers collisions cannot always be avoided; but I am glad that I am able to state, that during the past year none have occurred. If each would confine itself strictly to its duties, the proper authorities of each would be undisputed, and no difficulty would occur." The Mormons also were still preserving the shadow of the prospective government which they had set up earlier.[49]

On January 30 Doty wrote to the State Department that the federal officers in Utah had determined that the public interest required a proper person be sent to Washington to represent the actual condition of public affairs in Utah. They had selected Secretary Reed to go. It was obvious that Governor Doty wanted some representation in Washington other than that of Kinney, the delegate to Congress, who really represented the Mormons.[50]

The *Vedette* of December 17 kept the pressure on, complaining of the words at the Tabernacle the previous Sabbath: "The Saints were indulged to the hearts content of the most insanely prejudiced and intensely bigoted, by Elder Cannon and Brigham Young." The paper quoted Young: "The North prays that their swords may strike into the heart of every rebel, and I say amen, and the South prays that the North may be cut down on a thousand battle fields, and again I say amen." The *Vedette* claimed it had been "reliably informed" that from "an hundred throats" and from "bench to bench" there was ringing concurrence. They quoted Young again as he prophesied: ". . . in nine months Utah would be as free of Gentiles as the President's Message is of references to Utah." The paper editorialized: "We would, however, advise the great High Priest that it is dangerous to his reputation as a prophet to be thus eternally prophesying things which never come to pass." And of course the Gentiles remained, as did the Mormons.

On December 21 *Vedette* editor Charles H. Hempstead retired. The new editor proclaimed on December 23,

If professed prophets of the Lord will so forget the dignity of their calling to indulge Sabbath after Sabbath in ribald vulgarity, if men-leaders of the people, who are, as our correspondent truly says, "living evidence of the mistaken clemency of the Government," will insist on abusing and misjudging the Government, if "pardoned criminals" have the unblushing affrontry to preach treason to a deluded people, and endeavor uselessly to draft this people into conflict with the Government, for their selfish purpose, we intend to print their disloyal utterances and brand them as they deserve.

On December 30 the *Vedette* pointed with pride, mainly for the Gentiles, to the slow but sure advancement in every branch of industry throughout this Territory. . . . Notwithstanding all these evidences of progression, we have been, by the Tabernacle dictators, declared an "abominable nuisance," a "pandemonium," and denounced as everything but friends and protectors. The command has borne it patiently. The troops have listened to ribaldry and vulgarity as preached by Brigham and Heber [Kimball]; they have been threatened with annihilation, and blamed with violations of law and order. Yet they still remain, and they remain firm too. . . . The truth cannot be denied that every branch of agriculture and trade has prospered through the instrumentality of us Gentiles, as we are called.

On the last day of 1864, the *Vedette* persisted in the same theme, claiming that

Change, improvement and progress, are marked on all sides, and the Utah of today is no more what it was one short year ago, than light is unto darkness. In the city the transformation has been not merely remarkable and apparent, but truly wonderful. A spirit of enterprise has taken firm hold on all classes of people. The slow plodding routine of yore, has given place to activity and true life. . . . Gigantic mercantile structures have taken the place of the one story abodes of former years; the market has been enlarged . . . mercantile houses have trebled in number; while bakeries, shops, book stores, periodical stands, and the thousand and one places—the accompaniments of civilized communities—heretofore unknown in these parts, have multiplied on all hands. . . . It is apparent "a change has come o'er the spirit of the dreams" of the entire community. Real estate has advanced a hundred, and in some instances two and three hundred per cent, and, as a whole, the people are prosperous beyond any former period in their history. So long as the absurd and impossible doctrine of isolation governed, so long did the people feel the burthens of their situation in constrained poverty and voluntary oppression. Now, that the outer world begins to mingle with them, bringing hither capital, enterprise, energy, liberality, and the spirit of progress—surely there are none so blind and callous as not to see and appreciate the beneficent results. The people, whatever the leaders may say, begin to suspect that the "Devil is not so black as he is painted," that "unbelievers" in Joe Smith and Brigham Young—ungodly Gentiles—are not such beasts of prey as they have been told; that there is at least a little virtue outside of Zion, and that, perhaps, some "good may come out of Nazareth."

Brigham Young also had his year-end say when he wrote Elder Charles S. Kimball December 31: "We have a good many gentiles here this winter but our arrangements are such that they cannot carry out their evil schemes against us. The Lord sits in the heavens and laughs at man's puny efforts to thwart his purpose and to render his word into promises of non-effect, and He will visit them with fierce indignation in His own due time." [51]

NOTES

1. *Deseret News*, July 6, 1864.
2. J. Cecil Alter, *Early Utah Journalism* (Salt Lake City: Utah State Historical Society, 1938), p. 298.
3. Brigham Young Letters, California File, Huntington Library, letter of June 17, 1864.
4. O.R., vol. L, pt. 2, pp. 887–88.
5. *Ibid.*
6. *Dictionary of American Biography*, vol. XII, pp. 29–30; Warner, *Generals in Blue*, pp. 297–99; O.R., vol. L, pt. 2, pp. 850, 860. McDowell's controversial career is covered in many other sources.
7. O.R., vol. L, pt. 2, pp. 889–90.
8. *Ibid.*, pp. 893–94.
9. *Ibid.*
10. *Ibid.*, pp. 899–900.
11. *Ibid.*, pp. 901–2.
12. Brigham Young Letter Books, Church Archives.
13. Gustive Larson, "Utah and the Civil War," p. 74.
14. *Union Vedette*, July 14, 1864.
15. O.R., vol. L, pt. 2, p. 904.
16. *Ibid.*, pp. 909–10.
17. *Ibid.*, p. 910.
18. *Ibid.*, pp. 912–13.
19. *Ibid.*, p. 914.
20. *Ibid.*, pp. 916–17.
21. *Ibid.*, p. 923.
22. *Ibid.*, p. 932.
23. *Ibid.*, p. 966.
24. *Ibid.*, p. 979.
25. *Ibid.*, p. 980.
26. Brigham Young Letter Books, Church Archives.
27. O.R., vol. L, pt. 2, p. 999.
28. *Ibid.*, p. 1000.
29. *Union Vedette*, Aug. 17, 1864.
30. Eugene F. Ware, *The Indian War of 1864*, intro. and notes, Clyde C. Walton (Lincoln: University of Nebraska Press, 1960), pp. 148–49.
31. *Union Vedette*, Aug. 31, 1864.

32. *Ibid.*, Oct. 3, 1864.
33. *Ibid.*, Oct. 8, 1864.
34. *O.R.*, vol. L, pt. 2, p. 1011.
35. *Ibid.*, p. 1013.
36. *Ibid.*, p. 1015.
37. *Ibid.*, p. 1035.
38. *Ibid.*, pp. 1036–37.
39. *Ibid.*, p. 1101.
40. *Ibid.*, pp. 1100–1101.
41. *Ibid.*, p. 1103.
42. Brigham Young Letter Books, Church Archives.
43. *Ibid.*
44. *Ibid.*, Brigham Young to Daniel Wells and Brigham Young, Jr., Dec. 5, 1864.
45. *Journal of Discourses*, vol. XI, p. 26.
44. *Union Vedette*, Nov. 25, 1864.
47. Doty to Seward, Utah Territorial Papers, U.S. Dept. of State, Record Group 59, National Archives.
48. *Ibid.*
49. *Ibid.*
50. *Ibid.*
51. Brigham Young Letter Books, Church Archives.

The Saints and the Union Endure

As THE YEAR 1865 OPENED, the situation in Utah was considerably calmer. The telegraph, the *Deseret News*, the *Daily Telegraph*, and the *Union Vedette* all brought the news that the Civil War was finally drawing to a close. The interest in the Union's progress in the East was even more intense than heretofore. There was no possibility now, even in the minds of the most ardent Mormons, that the North and South were going to wear each other out so that the Latter-day Saints might take over. The North was obviously more than ever vigorous, prevailing, and triumphant.

General Connor was still in disfavor, as it were, for his proposed operations east of Salt Lake City. As it turned out, he was really not needed, at least not yet. The mining operations were still creating excitement and much prospecting, but the results of these enterprises had certainly not been rewarding. Except for an occasional incident, the Indians in Utah were quiet.

But further east the situation was more eventful. On January 3 General Connor sent San Francisco a carefully worded letter saying he understood his orders to render protection to the trails between Salt Lake City and Fort Kearny without regard to district or departmental lines. "Recognizing the great necessity of early action and the speedy punishment of the savages who had then recently depredated so seriously east of the Rocky Mountains, I entertained the opinion heretofore expressed that the orders contemplated the movement of a part of my troops to the scene of difficulty, if practicable or deemed advisable, but that no transfer of troops or change of command was intended."[1]

Connor related how he had halted his troops at Fort Bridger and found that there was no necessity for further movement east. As to the idea of raising troops in Utah, Connor stated that Governor Doty had declined to raise volunteers in the Territory.[2] It was just as well that no real efforts were made to raise volunteers in Utah, for the success of such a step would have been more than dubious.

General Connor told San Francisco on February 10 that he had learned by telegraph from Fort Laramie that the Indians had returned to the trails and, owing to their depredations, it was probable that communications by stage and telegraph with the East would not be resumed for some time.[3] This also may have been Connor's way of saying he was prepared to deal with the Indians, but was not being allowed to do so. On February 25 he informed San Francisco that he had removed his troops from Camp Connor or Soda Springs north of Salt Lake City, for the community was sufficiently thriving to protect itself, and the soldiers who had been stationed there were needed to guard the Overland Trail.[4] McDowell, who continued to have less than cordial relations with Connor, did not approve of the Irishman's action, but said that, as Connor was no longer under his orders, he forebore to say anything.[5] For, on February 27 Connor sent San Francisco his new orders from Washington, dated February 24, assigning the Territory of Utah and West Nebraska to the Department of the Missouri instead of to the Department of the Pacific.[6] Nevada and Camp Ruby remained in the Department of the Pacific and District of California.[7] Connor would henceforth be under and report to General Grenville M. Dodge, Department of the Missouri, and also under John Pope, now in command of the Military Division of the Missouri.

With Brigham Young the issues were still the same: statehood, removal of the army, protection of Mormon rights. He was putting less emphasis now on the somewhat shopworn idea that when North and South had fought to exhaustion, the Mormons would take over. It was clear that the Confederacy was dying and that the Union would be victorious. On January 2 he wrote to Kinney in

Washington: "Respecting our admission as a State, it will be as I have always said, when the Lord wishes us to become a State, we will be admitted, and man's efforts for us and against us will be overruled for the accomplishment of that end." Young pointed out that while one reason for refusing to admit Utah was its lack of population, yet Nevada was admitted with a population of only 35,000 to 40,000, certainly less than the estimate for Utah. Then, strangely, and with perhaps a tinge of sour grapes, Young told Kinney, "We do not care about being admitted as a state, and I think it advisable for you not to ask for our admission as a state, nor the establishment of a Land Office, nor for the Indians to be removed. Utah will be admitted after a while and by the right Congress."[8] It may be that Brigham Young had his tongue in cheek in this case. Utah was not admitted as a state until 1896.

The *Union Vedette*, with its ready and often caustic word, was at it again, on January 3, still hammering away at polygamy: ". . . the propagandists of polygamy openly advocate, and persistently practice, in defiance of public opinion, a system of licensed prostitution, obnoxious to decency and virtue, and totally subversive of the fundamental principles of civilization, thus, not only offending the known laws of the land, but outraging that common sentiment of Christianity on which rest the foundations of all good government." The paper contended that Young's sermons were "shameless records of the fact, abound in the tirades of abuse of that Government of whose clemency he has been an unworthy recipient, and whose forbearance he has long since ceased to deserve. . . . Open defiance of the law, scoffings at the sacrifices of patriotism are daily indulged, and blasphemous prayers breathed . . . that the devastation of war may continue in our land until the letter of a certain favorite Mormon prophecy shall be fulfilled." Returning to polygamy, the paper asked: ". . . can anything be imagined better calculated to arouse utter indignation and bring on a conflict truly irrepressible? For, surely, if polygamy be right, then modern civilization is all wrong. . . . We call upon the people of Utah, who we would fain believe are law abiding, to beware how they allow themselves to be led by the vicious and designing into crimes, from the results of which they will as surely find themselves unable to escape as their leaders will be to relieve them."

By February 6 the *Vedette* asserted that the Mormons in their "harangues . . . argue that the nation will continue the war until nearly all the men are killed—that the women and children will come here begging for bread—that they (the Mormons) will inherit all the riches and fullness of the land and control the destiny of the United States." A fanciful prognostication, as a Union victory was all but assured in early 1865.

The Union paper charged on February 15 that the Mormon leaders were raising the old accusation of federal harassment and oppression.

These leaders have in past days, now counted by years, employed the same cry of persecution. Since they have added treason, rebellion and polygamy to their evil practices; and all they desire "is to be let alone." They expect a mighty and powerful people to permit the foul ulcer of polygamy to remain upon the body politic. They expect that loyal men will listen year in and year out to the treason they preach and not resent it. They expect that their advocacy of the shedding of human blood for the remission of sin will be approved by the silence of the community. They are sadly mistaken. If we mistake not there is a moral power in Utah that cannot be crushed.

Meanwhile the *Deseret News* was relatively quiet in the ideological struggle. On February 1 it proclaimed that prosperity was being enjoyed on every hand. It continued to report adversely on the search for minerals, but did admit to progress in coal mining.[9] Over these months toward the end of the war, the paper's tone was considerably less raucous, and it seemed almost to ignore Camp Douglas.

Brigham Young was now concerned more with the *Union Vedette* than with Connor, who was moving eastward. He felt the *Vedette* was getting

unusually bitter of late . . . too bitter to hold out for long; they will exhaust themselves for want of fuel, for it is very difficult to keep up a one-sided warfare such as they are waging. . . . If we would quarrel with them or notice them, it would be encouraging, and they would zealously keep on, being fed by the opposition with which they were met; but it is very annoying, after they have exhausted every invective and every species of vituperation and slander to find no spot so vulnerable that they can cause us to wince in the least or to even express the most trifling anger or vexation. Such contemptuous indifference has more effect upon them than the most elaborate arguments and replies would have. . . .[10]

While the policy of passive avoidance was not as thorough as Young expressed, it was there, at least by 1865. Undoubtedly Young was waiting for the now inevitable end of the war to see what would happen.

The Mormon leader wrote more positively to James Street at San Francisco on January 17, 1865.

You probably are aware that there are certain individuals here who are seeking the injury of the citizens of this Territory, and to produce a rupture between the General Government and our people. The person who is now in charge of the Eastern Line—The Pacific Telegraph Company's Lines is one of the right hand men of Gen. Connor, who is the principal man of this clique, and without doubt uses his position to aid their schemes by reporting to them such items, whether true or false, as suits their purposes. Camp Douglas has, I understand, been recently put in communication with the wires East and West . . . and every telegram that passes on any of the wires goes through the office at that Post. To say the very least that can be said respecting that arrangement, it must be pronounced very unwise and improper, and calculated to operate injuriously against the interests of the Company.[11]

On February 2 Young wrote to Daniel Wells and Brigham Young, Jr., reporting on the legislature of the Territory and on the legislature of the rump state of Deseret. Things were quiet, although the *Vedette* "howls dreadfully and bitterly." The same day he advised Delegate Kinney of reports that the routes east were interrupted by Indians and added:

The folks on the Bench have not yet achieved the fame for which they have so long panted. The obscurity into which they are forced, despite all their efforts to produce the contrary effect, chafes them, and their organ the Vedette, howls dreadfully and bitterly [a favorite epithet that day, apparently], and threatens us with dire vengeance; but these utterances excite not the least attention among our people, except to increase the contempt which is entertained for those who make such threats, and among the outsiders, the meanness and vulgarity of its articles disgust many who would like to be its friends. The course which has been taken with them annoys them more than any other plan which could be adopted. If we would quarrel with them, or notice them, it would encourage them, for they would then think they were galling us, but when after they have exhausted every invective and every species of vituperation and slander, they find no spot so vulnerable as to cause us to wince in the least or to express the most trifling anger or vexation. It is very discouraging; such indifference has a better effect than the most elaborate arguments and replies. . . .[12]

On the occasion of the second inaugural of Abraham Lincoln as President, March 4, 1865, a strange event occurred in Salt Lake City. The city authorities, undoubtedly with the approval of Brigham Young, put on quite a celebration and invited the army to take part. Governor Doty also had his role in the observance, issuing a proclamation of celebration.[13] It can be surmised that this was a genuine patriotic display, or it can be surmised that there had been a change of policy on the part of the Mormons. Perhaps it was a little of both. For the war was slowing to a close in spite of the dire predictions of Church leaders. Perhaps it was time to make an accommodation; certainly it was no time for continued overt conflict.

The *Union Vedette* commented on March 3,

We are glad to hear that a cordial spirit has been manifested by the city authorities in forwarding this patriotic ceremony, and that the civilians are determined not to be left behind by the military in the race of loyalty. This is certainly a somewhat unusual occurrence in our experience here, but is none the less welcome on that account. None could possibly be more pleased than ourselves in witnessing manifestations on their part, of a spirit which shows that Mormons have an interest in the welfare of the Nation, and not in the downfall, that they consider themselves a part of the Republic, and that their hopes and fears, like our own, are bound up in its destiny.

Actually the celebration had been planned for some time. Brigham Young had written to Daniel Wells on February 28 regarding appointment of a committee "among the folks on the Bench" to celebrate the capture of Charleston and the inauguration of the President. The City Council had approved and citizens were to participate.[14]

Young later told Wells of the March 4 observance in considerable detail. It went off quietly, he said, with a long procession. He played down the role of the army, observing that there were no more than 250 soldiers in the parade. There were lengthy orations from the parade stands, particularly that of Judge Titus which was, according to Young, very dull. "In no other city in the Union could such a crowd of people, variously estimated at from five to ten thousand, have been kept together so patiently under such circumstances to listen to such a speech; the speaker would have been cried down. The weather was cold and the people had to stand in melting snow and water for upwards of two hours during the proceedings." Afterwards the City Council prepared a "collation" which was attended by a number of the officers, including Lieutenant Colonel Milo George, First Battalion Nevada Cavalry, in command temporarily because of the absence of Connor. Then on March 7 the City Council gave a ball and the officers, including Connor, attended. Young commented, again to Daniel Wells, "The General was profuse in his acknowledgement of the honor which had been done him. What a change do we here behold. You know how loftily they held their heads, and how much they hoped to accomplish when they came here." The garrison numbers had dwindled and Young was clearly of the belief that he and his people had been triumphant.[15]

The *Vedette* outdid itself in flamboyant symbolism on March 4 when it proclaimed of the war: "The fearful ordeal is now nearly over and the Nation stands before the world to-day triumphant and threatening, in its just anger, towards the hungry harpies of despotism, that sought to compass its downfall and tear the carcass of their victim when destroyed."

Of the March 4 celebration in Salt Lake City, the *Vedette* declared on March 6 that it was vastly different from previous such events.

The entire procession was about a mile in length and presented a very imposing appearance. As it moved along the streets, broad and straight of the Mormon capital, the sidewalks wherever it passed, the windows and even the house-tops being thronged by eager and in some instances, enthusiastic lookers-on. The Bands awoke the wintry echoes with inspiring strains of music, appropriate to the occasion, and what with the profusion of flags floating from many buildings and ornamenting the teams and sleighs of the processions, or borne by the occupants, and rosettes, streamers, and the thousand and one other devices, in all of which red, white and blue, were the pervading colors, the city wore a gala appearance, which seemed to be participated in by all parties, and it was evidently the determination, on all hands, to make it a city of general rejoicing. . . . On the whole, the ceremonies at the City Hall were an appropriate culmination of the day's proceedings. . . . Like the procession, it was a union of the civil and military authorities of Utah, and passed off with eminent satisfaction to all concerned.

The *Vedette*, still a little apprehensive, noted on March 8:

We have a great diversity of opinion expressed as to the motives which dictated the recent loyal demonstrations among the residents of Salt Lake City. Many are not prepared to believe in such miraculous conversions from former apathy, not to say secret aversion, with respect to the successful issue of our civil revolution, for, that such has not all along been the condition of public sentiment in Utah, it would be difficult to convince those, who have carefully watched the under currents of opinion among Mormons.

Despite their doubts, the Gentiles were willing to accept the improved relations.

In printing Lincoln's second inaugural address on March 8, the *Vedette* asserted: "If we have heretofore denounced the leaders of the Mormon Church, it has been because we believed, that their purposes were wrong—pernicious to the welfare of the people, who follow their teachings, and unfriendly to the Government, whose power we represent and whose dignity it is our duty to defend and uphold."

Lee's surrender at Appomattox on April 9 was reported in the issue of April 11, which shows how rapidly news of important happenings was received. The *Vedette* on April 12 said that on the very day the telegraph announced the downfall of rebellion, Brigham Young said the war would continue for four years longer.

Then, sadly, as it did to all the nation, came the news of Lincoln's assassination: "The wing of the Death angel broods over the Capitol and his shadow has fallen upon all the land. There is consternation in the public places and the hearts of the people are appalled with a sadness that is something more than sorrow. Our banners droop low and the cities are clothed in the habiliments of woe. Nature herself is hushed to silence as though in sympathy with the National bereavement."[16]

With black borders on its pages, the *Vedette* April 18 reported that in Salt Lake City all places of business were closed at once when the news arrived, flags went to half-mast, and many houses were hung with the emblems of mourning. The theater was closed. "The citizens have done themselves lasting honor on this sad occasion, and we acknowledge the display of deep feeling on their part with the gratitude it deserves." The flags on Brigham Young's residence and other houses were at half-mast, and the Mormon president's carriage went through the town covered with crepe. On Sunday the pulpit of the Tabernacle was similarly draped. The *Vedette* on April 21 reported on the ceremonies at the Tabernacle where an immense concourse gathered and "religious differences for the time were ignored and soldiers and civilians all united as fellow citizens in common observance of the solemn occasion." Both a Mormon elder and the chaplain of Camp Douglas gave eulogies.

As to the army, on April 6 Connor had written St. Louis headquarters, stressing once more his trials and tribulations in Utah Territory and giving his evaluation of the Mormons. However, his tone was a little milder than it had been. Connor outlined, probably for the benefit of his new department commander, the history of the past two-and-a-half years in Utah. He said he found in Salt Lake City "almost exclusively members of the Mormon Church," bitter and unrelenting in their hostility to the government. Non-Mormons, he claimed, were persecuted. "The so-termed sermons delivered in their tabernacles, boweries, and ward meetings were models of obscenity and treason. It appeared as though every effort was made by the advocates of polygamy to destroy all that native modesty characteristic of a woman, and to instill into the minds of the men the most bitter and unrelenting hatred toward our Government." In Mormon eyes the war would continue, Connor said, until both sides were exhausted and then the Mormons would be in control of destiny. "The officers and soldiers of my command were regarded as blacklegs and scoundrels, and were so designated by Brigham Young. . . . The Indians were, I firmly believe, incited to acts of hostility against the mails and immigrants, for the purpose of involving us in a war, and, as we were but few in numbers, thus hoping to get rid of us." Connor claimed he had exercised caution, but was determined to maintain the authority of the government "at any and all hazards." [17]

He then outlined his activities against the Indians and described his attempts to develop the mineral wealth of Utah with a view to bringing in a flood of emigrants and thus eventually to "break up a system of religion and government at once infamous and abhorrent to every refined mind. . . . It is now a settled fact that the mines of Utah are equal to any west of the Missouri River, and only await the advent of capital to develop them." He was still overestimating considerably the mineral potential. He pointed out that in setting up the *Union Vedette* much had been done "toward redeeming Utah from the 'one-man power' of the Mormon Church."[18]

Summing things up, Connor continued:

While I have every reason to know that the leaders of it [the Mormon Church] are disloyal and traitors at heart, I have no fear of their taking any steps to produce difficulties between them and the troops. They content themselves with gasconade and such petty annoyances as they may be able to inflict upon the Government, in refusing to furnish from their abundance, supplies, etc. They daily violate the acts of Congress in the practice of polygamy, in the passage of laws violating the organic act and of others wholly opposed to the spirit of our institutions. The secret of the power of these leaders lies in this one word—isolation. So long as they were able to keep their people from association with the outside world they were safe. To this end they employed every means possible to force Federal officers (not Mormons) out of the Territory, and they succeeded well until the advent of the troops giving protection to those not belonging to the church; the establishment of a free press; the discovery of extensive mines, and the subjection of the Indians have gathered quite a large population of loyal men, who form the nucleus around which gather all the elements opposed to this infamous evil of our age, clothed with the name of religion.[19]

Connor had not changed his basic opinion of the Mormons, but was trying to present the achievements of his command. He was actually patting himself on the back to his new superiors, and was not altogether without reason for pride. He flatly stated that "all these changes are in progress for the better, and to know that notwithstanding I had to encounter all the opposition of the Mormon Church, my policy has proved successful, and that but a few years will elapse before Utah will be redeemed from her infamy and degradation and contribute a loyal and healthy support to our common country, instead of being, as she now is, a foul and filthy ulcer upon the body politic." Further, he maintained, erroneously, the Indians were not likely to cause further trouble, having been "thoroughly whipped."[20]

General Dodge forwarded this summatory document to General Pope and the Division of the Missouri. Pope sent it on to Washington with the comment: "It throws great light upon the condition of the Mormon settlements and the objects of the rulers of Utah."[21]

Connor on May 4, 1865, received a message from Lieutenant General Grant, through Aide-de-Camp C. B. Comstock: "It is not believed that an institution like Mormonism can exist permanently in force and close communication with the civilized world. Our efforts should therefore aim to make such communication safe by thorough protection of Gentiles against Mormons, whether as transient visitors or permanent settlers, and trust mainly to the ordinary laws which govern civilization for the gradual removal of what is believed to be in opposition to those laws and which can derive vitality only from persecution."[22] Grant could not have been more in error about the permanency of the Mormon Church. That Grant had not studied the Utah situation is clear; he was but reflecting Connor's views.

As the war wound down, the new commander of the recently established West Sub-District of the Plains, Lieutenant Colonel Milo George, on May 4, 1865, wrote to the headquarters of the District of the Plains in Denver that there was a system of espionage and interference with affairs of non-Mormons by Brigham Young and Church authorities. He went into the details of several incidents of assault and interference. George felt the presence of military force was needed to guarantee the personal security of "those who may have become obnoxious to the church dignitaries and the objects of dangerous persecution." Therefore, he felt the troops should be kept at Salt Lake City. There was no pretense now; the principal purpose of the army's presence in the city was clear.[23]

Brigham Young was also summing up at war's end. He still advocated a policy of feeding the Indians rather than warring with them.[24] And then, on May 15, he wrote to his son and Daniel Wells,

There has been considerable feeling manifest of late in certain quarters because measures are being taken to check the increase of iniquity and to cleanse all nuisance from our city and streets. . . . The corrupt and all the workers of wickedness are disturbed and uneasy, and they raise an outcry through their organ the *Vedette* about my teachings and reproofs. They would really like now that the war east appears to be off the hands of the Government, to have attention drawn to us here, and troops to be sent to break us up. They openly avow their intention to break the power of the priesthood and to destroy our organization, and since the receipt of the news of the surrender of Generals Lee and Johnston and the capture of Jeff. Davis, they have been very exultant and their tone is more arrogant and defiant than it has been. But the Lord Almighty has not surrendered, if Lee and Johnston have; and they who think that they have but to bring sufficient human force to bear against us to destroy us and the Kingdom of God, will find out, to their confusion and ultimate shame and misery, that He still reigns and He has the power in heaven and on the earth to accomplish I Iis purposes and fulfil His world.[25]

In mid-summer of 1865, Speaker of the House Schuyler Colfax, prominent newsman and reporter Albert Richardson of the New York *Tribune*, and leading editor Samuel Bowles of the Springfield, Massachusetts, *Republican* visited Salt Lake City. Bowles later wrote of an interview with Brigham Young in which he quoted the Mormon leader as saying, "'Now that peace is established, let all be pardoned,'" but he also told Bowles that "early in or during the war he would have disposed of the rebel chiefs who fell into the hands of the Government without mercy or hesitation. Had he been President when Mason and Slidell [Confederate Commissioners to Britain and France] were captured, he would have speedily put them 'where they never would peep,' and negotiated with England afterwards." Bowles said Young uttered this sentiment "with such a wicked working of the lower jaw and lip, and such an almost demon-like spirit in his whole face, that, quite disposed to be incredulous on those matters, I could not help thinking of the Mountain Meadows Massacre, of recussant Mormons, of Danites and Avenging Angels, and their reported achievements."[26]

As to the Mormons in general, Bowles wrote, ". . . we all saw that the time had come for a new departure, for a new policy by the Government. The conflict of sects and civilization, growing up there in Utah, will soon solve the polygamous problem,—rightly and without bloodshed,—if the Government will make itself felt in it with a wise guardianship, a tender nursing, a firm principle."[27] He was full of praise for the accomplishments of General Connor, and added, "Mr. Colfax's reception in Utah was excessive if not oppressive. There was an element of rivalry between Mormon and Gentile in it."[28]

"The Mormons," he wrote, "are eager to prove their loyalty to the government, their sympathy with its bereavement, their joy in its final triumph—which their silence or their slants and sneers heretofore had certainly put in some doubt—and they leave nothing unsaid or undone now . . . to give assurance of their right-mindedness. Also they wish us to know that they are not monsters and murderers, but men of intelligence, virtue, good manners and fine taste." Bowles was optimistic regarding the mining opportunities.[29]

Describing Brigham Young during his visit, Bowles wrote: "He is a very hale and hearty looking man, young for sixty-four, with a light gray eye, cold and uncertain, a mouth and chin betraying a great and determined will—handsome perhaps as to presence and features, but repellent in atmosphere and without magnetism. In conversation, he is cool and quiet in manner, but suggestive in expression; has strong and original ideas, but uses bad grammar. He was rather formal, but courteous, and at the last affected frankness and freedom, if he felt it not."[30]

In a later account, combining both his 1865 and an 1868 trip, Bowles wrote that "Brigham Young is the head of everything; all tributes pour into him; all authority flows from him as the center of church and state. He dispenses favor; he administers justice and injustice; he receives the revenues, and he spends them,—both without any apparent accountability; the best farms are his; the largest saw-mills, the most prospering manufactures; of all the good things, whether women, or lands, or forests, coal mines, or contracts, he has, if not the monopoly, certainly the first choice, and the disposition of all."[31]

The U.S. Army still occupied Camp Douglas and there were still suspicions as to the Mormons' loyalties. Major General John Pope, in command of the Department of the Missouri, in a general survey as to conditions in his vast department, particularly regarding Indians, wrote to Washington on August 1, 1865:

All of the tribes of Indians east of the mountains, and many west, are in open hostility. . . . Protection is thus required along 3,500 miles of road, nearly all of which lies in an uninhabited country, and yet over which are daily passing the U.S. mails to the Territories and the Pacific, crowds of immigrants, and great trains of supplies for the mining regions, as well as individuals and small bodies of travelers. The threatened difficulties with the Mormons in Utah also demand attention, and the civil officers appointed for that Territory by the government, as well as the citizens of the United States now there and going there, absolutely need military protection to enable them to remain in the Territory at all.[32]

Probably Pope exaggerated in the case of the Mormons, but his words do show the army's continued concern.

Thus the Civil War era came to an end in Utah Territory, as it did in the rest of the nation, to which Utah now more than ever belonged. It ended with no sensational events in Utah. No date marked a radical change in the Territory, nor was there an immediate alteration in leadership. There were two real victors and no real loser, unless it was the Indians. The Church of Jesus Christ of Latter-day Saints thrived and continued to do so, if somewhat altered. Still, many of the troublesome issues remained. The United States, in the painful throes of Reconstruction, was put back together, also altered. The lines of communication with the West had been sustained by the Union in Utah, except for occasional Indian interruptions. The honor and integrity of the nation were preserved, the Indians in Utah were somewhat restrained, and over all there was an enhanced sense of unity.

Brigham Young and his Latter-day Saints remained in control, but grew more mellow and flexible in the face of the inevitable. Young continued to rule the Church and, in reality, Utah, with his usual pragmatism and astuteness, until his death in 1877. There were, of course, apostates, but not in sufficient quantity or strength to be a major threat to the Church. The backbone of the faith and of Young's power and authority was a maleable and devoted populace. This was the rock on which the Church and the theocratic state of Utah had to be built. The Civil War years with their vicissitudes had not decreased Young's authority or his faith. He had often been wrong in his predictions during the war years. The exhausted nation had not flocked to Zion from the North and South after tearing each other apart, as he so often prophesied. The army had not been withdrawn, the United States did live, and

Lincoln had proved that a leader could carry out the principles of the Constitution so often extolled by Young and the Mormons.

The inaccuracy of Young's predictions did not detract from his dominion over his followers. He was proving that a religious-political state could exist successfully within the United States. He had consistently defended the rights of his people, but with sufficient pliancy and skill to enable the Church to continue, not only to exist, but to grow, expand, and further develop. For the converts were continuing to arrive. He had trod a narrow, shrewd, and careful course in his actions, if not always in his words, during the war years. And it was always the results, not the contradictions in the record, that concerned Brigham Young.

Governor Doty, who had kept to a middle course in the conflict between the Mormons and the federal presence in the Territory, died in June, 1865. He had been able, liberal, and tolerant, in conspicuous contrast to most of the other often incompetent federal officials in Utah. As Indian agent, always a difficult role, he had been a success. As governor, he had taken some of the sharp edges off the Utah politicians and leaders on both sides. Speaker of the House of Representatives Colfax, in Utah at the time of Doty's death, summed him up with accuracy when he wrote that the governor was "A most judicious executive and the best this Territory ever had, who performed his delicate and responsible duties with firmness and yet with discretion."[33] Perhaps a measure of his success was seen the day of his funeral: the city of Salt Lake was draped in mourning.[34]

As commander of the District of the Plains in 1865, which included the merged districts of Utah, Colorado, and Nebraska, General Connor campaigned in the unsuccessful Powder River Indian expedition against Sioux, Cheyenne, and Arapaho. As a result of this abortive and controversial campaign, Connor was removed from command. Somewhat bitter, he went back to Utah and resumed his command there. On March 13, 1865, he had received the brevet rank of major general of volunteers, and on April 30, 1866, he was honorably mustered out of the volunteer army. He turned down a colonelcy in the U.S. regulars.[35]

But Connor continued a very active life both in Utah and in California, with his principal residence in Utah. Both in and out of the army, Connor facilitated the melding of Utah into the mainstream of the Union. It probably did not seem ironic to Connor that he stayed in Utah despite his wartime vituperation and contumely against the Mormons. He was always a man with an eye to opportunity. Although his idea of watering down Mormonism by an influx of miners seeking mainly for precious metals failed in the long run, he himself never gave up the idea of mineral wealth. In Utah he founded several smelting companies and invested in mines. A capable general, he cannot be said, on balance, to have been entirely successful either as a businessman or politician, though he was clearly dedicated to Utah in his own way.

Connor continued to be the leader of the anti-Mormon movement, and he did become involved in politics in the immediate postwar years. It was a long while before the 10–15 percent Gentile population of Utah in the 1860s grew large enough to be a political power, but Connor tried to give the minority a voice in public affairs. For it was clear that under the territorial system, with federal appointments and some financial advantages, the minority had more political influence than its small percentage of the population would seem to merit.

Connor did introduce electric lights into Utah, owned the first steamboat on Great Salt Lake, as well as a schooner, and was termed, with justification, the "First Gentile of Utah."[36] Connor seemed to be a natural soldier, with some of the attributes of an accomplished administrator, although at times he was undoubtedly too heavy-handed and too willing to think and write the worst of the Saints. His handling of Indian affairs was generally effective in keeping communications and transportation open. Had he not had a sense of public relations—when to be intransigent and when to be pliant—Utah could easily have become an armed battleground between federal authorities and the Mormons, with all the complications and tragedy inherent in such a conflict. Perhaps his ambition and impetuosity sometimes got the better of his perspective, but, in the broader picture, his contribution to his new homeland was considerable.

General Connor died in 1891 and was buried at Camp [now Fort] Douglas. By the time of his death, substantial understanding and amelioration of passions were being expressed in the *Deseret Evening News*. His obituary, which ignored his many controversies with the Mormons, was headed: "Conquered at Last." The paper said of Connor that "He was a natural soldier, and would, no doubt, have gained great military prestige if his lot had been cast in wider fields with larger opportunities for the exercise of his military talents. He was a man with much force of character. His faults were those of common humanity. . . . General Connor will remain a notable figure in Utah history and he will be remembered as a brave and gallant soldier."[37]

There was always something of the restless soldier of fortune in Connor; he was continually seeking, with intensity and drive, but not always finding, not always successfully completing his many assigned tasks or fulfilling his personal dreams.

Both during the war and afterwards, there seems to have grown up a certain mutual respect between Brigham Young and General Connor, both indisputably men of character and principles. In 1871 Brigham Young and others were arrested for "lascivious cohabitation." Connor is said to have offered to furnish $100,000 bond for the Mormon leader.[38] Young later was reported to have said, "Men have been here before him; to our faces they were our friends; but when they went away they traduced, villified and abused us. Not so with Connor. We always knew where to find him. That's why I like him."[39]

In sum, it can be postulated that Connor was headstrong (though not to the point of recklessness), that he was opinionated in the extreme, and always controversial. There is some indication that his almost monomaniacal harping on and exaggeration of what he thought were Mormon "evils" may have been an unconscious effort to build up the importance of his own duties. Obviously he yearned for service in the more spectacular theaters of war where his Celtic passions and pugnacity could find much more obtrusive exposure. He seemed to enjoy the continual jousting with Brigham Young. As his statements grew more and more shrill, the army and general government had seen fit to put some restraints upon him, difficult as this was to do to a man of Connor's near-paranoid fanaticism regarding the Latter-day Saints. It seems certain that at times he misapprehended the purpose of his assignment in Utah.

Yet his toughness, combined with a degree of flexibility when pragmatism dictated it, his willingness to work for peace with both the Indians and the Mormons, in the long run worked. Connor had a job to do, was determined to do it as he saw it, and in the main he was a credit to the leadership of the United States in the crisis years of the Civil War.

As to Abraham Lincoln, from the extant records it seems that the President had little directly to say in writing about the Mormons. Yet we know from the letters of the Utah territorial delegates and others that he was aware of what was transpiring in Utah, and in his careful way worked around the thorny aspects of the situation. He and the federal officials had more important events to be concerned with, but the problems of the West and Utah were not neglected in Washington. Lincoln can be blamed, but no more than most nineteenth-century presidents, for the appointment of political hacks to high territorial posts. But a more judicious selection of appointees probably could not have been expected during the hectic and tension-ridden days of the Civil War.

The Mormons themselves were suspicious of Lincoln and critical, particularly in the early days of his presidency. It is possible that they held him in even greater disfavor than remaining written documents indicate. There was a slow evolution toward a favorable viewpoint, which seemed to accelerate after Lincoln's story about "ploughing around them" gained currency. With the second inaugural and the assassination, Lincoln's image among the Mormons reached a new high, and the martyred President now resides firmly in the pantheon of Mormon heroes.

It is evident that the Mormon Church remained viable, powerful, independent, and very much alive, although it had to bend at times to change its position. It will undoubtedly continue to do so. By 1865 the Mormon Church, and therefore Utah, was moving toward "Americanization." The self-sufficient, entirely local self-rule and economic independence of the Mormons were of necessity beginning to break down. The opening of the West, east-west communications, technological advances, and the Civil War had proven that this policy of isolation had to end. The coming of the railroad in 1869 would further erode Mormon insularity. Yet there were compensations for the Mormons. Always alert to business opportunities if they did not interfere with Church policy, the Mormons obviously profited from the emigrants, the telegraph, and the stage lines. There were even economic benefits from their supposed enemies—"the army of occupation" and the miners.

The emigrants and stage users were transient and were not a serious threat to the purity of the Church and the community. The army and miners were somewhat more permanent and thus constituted an increased threat. This threat had to be and was met, somewhat reluctantly, by facing the inevitable with vision and enterprise.

It is obvious that the federal authorities and most of the northern populace did not understand the Mormon position, and probably could not have been expected to do so in view of the emotionalism generated in the 1860s at the mere mention of Mormonism or polygamy. That there was during the Civil War no overt action by the Mormons that could be called treasonous or pro-Confederate is also obvious after the fact, but in the overheated crisis days of the conflict even rumors of disloyalty were taken seriously. And the widely accepted image of the Church which has been created over the years, particularly in print, gave some ground for suspicions, founded or not. The North could take no chances with a population that might possibly turn out to be perfidious, given the vital geographical position of Utah and Salt Lake City. Furthermore, the Union had to be vigilant in the light of rumors, again overblown, of a threat of Confederate invasion of Utah from Texas and New Mexico. And there was anxiety, in the end needless, over the alleged dangers to California.

Talk of foreign invasion, Confederate takeover, even the setting up of an independent nation were rife in California during the war. Political policies and military operations often have to be undertaken, not in the light of reality, but in the mist of what appears to be, whether accurate or not. It is clear that if the communications through Utah had been disrupted, the Union would have had enormous difficulty in rerouting the telegraph and the trails farther to the north.

The Mormon Church once more had conquered adversity and withstood assaults upon it. Yet the events and the bitter words of the 1860s pale when compared with the cruel and unwarranted persecutions they had survived in the past.

Utah Territory and its people were now at least somewhat integrated into the nation and faced a future of development from within and without. Isolation was being eroded, albeit slowly. All the antagonism and invective aside, a form of reconstruction had taken place in the West and in Utah during the war, and it was continuing. Both sides had waged a war, more of words than of overt action. Nevertheless, a kind of internal warfare it had been, with strategy and tactics of invective and psychological skirmishing instead of bullets and shells. Victories had been gained and defeats sustained by both sides, but in the end the march of events, both in Utah and elsewhere, had brought about unwritten and sometimes subtle compromises.

It is in fact surprising that there was so much compromise, though it is seldom given that name. But compromise it was, nevertheless, largely unspoken and unnegotiated. Yet the principles of Connor and Brigham Young remained unshakable, and both, despite obvious faults, served their faiths and their nation well. It was not a case of ineptitude or lack of leadership on either side; it was, instead, perhaps a case of too much leadership from the top, one buttressed with the power of religious faith, and the other with the power of the army and the government. Both men deserve much credit for avoiding the armed conflict that would have been disastrous to both Church and state.

To some it is strange that Utah and the Mormons did remain loyal in view of their past persecutions. But, there was nothing better offered to the Mormons by the Confederacy. They were realists, most of the time, and reality was the United States. And that reality included the rights of the Mormons and their religious-political state, both within the Union and within the Church, rights guaranteed to all Americans. Treasonous and rebellious they were not, but polygamous they were, and this, almost singly, was the reason the Mormons had been harassed and were viewed with almost universal suspicion.

It is highly probable that if, upon passage of the federal anti-polygamy law in 1862, the Church had disavowed the institution, Utah would have become a state during the war; with polygamy intact statehood was impossible. The Mormons themselves appeared, or wanted to appear, unable to understand this attitude on the part of the rest of the country. There were also misgivings among non-Mormons over the close ties of the Latter-day Saints Church and the state in the Utah Territory. But even that probably would have been overlooked had it not been for polygamy. And it must be remembered that the Mormons were not really aligned with any political party. They constituted in a sense their own party and held a tight control over elections.

As we have seen, there is no reliable evidence that the Mormons had any significant relations with the Confederacy. The myths and rumors of emissaries coming to Utah from the South, which have persisted over the years, have little substance as far as research shows. The generally held opinion in the North, both in the 1860s and in the years following, never seemed able to advance beyond the concept that if the Latter-day Saints appeared to be disloyal, they must, ipso facto, be pro-Confederate. They had to be all one thing or the other. While in some ways the Mormon Church, consciously or unconsciously, seemed to foster this image of disloyalty, it was an inaccurate image. The often repeated theory of Mormon leaders that the North and South would fight to exhaustion and then their people turn to Zion as a last refuge could be interpreted as subversive of the Union, whereas it was, at worst, naive. This seeming disloyalty, which in its broadest sense was really loyalty to the principles of the United States, needs understanding. The Mormon passion for self-decision and self-government in everything, both religious and secular, made them, perhaps, admire the South. But in the long run both North and South had opposed the Mormons' faith and persecuted their people. Both North and South were, in the Mormon view, trying to destroy the Constitution which was to them a sacred document, as they so tirelessly professed. The Church had not given up its independence, yet the process of the melding of the Saints into the nation had begun and had gained momentum. By 1870 the shadow government of the "State of Deseret" had quietly faded away.

The Mormons were loyal—loyal to the United States and to the Constitution as they saw it, loyal to Brigham Young, to their Church, and to their God. That there were at times conflicts in this loyalty there can be no doubt, but it was loyalty that won out in the long haul.

Despite some Mormon rhetoric, there was no federal attempt nor intention to destroy the Mormon Church. If this had been federal policy, it could easily have been done, albeit at great cost, and with tragic results. There had been no organized or unorganized Copperhead movement in Utah. The very occasional shouts for Jefferson Davis in drunken revelry or in anger were mostly voiced by transients and Gentiles, often miners heading elsewhere. There never were the pro-secessionist, peace-democrat, or similar movements of an anti-Union character in Utah. In fact, there was never as much anti-Union, pro-Confederate sentiment in Utah as existed in the neighboring lands of Arizona, Nevada, Montana, or Colorado.

It is greatly to the credit of the American people, even under the unprecedented stress of civil war, that the ideas of tolerance and human freedom had triumphed, altered, perhaps, but still victorious.

There was in Utah, to be sure, the attempt to water down the power of the Church by bringing in non-Mormons or Gentiles to seek gold and silver in the not-very-productive mines. But this movement had a long way to go to achieve any appreciable dilution of the population. The army, which really meant the Californians, brought in an anti-Mormon faction, but its tenure was transitory. The Mormons had a firm grip on affairs in Utah, one which they did not loose.

In the long run, despite Mormon opposition, the bringing in of the volunteer army in 1862 and the establishment of Camp Douglas was a wise move on the part of the Union. The Union could spare the small number of troops and the telegraph and the trails were protected. The secondary though never officially stated purpose, of watching the Mormons, also seemed prudent in the light of the times, although Connor took it upon himself to carry it too far. It might have been better to have tried to raise official U.S. volunteers in Utah, but that would have had little chance of success given the posture and control of the Church. The experiment of using the Utah people as Mormon militia had been successfully tried in 1862 on a short term basis but those temporary troops were in reality controlled by Brigham Young and not by the federal government. There had been in Utah no draft and only feeble efforts at enlisting citizens into the federal volunteer army.

While the role of Utah during the war years is generally neglected, with at most a passing mention in Civil War and western history, it was consequential in the broader overview of the Civil War. For intimately linked with it were questions of religious liberty versus national loyalty, some rather touchy legalities, the essential maintenance of transcontinental communications, the problem of the Indians, and the uninterrupted tide of national development. Yet Utah Territory appeared on the surface to be a mere backwash of the Civil War and was so considered at the time—when it was considered at all. The issues of that localized conflict were in no way comparable to the war in the East. Still, Utah Territory was a key part of the nation and the nation's history by the mere accident of geography. There are lessons to be learned from its peculiar role, its unique position and distinctive institutions, its singular struggle, and its dominant and colorful personalities.

What had occurred, and even what had *not* occurred, in Utah and the mountain West are a part of the Civil War story. There would be troubles to come in Utah, but the course had been set. There had been little bloodshed except in the Indian fights; no battles, except of words, had afflicted the contending factions. The integrity of the West as a part of the nation, of Utah, and of the Mormon Church had been preserved. Perhaps it can be said that it was no longer "the Saints *and* the Union," but "the Saints *in* the Union."

NOTES

1. *O.R.*, vol. L, pt. 2, p. 1112.
2. *Ibid.*
3. *Ibid.*, p. 1131.
4. *Ibid.*, p. 1145.
5. *Ibid.*
6. *Ibid.*, p. 1147.
7. *Ibid.*, p. 1148.
8. Brigham Young Letter Books, Church Archives.
9. *Deseret News*, Jan. 25, 1865.
10. Brigham Young Letter Books, Church Archives, Brigham Young to Daniel Wells and Brigham Young, Jr., Jan. 12, 1865.
11. Brigham Young Letter Books, Church Archives.
12. *Ibid.*
13. Tullidge, *History of Salt Lake City*, p. 332.
14. Brigham Young Letter Books, Church Archives, Brigham Young to Daniel Wells and Brigham Young, Jr., Feb. 28, 1865.
15. *Ibid.*, Mar. 13, 1865.
16. *Union Vedette*, Apr. 17, 1865.
17. *O.R.*, vol. L, pt. 2, pp. 1184–85.

18. *Ibid.*
19. *Ibid.*
20. *Ibid.*, p. 1186.
21. *Ibid.*
22. *Ibid.*, p. 1221.
23. O.R., vol. XLVIII, pt. 2, pp. 315–16.
24. Brigham Young Letter Books, Church Archives, Brigham Young to President Orson Hyde, Apr. 16, 1865.
25. Brigham Young Letter Books, Church Archives.
26. Samuel Bowles, *Across the Continent* (Springfield, Mass.: Samuel Bowles, 1866), p. 113.
27. *Ibid.*, p. vi.
28. *Ibid.*, pp. 28, 83.
29. *Ibid.*, p. 95.
30. *Ibid.*, p. 86.
31. Samuel Bowles, *Our New West* (Hartford, Conn.: Hartford Publishing, 1869), p. 215.
32. O.R., vol. XLVIII, pt. 2, pp. 1150–51, Aug. 1, 1865.
33. Larson, "Utah and the Civil War," p. 77.
34. Bancroft, *Utah*, p. 622; *Deseret News*, June 21, 1865.
35. For summaries see *Dictionary of American Biography*, vol. IV, pp. 352–53; Warner, *Generals in Blue*, pp. 87–88; Rogers, *Soldiers*, p. 146ff.; Utley, *Frontiersmen in Blue* (New York: Macmillan, 1967), pp. 322–32.
36. Whitney, *History of Utah*, vol. II, p. 215; Bancroft, *Connor*, p. 27.
37. *Deseret News*, Dec. 18, 1891, as in Journal History, Dec., 1891.
38. Whitney, *History of Utah*, p. 113.
39. Salt Lake *Times*, Dec. 18, 1891, as given in Rogers, *Soldiers*, p. 250.

Bibliography

I
Manuscripts

Ackroyd, Walter. Record. Church Archives, Church of Jesus Christ of Latter-day Saints, Salt Lake City, Utah.

Bernhisel, John M. Papers. Church Archives, Church of Jesus Christ of Latter-day Saints, Salt Lake City, Utah.

Cutting, A. Howard. Journal of a Trip by Overland Route from Illinois to Sacramento, 1863. California File, Huntington Library, San Marino, Cal.

Governors' Papers. Utah State Archives, State Capitol, Salt Lake City, Utah.

Hooper, William. Letter. Church Archives, Church of Jesus Christ of Latter-day Saints, Salt Lake City, Utah.

Journal History. Church Archives, Church of Jesus Christ of Latter-day Saints, Salt Lake City, Utah.

Letters of Application and Recommendation during the Administrations of Abraham Lincoln and Andrew Johnson, 1861–1869. U.S. Department of State. Record Group 59, National Archives, Washington, D.C. Also microfilm M650, National Archives and Records Center, Denver, Colo.

Letters Received. U.S. Department of the Interior. Office of Indian Affairs. Record Group 75, National Archives, Washington, D.C. Also in National Archives and Records Center, Denver, Colo.

Lincoln, Abraham. Papers, including Robert Todd Lincoln Papers. Library of Congress, Washington, D.C.

Nevins, Allan. Research notes, "Utah and the Union." Allan Nevins Papers, Columbia University Library, New York City.

Taylor, John. Papers. Special Collection, Marriott Library, University of Utah, Salt Lake City.

Telegrams and Letters Received, 1861–65. U.S. War Department, Division and Department of the Pacific. Record Group 93, National Archives, Washington, D.C.

Utah Territorial Executive Papers. Utah State Archives, Salt Lake City.

Utah Territorial Legislature Debates. Utah State Archives, Salt Lake City.

Utah Territorial Papers. U.S. Department of State. Record Group 59, National Archives, Washington, D.C. Also microfilm in National Archives and Records Center, Denver, Colo.

Woodruff, Wilford. Journals. Church Archives, Church of Jesus Christ of Latter-day Saints, Salt Lake City, Utah.

Wootton, Francis. Appointment Files. U.S. Department of State. Record Group 59, National Archives, Washington, D.C.

Young, Brigham. Letter. Private Collection of Theron Luke, Provo, Utah.

Young, Brigham. Letters. Beinecke Rare Book and Manuscript Library, Yale University, New Haven, Conn.

Young, Brigham. Letters. California File, Huntington Library, San Marino, Cal.

Young, Brigham. Letter Books. Church Archives, Church of Jesus Christ of Latter-day Saints, Salt Lake City, Utah.

Young, Brigham. Office Journal, 1858–63. Church Archives, Church of Jesus Christ of Latter-day Saints, Salt Lake City, Utah.

Young, Brigham. Brigham Young Folder. Miscellaneous Manuscripts, Library of Congress, Washington, D.C.

II
Printed Official Records

Congressional Globe. U.S. Congress. Senate. Washington, D.C., 1860–65.

Dole, William P. "Report of the Commissioner of Indian Affairs," Nov. 26, 1862. *Executive Documents.* U.S. Congress. House of Representatives. 37th Cong., 3rd sess., 1862–63. Washington, D.C., 1863.

Doty, James Duane, Acting Superintendent of Indian Affairs, Utah Territory. "Report of James Duane Doty," Oct. 24, 1863, in "Report of the Commissioner of Indian Affairs." *Executive Documents.* U.S. Congress. House of Representatives. 38th Cong., 1st sess., 1863–64. Washington, D.C., 1864.

Harding, Stephen S. "Message to the Territorial Legislature of Utah,"

Dec. 8, 1862. *Senate Miscellaneous Document, No. 37.* U.S. Congress. Senate. 37th Cong., 2nd sess., 1862. Washington, D.C., 1863.

Kinney, John F. *Speech of Hon. John F. Kinney of Utah upon the Territories and the Settlement of Utah,* Mar. 17, 1864. U.S. Congress. House of Representatives. Washington, D.C., 1864.

Orton, Richard H., Adjutant General of California. *Records of California Men in the War of the Rebellion, 1861 to 1867.* Sacramento, Cal.: State Printing Office, 1890.

"Report of the Committee on Territories," Feb. 13, 1863. *Senate Committee Report, No. 87.* U.S. Congress. Senate. 37th Cong., 2nd sess., 1863. Washington, D.C., 1863.

Report of the Secretary of War. U.S. War Department. 37th Cong., 2nd sess., 1861–62. Washington, D.C., 1862.

U.S. Department of the Interior. Office of Indian Affairs. *Annual Report of the Commissioner of Indian Affairs.* Washington, D.C., 1862–65.

War of the Rebellion, a Compilation of the Official Records of the Union and Confederate Armies. Washington, D.C., 1880–1900.

III
Major Newspapers

Daily Alta Californian, Sacramento, Cal.
Deseret News, Salt Lake City, Utah.
Millennial Star, Liverpool, England.
Napa County Reporter, Napa City, Cal.
San Francisco *Bulletin.*
San Francisco *Chronicle.*
Union Vedette, Camp Douglas, Utah.

IV
Books, Collected Works, Pamphlets, Articles

Alexander, Thomas G. *A Clash of Interests, Interior Department and Mountain West 1863–96.* Provo, Utah: Brigham Young University Press, 1977.

———. "A Conflict of Perceptions: Ulysses S. Grant and the Mormons." *The Ulysses S. Grant Association Newsletter* (Carbondale, Ill.), 8 (July, 1971), 29–42.

———, and Leonard J. Arrington. "Camp in the Sagebrush: Camp Floyd, Utah, 1858–1861." *Utah Historical Quarterly,* 34 (Winter, 1966), 3–21.

Allen, James B., and Glen M. Leonard. *The Story of the Latter-day Saints*. Salt Lake City: Deseret Book Co., 1976.

Alter, J. Cecil. *Early Utah Journalism*. Salt Lake City: Utah State Historical Society, 1938.

———. *Utah, the Storied Domain*. Chicago: American Historical Society, 1932. 3 vols.

Anderson, C. LeRoy. "The Scattered Morrisites." *Montana, the Magazine of Western History*, 26 (Autumn, 1976), 52–69.

———, and Larry J. Halford. "The Mormons and the Morrisite War." *Montana, the Magazine of Western History*, 24 (Autumn, 1974), 42–53.

Anderson, Nels. *Desert Saints, the Mormon Frontier in Utah*. Chicago: University of Chicago Press, 1942, 1946.

Arrington, Leonard J. *Great Basin Kingdom, an Economic History of the Latter-day Saints*. Cambridge, Mass.: Harvard University Press, 1958.

———, and Thomas G. Alexander. "The U.S. Army Overlooks Salt Lake Valley, Fort Douglas 1862–1965." *Utah Historical Quarterly*, 33 (Fall, 1965), 327–50.

———, and Davis Bitton. *The Mormon Experience, a History of the Latter-day Saints*. New York: Knopf, 1979.

Bancroft, Hubert Howe. *Biographical Sketch of General P. E. Connor*. San Francisco: n.p., 1887. Microfilm of typescript of pamphlet in Bancroft Library, University of California, Berkeley.

———. *History of Utah, 1540–1887*. San Francisco: History Co., 1890.

Barrett, Gwynn. "John M. Bernhisel, Mormon Elder in Congress." Ph.D. diss., Brigham Young University, Department of History, Provo, Utah, 1968. Copy in Church Archives, Church of Jesus Christ of Latter-day Saints, Salt Lake City, Utah.

Barta, Edward J. "Battle Creek, the Battle of Bear River." Master's thesis, Department of Education, Idaho State College, 1962. In Library, Idaho State University, Pocatello.

Beller, Jack. "Negro Slaves in Utah." *Utah Historical Quarterly*, 2 (Oct., 1929), 122–26.

Biographical Directory of the American Congress 1774–1961. Washington, D.C.: Government Printing Office, 1961.

Bitton, Davis. *Guide to Mormon Diaries and Autobiographies*. Provo, Utah: Brigham Young University Press, 1966.

Bowles, Samuel. *Across the Continent*. Springfield, Mass.: Samuel Bowles & Co., 1866.

———. *Our New West*. Hartford, Conn.: Hartford Publishing Co., 1869.

Brand, Carl Fremont. "History of the Know Nothing Party in Indiana."

Indiana Magazine of History, 18 (June, Sept., 1922), 177–207, 266–306.

Brooks, Juanita. *The Mountain Meadows Massacre.* Norman: University of Oklahoma Press, 1962.

Bullough, Vern L. "Polygamy: An Issue in the Election of 1860?" *Utah Historical Quarterly*, 29 (Apr., 1961), 119–26.

Burton, Richard F. *The City of the Saints, and Across the Rocky Mountains to California, 1860.* New York: Harper & Brothers, 1862.

————. *The Look of the West, 1860: Across the Plains to California.* Lincoln: University of Nebraska Press, 1963.

Caldwell, Gaylon L. " 'Utah Has Not Seceded': A Footnote to Local History." *Utah Historical Quarterly*, 26 (Apr., 1958), 171–75.

Cannon, Frank J., and George L. Knapp. *Brigham Young and His Mormon Empire.* New York: Fleming H. Revell Co., 1913.

Carman, Harry J., and Reinhard M. Luthin. *Lincoln and the Patronage.* New York: Columbia University Press, 1943.

Colton, Ray C. *The Civil War in the Western Territories.* Norman: University of Oklahoma Press, 1959.

Cooley, Everett L. "Carpetbag Rule, Territorial Government in Utah." *Utah Historical Quarterly*, 26 (Apr., 1958), 107–20.

Creer, Hargrave. *Utah and the Nation.* Seattle: University of Washington Press, 1929.

Daines, Franklin. "Separation in Utah, 1847–1870." In *Annual Report of the American Historical Association for 1917.* Washington, D.C., 1920.

Daughters of Idaho Pioneers. *History of the Development of Southeastern Idaho.* N.p., 1930.

Dawson, John W. "Charcoal Sketches of Old Times in Fort Wayne." Ed. Alene Godfrey. Prepared by Staff of the Public Library of Fort Wayne and Allen County, 1958. Repr. from *Old Fort News*, Jan.–Mar., 1959. Pub. by the Allen County–Fort Wayne Historical Society, Fort Wayne, Ind.

Edwards, Glenn Thomas, Jr. "The Department of the Pacific in Civil War Years." Ph.D. diss., Department of History, University of Oregon, 1963; printout, University Microfilms, Inc., Ann Arbor, Mich., 1964.

Ellsworth, S. George. *Utah's Heritage.* Santa Barbara, Cal., and Salt Lake City: Peregrine Smith, 1972.

Esshom, Frank. *Pioneers and Prominent Men of Utah.* Salt Lake City: Utah Pioneers Book Publishing Co., 1913. 2 vols.

Etulain, Richard W. "A Virginian in Utah Chooses the Union: Col. Philip St. George Cooke in 1861." *Utah Historical Quarterly*, 42 (Fall, 1974), 381–85.

Evans, Max J., and Ronald G. Watt. "Sources for Western History at the

Church of Jesus Christ of Latter-day Saints." *Western Historical Quarterly*, 13 (July, 1977), 303–12.

Fisher, Margaret M. *Utah and the Civil War, Being the Story of the Part Played by the People of Utah in That Great Conflict with Special Reference to the Lot Smith Expedition and the Robert T. Burton Expedition*. Salt Lake City: Deseret Book Co., 1929.

Fiske, Chad J. *A Mormon Bibliography 1830–1930*. Salt Lake City: University of Utah Press, 1978.

Franklin County (Idaho) Historical Society. *The Passing of the Redman*. Preston, Idaho, 1917.

French, Etta Reeves. "Stephen S. Harding: A Hoosier Abolitionist." *Indiana Magazine of History*, 27 (Sept., 1931), 207–9.

Furniss, Norman F. *The Mormon Conflict 1850–1859*. New Haven, Conn.: Yale University Press, 1960.

Gibson, Harry W. "Frontier Arms of the Mormons." *Utah Historical Quarterly*, 42 (Winter, 1974), 4–26.

Gottfredson, Peter. *History of Indian Depredations in Utah*. Salt Lake City: Skelton Publishing Co., 1919.

Gowans, Fred R. "Fort Bridger and the Mormons." *Utah Historical Quarterly*, 42 (Winter, 1974), 49–68.

———, and Eugene E. Campbell. *Fort Bridger, Island in the Wilderness*. Provo, Utah: Brigham Young University Press, 1975.

Greeley, Horace. *An Overland Journey from New York to San Francisco, in the Summer of 1859*. New York: C. M. Saxton, Barker, 1860.

Griswold, B. J. *The Pictorial History of Fort Wayne, Indiana*. Chicago: Robert O. Law Co., 1917.

Hance, Irma Watson, and Irene Warr. *Johnston, Connor, and the Mormons: an Outline of Military History in Northern Utah*. N.p.: ca. 1962.

Hansen, Klaus. *Quest for Empire: The Political Kingdom of God and the Council of Fifty in Mormon History*. East Lansing: Michigan State University Press, 1967.

Hart, Newell. "Rescue of a Frontier Boy." *Utah Historical Quarterly*, 33 (Winter, 1965), 51–52.

Hebard, Grace Raymond. *Washakie*. Cleveland, Ohio: Arthur H. Clark Co., 1930.

Heitman, Francis B. *Historical Register and Dictionary of the United States Army*. Washington, D.C.: Government Printing Office, 1903. 2 vols.

Hewitt, Randall H. *Across the Plains and over the Divide*. New York: Argosy-Antiquarian, 1964 ed.

Hickman, Bill. *Brigham's Destroying Angel: Being the Life, Confession and Startling Disclosures of the Notorious Bill Hickman. . . .* Salt Lake City: Shepard Publishing Co., 1904.

Hirshson, Stanley P. *The Lion of the Lord, a Biography of Brigham Young.* New York: Knopf, 1968.

Historical Statistics of the United States. Washington, D.C.: U.S. Dept. of Commerce, 1960.

History of Brigham Young, 1847–1867. Berkeley, Cal.: MassCal Associates, 1964, 1966.

Howe, Henry. *Times of the Rebellion in the West.* Cincinnati, Ohio: by the author, 1867.

Hubbard, George U. "Abraham Lincoln as Seen by the Mormons." *Utah Historical Quarterly,* 31 (Spring, 1963), 92–108.

Hunt, Aurora. *The Army of the Pacific.* Glendale, Cal.: Arthur H. Clark Co., 1951.

Hunter, Milton. *Brigham Young, the Colonizer.* Independence, Mo.: Zion Printing and Publishing Co., 1945.

Jenson, Andrew. *Church Chronology, a Record of Important Events.* Salt Lake City: Deseret News Press, 1899.

———. *Encyclopedic History of the Church of Jesus Christ of Latter Day Saints.* Salt Lake City: Deseret News Publishing Co., 1941.

Johnson, Allen, and Dumas Malone, eds. *Dictionary of American Biography.* New York: Scribner, 1946. 20 vols.

Journal of Discourses Delivered by President Brigham Young, His Two Counsellors, the Twelve Apostles, and Others. Reported by G. D. Watt and J. V. Long. Ed. George Q. Cannon. Liverpool: Cannon, repr. ed., 1964.

Keleher, William. *Turmoil in New Mexico 1846–1868.* Santa Fe, N.M.: Rydal Press, 1952.

Kibby, Leo P. "Patrick Edward Connor, First Gentile of Utah." *Journal of the West,* 2 (Oct., 1963), 425–26.

Kirby, J. Randolph. "Fort Wayne Common School Crusaders: The First Year for Free Schooling, April 1863–March 1864." *Old Fort News* (Fort Wayne, Ind.), 42 (Jan., 1979), 1–31.

Lamar, Howard R. *The Far Southwest, 1846–1912.* New Haven, Conn.: Yale University Press, 1966.

———. "Statehood for Utah: A Different Path." *Utah Historical Quarterly,* 39 (Fall, 1971), 307–27.

Larson, Gustive Olof. *The "Americanization" of Utah for Statehood.* San Marino, Cal.: Huntington Library, 1971.

———. *Prelude to the Kingdom, Mormon Desert Conquest.* Francestown, N.H.: Marshall Jones Co., 1947.

————. "Utah and the Civil War." *Utah Historical Quarterly*, 33 (Winter, 1965), 55–77.

Lewis, Oscar. *The War in the Far West 1861–1865*. Garden City, N.Y.: Doubleday, 1961.

Lincoln, Abraham. *The Collected Works of Abraham Lincoln*. Ed. Roy P. Basler, New Brunswick, N.J.: Rutgers University Press, 1953. 8 vols. plus index. Supplement, Westport, Conn.: Greenwood Press, 1974.

Linn, William Alexander. *The Story of the Mormons, from the Date of Their Origin to the Year 1901*. New York: Macmillan, 1902; repr. New York: Russell & Russell, 1963.

Long, E. B. "The 'Terrible Combat' at Bear River." *Civil War Times Illustrated*, 15 (Apr., 1976), 4–10, 40–43.

————. *The Civil War Day by Day: An Almanac 1861–1865*. Garden City, N.Y.: Doubleday, 1971.

Luce, W. Ray. "The Mormon Battalion: A Historical Accident." *Utah Historical Quarterly*, 42 (Winter, 1974), 27–38.

Ludlow, Fitz Hugh. "Among the Mormons." *Atlantic Monthly*, 13 (Jan.–June, 1864), 479–95.

————. *The Heart of the Continent, a Record of Travel across the Plains and in Oregon*. New York: Hurd and Houghton, 1870.

Lythgoe, Dennis L. "Negro Slavery and Mormon Doctrine." *Western Humanities Review*, 21 (Autumn, 1967), 327–38.

————. "Negro Slavery in Utah." *Utah Historical Quarterly*, 39 (Winter, 1971), 51–54.

McLaws, Monte Burr. *Spokesman for the Kingdom: Early Mormon Journalism and the Deseret News, 1830–1898*. Provo, Utah: Brigham Young University Press, 1977.

Madsen, Brigham D. *The Bannock of Idaho*. Caldwell, Idaho: Caxton, 1958.

————. "Shoshone-Bannock Marauders on the Oregon Trail 1859–1863." *Utah Historical Quarterly*, 35 (Winter, 1967), 4–9.

Miers, Earl Schenck, ed. *Lincoln Day by Day, a Chronology 1809–1865*. Washington, D.C.: Lincoln Sesquicentennial Commission, 1960. 3 vols.

Morgan, Dale Lowell. *The Great Salt Lake*. Indianapolis, Ind.: Bobbs-Merrill Co., 1947.

————. "The State of Deseret." *Utah Historical Quarterly*, 8 (Apr., July, Oct., 1940), 67–239.

Mulder, William, and A. Russell Mortensen, eds. *Among the Mormons, History Accounts by Contemporary Observers*. New York: Knopf, 1958.

National Almanac and Annual Record for the Year 1863. Philadelphia: George W. Childs, 1863.

National Cyclopaedia of American Biography. New York: James T. White & Co., 1900–1907.

Neely, Mark E., Jr. "President Lincoln, Polygamy, and the Civil War: The Case of Dawson and Deseret." *Lincoln Lore* (Louis A. Warren Lincoln Library and Museum, Lincoln National Life Foundation, Fort Wayne, Ind.), nos. 1644, 1645, Feb., March, 1975.

Neff, Andrew Love. *History of Utah, 1847–1869.* Salt Lake City: Deseret News Press, 1940.

Nibley, Preston. *Brigham Young, the Man and His Work.* Salt Lake City: Deseret News Press, 1936.

Nichols, David A. *Lincoln and the Indians.* Columbia: University of Missouri Press, 1978.

O'Dea, Thomas F. *The Mormons.* Chicago: University of Chicago Press, 1957.

Papanikolas, Helen Z. *The People of Utah.* Salt Lake City: Utah State Historical Society, 1976.

Pedersen, Lyman C., Jr. "The Daily Union Vedette: A Military Voice on the Mormon Frontier." *Utah Historical Quarterly,* 42 (Winter, 1974), 39–48.

Peterson, Charles S. *Utah, a Bicentennial History.* New York: W. W. Norton, and Nashville, Tenn.: American Association for State and Local History, 1977.

Poll, Richard D. "The Mormon Question, 1850–1865: A Study in Politics and Public Opinion." Ph.D. diss., University of California, 1948.

——. *Utah's History.* Provo, Utah: Brigham Young University Press, 1978.

Pomeroy, Earl S. *The Territories and the United States, 1860–1890.* Studies in Colonial Administration. Philadelphia: Oxford University Press, 1947.

Potterf, Rex M. "John W. Dawson, Herodotus of Fort Wayne." *Old Fort News* (Fort Wayne, Ind.), 32 (Summer, 1969), 1–14.

Prairie Farmer (Chicago), May 9, 1863.

"Redwood City's Lathrop House, 1863–1969." San Mateo, Cal.: San Mateo County Historical Association, 1969. See also untitled memo from San Mateo County Historical Association on Connor family.

Richardson, Albert D. *Beyond the Mississippi.* Philadelphia: American Publishing Co., 1867.

Roberts, Brigham Henry. *A Comprehensive History of the Church of Jesus Christ of Latter-day Saints, Century I.* Salt Lake City: Deseret News Press, 1930. 6 vols.

Rockwell, Wilson. *The Utes, a Forgotten People.* Denver, Colo.: Sage Books, 1936.

Rogers, Fred B. *Soldiers of the Overland*. San Francisco: Grabhorn Press, 1938.

Smith, Joseph. "A Revelation and Prophecy: by the Prophet, Seer and Revelator." Speech given Dec. 25, 1832. Orig. in the broadside *Pearl of Great Price* (Liverpool: n.p., 1851). Repr. as a pamphlet by the Utah Historical Society, Salt Lake City, n.d.

Stanwood, Edward. *A History of the Presidency from 1788 to 1897*. Boston: Houghton Mifflin Co., 1912. 2 vols.

Stegner, Wallace Earle. *Mormon Country*. New York: Duell, Sloan & Pearce, 1942.

———. *The Gathering of Zion*. New York: McGraw Hill, 1964.

Stenhouse, Thomas B. H. *The Rocky Mountain Saints*. New York: Appleton & Co., 1873.

Steptoe, Edward. "An Unwritten Page of Utah's History: How Brigham Young Was Arrested for Polygamy." *Overland Monthly*, 2nd ser., vol. 28 (Dec., 1896), 677–80.

Tegeder, Vincent G. "Lincoln and the Territorial Patronage: The Ascendancy of the Radicals in the West." *Mississippi Valley Historical Review*, no. 35 (June, 1948), 86–89.

Thornbrough, Emma Lou. *Indiana in the Civil War Era, 1850–1860*. Indianapolis: Indiana Historical Bureau and Indiana Historical Society, 1965.

Trenholm, Virginia C., and Maurine Carley. *The Shoshones: Sentinels of the Rockies*. Norman: University of Oklahoma Press, 1964.

Tullidge, Edward W. *History of Salt Lake City*. Salt Lake City: Star Printing Co., Edward W. Tullidge, pub. and prop., 1886.

Utley, Robert M. *Frontiersmen in Blue: The United States Army and the Indian, 1848–1865*. New York: Macmillan, 1967.

Waite, Mrs. C. V. *The Mormon Prophet and His Harem: An Authentic History of Brigham Young, His Numerous Wives and Children*. Cambridge, Mass.: Riverside Press, 3rd ed., 1867.

Ware, Captain Eugene F. *The Indian War of 1864*. Intro. and notes, Clyde C. Walton. Lincoln: University of Nebraska Press, 1960.

Warner, Ezra J. *Generals in Blue*. Baton Rouge: Louisiana State University Press, 1964.

Watters, Gary L. "Utah Territory." In *The Western Territories in the Civil War*, ed. LeRoy H. Fischer. Special issue, *Journal of the West*, 16 (Apr., 1977), 44–56.

Werner, M. R. *Brigham Young*. New York: Harcourt Brace, 1925.

Whipple, Maurine. *This Is the Place, Utah*. New York: Knopf, 1945.

Whitney, Orson P. *History of Utah*. Salt Lake City: Cannon & Sons Co., 1893. 4 vols.

Winther, Oscar O. *The Great Northwest.* New York: Knopf, 1950.

Young, Levi Edgar. *The Founding of Utah.* New York: Scribner, 1923–24.

Zimmerman, Charles. "The Origin and Rise of the Republican Party in Indiana from 1854 to 1860." *Indiana Magazine of History*, 13 (Sept., Dec., 1917), 211–69.

Index